Globe Law and Business

Advising the Wealthy Client

A Handbook for Working with the Ultra Wealthy

Consulting Editor **Barbara R Hauser**

Consulting editor
Barbara R Hauser

Managing director
Sian O'Neill

Advising the Wealthy Client: A Handbook for Working with the Ultra Wealthy
is published by

Globe Law and Business Ltd
3 Mylor Close
Horsell
Woking
Surrey GU21 4DD
United Kingdom
Tel: +44 20 3745 4770
www.globelawandbusiness.com

Advising the Wealthy Client: A Handbook for Working with the Ultra Wealthy

ISBN 9781787423305
EPUB ISBN 9781787423312
Adobe PDF ISBN 9781787423329
Mobi ISBN 9781787423336

Table of contents

Introduction

Barbara R Hauser
Independent family adviser

This was a fun book to put together! The charge was to assemble some of the best thinking about the issues of concern to the very wealthy client. We use the understated general term 'wealthy' deliberately. The advice we have collected will be useful to those working with the world's billionaires and working with those who have several million. They are increasing in numbers, but there didn't seem to be any organised advice for them. Now there is, and we hope you enjoy going through the variety of topics.

The book begins with a thoughtful analysis of the current role played by private fortunes. Joseph Field steps through the various societal and political minefields, many of which negatively impact private wealth. Governments seeking additional revenue have made secrecy nearly impossible. The growing wealth gap tarnishes the idea of surplus private wealth. Nonetheless Joseph closes with a wise thought: "The techniques may have changed and may change even more, but if families can identify where they want to be 20 or 50 years from now, the chances of survival should be good".

The next chapter is a granular one on comprehensive consolidated balance sheets, by the CIO of a large family office in the Gulf region. Asher Noor warns that the place to start is at the beginning, with a careful and accurate inventory of the client's various holdings. He steps through what it should contain and how it should be organised. In my experience this is a crucial step that is often overlooked.

After organising the inventory, the next event is likely to be the purchase of a substantial home. The author Jeremy McGivern, who works only with buyers, has dealt with many such purchases in the London market. He offers advice ranging from the tax and technical to the prosaic and practical. He has a number of valuable tips for buyers on how to negotiate the purchase price, and he closes with a challenge: "You have the choice – follow the boring, disciplined approach that *works* or try the haphazard approach adopted by most buyers and hope you get lucky. Which will you take?"

A topic of great concern to the wealthy client is risk, of all types. We begin that topic with a chapter by Linda Bourn on "Risk assessment and strategic insurance planning". Linda has developed an expertise in all forms of insurable risks. She urges clients to consider all of the family members and all the types of risk. She provides a very detailed annual risk assessment process that can be applied to the diversity of risk exposures faced by wealthy clients.

Taking a targeted focus on risk itself, John Deverell argues that what is needed is a "prepared mind". There should be a thoughtful risk assessment process, but he warns that "while risk registers typically include a column for 'likelihood' and another column for 'impact', they usually – and in my opinion wrongly – omit to have a column for risk velocity". He makes the point that while many risks are comparatively "slow burn", "things can go wrong very quickly". He includes some cases to illustrate his point.

In current times of omnipresent social media, the reputational risk has become a sober and challenging subject. Charlie Bain, the author of the chapter on reputational risk, warns of the ability of others to spread damaging information, true or not. He notes that "[a] reputational crisis happens quickly and, a bit like a fire, spreads if you haven't prepared properly and so know what to do". He acknowledges how easily false information can be posted, and concludes with: "It is a deeply worrying thing to say that you should know your digital profile as well as you know yourself or your business, but it has never been so true".

Another area of risk is the threat to a client's wealth that can come from divorce and a variety of marital claims. In the chapter on "Protection from marital claims", Amy Radnor begins with the observation that "[i]n the wider context of wealth protection, divorce and family breakdown is a time of particular vulnerability for individuals, trustees and family offices". For a number of reasons, the approach of the English courts can lead to the jurisdiction or forum 'shopping' seen in many high profile cases. English divorce awards are often based on 'need', which is an elastic and subjective concept. Amy discusses the increased use of prenuptial and postnuptial agreements to counter these claims and Rose Spencer-Longhurst explores the use of trust structures as a means of protecting assets in the event of marital breakdown.

Some wealthy clients are simply moving to another jurisdiction, perhaps with more flexible laws, lower taxes or better quality of life. As Nicola Saccardo explains in his chapter on "Choice of residence", the increase in the mobility of wealthy clients has led to several countries introducing new regimes meant to attract wealthy clients, thus creating competition among jurisdictions. Nicola gives a helpful checklist of the factors that should be considered in choosing a place of residence. He includes descriptions of the many jurisdictions' new laws intended to entice wealthy clients.

Given that most wealthy clients have assets in more than one jurisdiction, Jeremy Arnold, in his chapter on "Managing taxes", gives excellent advice on how to manage all of the various taxes. He covers all types of taxes, and their structures and penalties, and includes the increasing number of required disclosure laws. He concludes that: "The challenge for those people who advise the wealthy client is to get the advice right and also to be able to explain that advice to the client in a way that can be understood. Often the right answer may not be immediately apparent or the client will be faced with options and choices. The skilled tax adviser will be able to exercise judgement in helping the client reach the right decision".

In most jurisdictions, the wealthy client will have one or more trust agreements. In their chapter "Reviewing the trust agreement", Gail Cohen and Gerard Joyce have provided a very practical and thorough outline of the provisions that should be looked at. They note at the outset that they discuss the elements necessary to appropriately review all trusts, "regardless of the trust's jurisdiction. From time to time, however, provisions applicable solely to US-centric trusts will be specifically mentioned as well as provisions that are specific to cross-border trusts". At the end of the chapter they include a master checklist to use for the review of any trust.

When wealthy clients have a number of trusts, they often begin to ask about creating their own private trust company. Todd Mayo, in his chapter "Consider creating a private trust company", provides extensive detail of the pros and cons of creating a private trust company. He includes a consideration of the number of competing jurisdictions that have their own laws intended to attract wealthy clients. Todd includes very practical advice on the proper management of a private trust company.

In my chapter "Consider a family office", I consider the wealthy client who could benefit from creating an organised staff to handle their various needs. I also refer the reader to *Family Offices: The STEP Handbook for Advisers*, 2nd edition (2019) and a Special Report, *Setting Up a Family Office* (2020), both published by Globe Law and Business. My general advice to clients who are interested in creating a single family office is a simple series of questions. Begin by asking which services the client would like, which will then determine the need for staff in number and in type, which in turn will determine the size of an office. There are also questions about where it should be located, and the factors that are relevant to that decision.

As part of the human condition we have included the chapter "Managing declining capacity", by Keith Drewery. Keith gives advice on a number of issues that come up when the wealthy client seems to have reached a stage of diminished capacity, a topic that is not often addressed. Keith focuses on the many aspects of this condition and gives extensive advice on how best to address each of the areas that is affected.

Next we have a chapter on "The philanthropy framework", by Melissa Berman of Rockefeller Philanthropy Advisors. She explains a new framework they have developed in response to changing philanthropy habits around the world. The framework has three core elements:

- Charter, the organisation's scope, form of governance and decision-making protocol;
- Social compact, its implicit or explicit agreement with society about the value it will create; and
- Operating model, the approach to the resources, structures and systems needed to implement strategy.

They explain how the framework is implemented, and close with a statement of its purpose, which is "to enable their clients to articulate their role in society, their operational strategies and their relationships to others to more effectively implement change".

After discussing the various elements of advice for the wealthy client, we turn to Natasha Pearl and her chapter on the "The essential infrastructure for wealth preservation". She challenges the conventional wisdom that wealth preservation is almost wholly dependent on investment management, explaining how lack of infrastructure can doom even well-crafted wealth plans. She gives multiple examples of the consequences of deficient infrastructure, offering a master checklist to evaluate, and an approach to improve, the wealthy client's infrastructure.

We close with a look to the future. In his innovative chapter "The future of finance", Craig Pearson suggests the possibility that many of today's assumptions will no longer apply. It is a perfect bookend to the opening chapter by Joseph Field.

We hope that you enjoy this compilation of experts in these fields, all geared to giving great advice to the wealthy client.

An overview of the global situation for private wealth

Joseph A Field
Pillsbury Winthrop Shaw Pittman LLP

It was the best of times, it was the worst of times, it was the age of wisdom, it was the age of foolishness, it was the epoch of belief, it was the epoch of incredulity, it was the season of light, it was the season of darkness, it was the spring of hope, it was the winter of despair.

Charles Dickens – *A Tale of Two Cities*

1. Introduction

Some 225 years ago, the aristocracy of France was all but destroyed in a Reign of Terror as part of a revolution which Dickens described as "the spring of hope [and] ... the winter of despair".

Most of us are not living in revolutionary times, but some of us are. We are all living within a continuum where, at one end, there is great hope for the conquest of disease, the enrichment of peoples everywhere and technology which serves to bring us all together. At the same time, we are witness to a peacetime which is not peaceful and where human rights are under constant assault. Politics seems to have run amok in many parts of the world, fuelled to a large extent by the thought that government is not the servant of the people and that opportunity for some is just more misery for others. The world seems far less stable and far less safe than it did at the height of the Cold War. The Middle East is in constant turmoil, with foreign states putting the boot to civilian populations who starve and die. Repression in Hong Kong and Korea and even India only slightly eclipse scandals and police states elsewhere. Latin America, seemingly, is a volcano waiting to erupt. Today, even in the United States, racial tensions threaten the very core of American society.

To understand what wealthy families are going to need in these turbulent times, it is important to recognise four important drivers and how those affect families and their wealth.

- Globally, we are experiencing a variety of political and social upheavals that have created an environment of dramatic

change. Rapid wealth creation and accumulation are happening at the same time as increased income inequality, population growth and disruptions due to changing climate. This has led to legislative and regulatory reactions, political extremism and overall instability. Hong Kong may have just disappeared as an independent economic and political jurisdiction.
- COVID-19, an unexpected and horrific pandemic, has fallen upon us and has limited travel and caused chaos in the economic markets. The implications of such an event are hard to fathom at this point, but certainly global families will change the way they think, invest and even congregate.
- Decision making within families is changing; younger generations are increasingly involved with the profile of family investment.
- Privacy is becoming harder to maintain, and therefore more prized. Preserving privacy requires more thoughtful approaches in a world where bank secrecy – for many reasons – is gone and cyber security is an increasingly important and complex topic.

A more connected and technology-enhanced world has contributed greatly to wealth creation. The number of wealthy people is expanding in almost geometric proportions. In China, there are more dollar millionaires than in the United States, but exchange controls make it virtually impossible for this new wealthy class to spend and often to invest abroad. The number of billionaires being minted in Silicon Valley is growing at a very rapid rate and many of them will eventually return home to countries like China and India, enriched with ideas and a much more global perspective. The *Huffington Post* reported on 28 December 2019 that the wealth of the world's 500 richest individuals grew by 25% in 2019.

At the same time, the gap in income inequality has grown. This gap, coupled with population increase and the effects of climate change, creates implications for wealthy families in myriad forms, depending on where they are located. This results, in some places, in:
- more regulation aimed at redistributing wealth;
- public opinion turning more dramatically against wealth; and
- overall instability mandating families to look at safer havens.

Confrontation between rich and poor takes on many forms. It can be seen in the emergence of extremist regimes in many European, Asian and Latin American countries. It has led to riots in France and to a broad populist resistance to immigration policies in many other European countries. Mass migrations from Africa to Europe are taking place, and we are all too familiar with President Trump's continuing desire to build a wall between the United States and Mexico. Racial tension in the US has led to massive demonstrations and an attack on the very core of the law and order system.

Increasingly, fear is becoming a motivator for international wealthy families. Serious political unrest in Buenos Aires, Beirut or Hong Kong tends to make people uncomfortable. Threats to property in Rio or to persons in Mexico City, or kidnapping for ransom in many places, mean that families are much more inclined to invest in foreign countries, either to provide an anchor to the wind or to diversify the family investment base.

At the same time, a significant feature in the creation of great new fortunes includes the enrichment of a much younger class of the very wealthy. For many of them, there is a change in thinking whereby socially responsible and impact investing have replaced traditional notions of gifting and charity to a significant degree, and much more emphasis is placed on investing in socially responsible companies from a purely economic perspective than had been the case previously. Even among more traditionally wealthy families, the pledge of Bill Gates and Warren Buffett to donate most of their wealth has a lot of families thinking about following similar paths.

2. The slow death of privacy?

Against this backdrop we need to recognise that we are living in much more of a global village and some of the traditional pillars of privacy are falling by the wayside. Tax evasion, which was viewed as almost a sport by some very wealthy families in many countries, is now a very serious crime, and governments are enforcing these laws with vigour. The very rules which attack the illicit hiding of wealth make it much more difficult for those who simply wish to preserve family privacy to do so. In the United Kingdom, a failure to demonstrate the source of funds can lead to the seizure and eventual forfeiture of expensive homes.

The notion of preserving privacy through bank secrecy is gone. What was once viewed as a positive tool for protecting the patrimony of people threatened by oppression has come to be viewed in the last 10 years as a sinister curtain to protect those who do not wish to pay their fair share of taxes. Bank secrecy became a focus of the world's most sophisticated countries and many international agencies. Finally, even the Swiss eliminated legislation permitting this.

Privacy has fallen victim to the wholesale attack against tax evasion and the use of offshore havens and is under constant threat from cyber pirates.

During the last decade or so, politicians, the press and society have attacked the wealthy as people who do not play by rules mandated to others. Many countries now villainise the accumulation of wealth over generations by imposing wealth taxes. Senator Elizabeth Warren has included a wealth tax as one of the main planks in her platform. There are also countries which impose supertax rates on the highest earners.

It is interesting to note that when money laundering rules first came into effect at the beginning of this century, predicate crimes were limited to drug trafficking and terrorism; tax evasion was not a qualifying offence. Today, tax evasion is the moving force of such regulation, but it is not the sole driver. Transparency is the word which predominates the regulation of financial affairs and privacy seems to have fallen completely by the wayside.

Indeed, in the course of the last few years, a great deal of attention has been paid by the press and a number of regulatory agencies and national governments to the 'Panama Papers' and the 'Paradise Papers', which were client files from a Panamanian law firm and a Bermuda trust company setting out data on the accounts and financial affairs of their wealthy clients. In Panama, some irregularities were found, but in Bermuda, none were discovered. The salient point, which is not often raised in the press, is that in both cases the documentation was stolen and the information was sold to governments or news agencies who paid for them. The press often publishes stories about how wealthy families live in great luxury in tax havens and imply that there is something sinister or illegal about this. In nearly all cases, there is nothing illegal about this and the families in question are fully compliant with the law, but that does not sell newspapers.

The world is changing rapidly. With advances in artificial intelligence and machine learning, it will be increasingly difficult for families to maintain what privacy they have left. Data theft is a serious problem. Data protection is now a more prominent part of European law (under the updated General Data Protection Regulation), and those who breach these rules are subject to severe criminal sanctions in the European Union. The State of California has also just enacted rigorous data protection legislation. The disappearance of barriers to family information remains an ongoing serious threat, in Europe and elsewhere in the world. While some laws protect the privacy of personal data, others do not.

3. Tax policy becomes an invasive tool

The other main impediment to protecting information related to family wealth is in fact statutory. In 2010, the United States promulgated the Foreign Account Tax Compliance Act. This act was created to obtain information on American citizens and residents with respect to foreign bank accounts, to ensure they were reporting this information to the US Treasury and that taxes were paid. The act is not a tax, *per se*; it imposes no penalties on taxpayers. Indeed, the responsibility for filing information returns with the US Treasury lies solely with foreign financial institutions. All the costs for implementing the act are borne by these foreign financial entities.

For many countries outside the United States, the Foreign Account Tax Compliance Act was first seen as a tool for interfering in their domestic financial affairs; a further intrusion by the US Government, using a 'long-arm' statute that reached beyond the US border to effect US laws and policy. In many nations, the act was at odds with local banking and personal privacy regulation, and Canada and Israel even threatened litigation. However, after much discussion and review, a vast number of foreign governments found the concept extremely attractive. In May of 2014, some 47 countries signed on to the Standard for Automatic Exchange of Financial Account Information, otherwise known as the Common Reporting Standard (CRS).

Today, about 110 countries are party to the CRS system. They represent almost every major country in the world, except the United States (which already had the Foreign Account Tax Compliance Act). CRS has one aspect which is very different from the US act, in that it provides for the *automatic* exchange of information among all member nations. Information began to be collected and processed last year. However, CRS was hurried into existence, and many of the standards in terms of judging how countries will apply the rules simply do not exist. Even the date from which information shall be collected is unclear in many countries. While there are several technical problems still outstanding, information-gathering and analysis proceed apace. Over five million reports were posted in the UK in the first year; it is hard to say what China or Russia will do with the reports they receive. As many nations – from Germany to China to Mexico – greatly tighten their tax enforcement, CRS carries with it potential for the imposition of a whole new range of criminal penalties, and even where penalties do not apply, the spectre of disclosure of sensitive family data to myriad governments is highly unappetising to many.

4. Some disturbing new rules

In January 2018, the Organisation for Economic Cooperation and Development (OECD), an international organisation sponsored by the G-20 and headquartered in Paris, proposed new rules for those who attempt to avoid CRS. Part of this measure is to impose criminal sanctions against lawyers, accountants, bankers and other advisers who may counsel clients on how to avoid CRS, either intentionally or inadvertently. While the US is not part of the CRS system, American advisers should think twice about helping their international clients on how to avoid the reporting which may be required under CRS. Ironically, the OECD may be launching a form of reverse long-arm statute against the United States.

In April 2018, the European Union proposed Anti-Money Laundering Directive 5. By the terms of this directive, which is now law in most EU states, there will be an EU-wide registry of beneficial ownership of legal entities. In many countries, this will extend to beneficiaries of trusts. While there are some exceptions, the thrust and the mood of the body politic in Europe is clear, and such measures are likely to be adopted in many other places.

In late 2018, the EU Code of Conduct Group proposed, and almost all offshore jurisdictions adopted, laws on enhanced economic substance requirements within the jurisdiction in question for offshore companies. Failure to comply could lead to the de-registration of such a company and, in extreme cases, criminal sanctions. Again, legislation was enacted too quickly and the definition of what constituted proper and improper economic substance was vague. The concept of requiring corporate substance was first enacted in the United States as a tax tool for preventing artificial corporate structures from being used to avoid tax. Ironically, most, if not all, of the countries which adopted the EU-mandated legislation at the end of 2018 have little or no income tax.

Clearly, with all this new regulation, a primary target is wealthy families, and, in the eyes of many governments and international organisations, offshore companies and trusts are a facile method for hiding illicit funds.

5. Privacy and cyber security

Placing funds in a bank secrecy jurisdiction to protect privacy is no longer an option. Comparatively little can be done to protect information about assets from governments, or indeed private parties who wish to glean data on the wealth or financial affairs of families.

Cyber security is a pressing issue; not only in terms of the legitimate protection of information from governments or the curious, but also due to the real and growing threat that family assets are subject to exposure and theft. Over the last few years, global families have become acutely aware of the dangers of being exposed to hacking and data theft. Many now devote substantial resources to protecting their information. Encryption of data is commonplace and cyber security is often a high line item on the agenda of many families.

Another relatively new issue is the question of cryptocurrency. Bitcoin has had something of a rocky ride, while governments and inter-governmental authorities are trying hard to define what cryptocurrency really is and how they propose to regulate and tax it. At the same time, families are exploring how this phenomenon can be used as an investment vehicle and as a technique for keeping assets private.

6. What are families doing?

One aspect of the increased ability to communicate and to operate from any place is that internet-connected families are more mobile, both in terms of where they live or locate a family office, and in terms of where they invest. Today, families are thinking globally to make investments which make sense in terms of their investment objectives, or which may provide some real tax benefit. Changes in the US tax law at the end of 2017 caused many American businesses, including family businesses, to consider bringing profits back to the United States. In Europe, over the last few years, holding company rules have made it easier to invest throughout the European Union. Even Brexit has caused many families in the UK to think defensively and to consider establishing operations in the EU, or farther afield. Tensions in Asia have made families throughout the region rethink policies of investing primarily in Asia. Singapore and Switzerland have been major beneficiaries of regional funds being on the move. To some extent, in our experience, the United States has been a significant recipient of foreign investment from all over the world because of its strong economy, the size of the American market and the freedom to invest in almost anything.

A by-product of this tension between political upheaval and shifting tax policies is that a whole cottage industry has developed around changing residence and acquiring a new, or second (or third), nationality.

Many families established themselves in tax havens over quite a long period of time, and places like Bermuda, the Bahamas, the

Cayman Islands, the Channel Islands and the Isle of Man offered shelter and special advantages at a low tax cost.

For several generations, the United Kingdom with its remittance basis of taxation has attracted highly paid executives and very wealthy families to take advantage of a system whereby they could live in the UK at minimal or no tax cost. The system created a lot of jobs in the UK, and it was a boon to the London real property market and the City of London. However, over the last few years, new restrictions have been imposed on the acquisition of UK real estate and the benefits of the remittance basis have been reduced.

In response to this, several jurisdictions have decided that there is real benefit in offering tax advantages to the wealthy and have jumped into the fray. They are now actively attracting wealthy foreign investors to establish themselves in these countries. Noteworthy among these are Singapore, Switzerland and Italy, with Portugal and, to a degree, Spain being very much in play. Unlike the remittance basis of taxation, wealthy foreigners in Singapore can easily limit their exposure to tax by earning most of their wealth outside the country, which has a territorial system of taxation. In Italy, the newly arrived resident (who may even be Italian) pays a flat fee on all foreign income, which he can either keep offshore or remit to Italy. Such regimes are very popular and certain countries provide cultural affinity to investors from former colonies (eg, Portugal for Brazil and Spain for much of the rest of Latin America).

Another subject which has attracted substantial interest and investment is the acquisition of new or additional passports. Often referred to as 'Nationality by Investment', a significant number of countries have made it possible for foreigners to become nationals (and obtain passports) by investment in government or commercial projects. The process is often rapid. The price varies with the location and opportunities which may be available. The cost in the Caribbean is often lower than in a select number of EU jurisdictions, which offer complete freedom of establishment throughout the EU. The only question is how long will the EU, the United States or other major jurisdictions permit the acquisition of nationality in this way. Some 30 years ago, Ireland had a similar programme, but it was eliminated after pressure from other EU nations.

7. A few conclusions

Obviously, all families are different and I can only speak to our own experience, but the attitude of families has changed greatly over the last few years when it comes to protecting and preserving their wealth. There are of course still many cultural and family constraints which guide how families will behave. Furthermore, the age of wealthy patriarchs and matriarchs is coming down rapidly, and inherited wealth as a percentage of global wealth is far less than it used to be. While many of the issues confronting a family may be particular to them, there are nonetheless several general trends we have observed over the past few years.

7.1 Younger generations involved in the management and preservation of wealth

Families are highly interested in preserving privacy and wealth, but in some circles, the approach has changed. Information used to be kept from younger generations, particularly in Asia and the Middle East, but this is evolving rapidly; in part because of globalisation and the nature of social change and in part because it is much easier for younger generations to find out what they own. Also, many families have found that engaging younger generations sooner provides for a more understanding, experienced and sophisticated rising class within the family. Fewer mistakes are likely to be made if they already understand the family dynamic when they rise to a position of authority. Much more attention is being paid to impact investing and to planned charitable giving, even where taxation may not be an issue.

7.2 Discreet ownership

With the cyber tools available to everyone, keeping matters away from prying eyes is becoming much more difficult. Cyber security has become a more prominent and more common issue among wealthy families everywhere. Protecting the family's private affairs is still of great importance, but the techniques have changed and reliance on electronic programs and the outsourcing of certain skills plays a much more important part today than it did even five years ago.

7.3 Taxation and patrimony

In 1947, in the case of *Commissioner v Newman*, Judge Learned Hand opined that, "Over and over again courts have said that there is nothing sinister in so arranging one's affairs as to keep taxes as low as possible. Everybody does so, rich or poor; and all do right, for nobody owes any public duty to pay more than the law demands: taxes are enforced exactions, not voluntary contributions. To demand more in the name of morals is mere cant".[1] With increasingly draconian efforts to impose minimum taxation on everyone and, in many countries, to impose higher obligations on the wealthy, people tend to forget the words of Judge Hand. While not every wealthy family is prepared to move to Italy to reduce its taxes, a great number do. For wealthy families, tax planning is something that may involve the minimisation of income taxation, but more often the primary goal is to achieve a tax plan to preserve a family's wealth in real terms over generations. While there are families that are prepared to give away most of what they have, they usually still provide enough for their children to have a home and a basic lifestyle.

7.4 Planning for the future

This is a major topic of discussion at almost all family gatherings. However, the issues are no longer confined to succession and governance. Times are changing at a very rapid pace, and many families are concerned about how to be sure that they are prepared to address the future. To this end, family meetings today often include outside advisers to address a variety of issues. In many cases, family members will often seek work experience outside the family's core area of interest, and often in a remote geographical location. Globalisation is here to stay, and we are moving at a much more rapid pace, but the institution of the family has been around a long time. The techniques may have changed and may change even more, but if families can identify where they want to be 20 or 50 years from now, the chances of survival should be good.

1 *Commissioner of Internal Revenue v Newman*, 159 F.2d 848 (2d Cir. 1947), https://law.justia.com/cases/federal/appellate-courts/F2/159/848/1565902.

Organising a consolidated balance sheet for the wealthy

Asher Noor
AlTouq Group

1. Introduction

Two farmers met. They were comparing the size of their lands. The first farmer to demonstrate the vastness of his lands bragged that if he drove his tractor from dawn onwards, he would still be on his land by dusk time. The other farmer was unfazed and remarked that he too once had a tractor like that!

Wealthy clients, too, usually struggle to articulate the exact quantum of their wealth. While discretion might have a lot to do with it, even behind closed doors many wealthy clients find it exceedingly difficult to put an accurate number to their wealth.

Those who do hazard a guess might naively or erroneously omit to take accurate account of the liabilities that come along with the assets they tally up, let alone the trappings of liquidity profiles and collateralisation or the ownership conundrum of club deals and the contingent nature of some assets and liabilities. Add to it the liberal mixture or hybrid nature of family versus investment assets or sentimental and generational custodianship of certain other possessions and the counting suddenly becomes quite complicated. It certainly is important to distinguish between the paper rich and the truly wealthy.

2. The dilemma

When it comes to advising the wealthy who for the first time are thinking of professionalising and institutionalising, the starting point is usually a series of conversations that help firm up the scope (including the resolve to proceed). In such conversations between the wealthy client and the wealth adviser, the concern that comes up every time is the lack of an accurate, consolidated, bird's-eye view of their net wealth (ie, assets minus liabilities). In other words, an inventory of what the wealthy client owns and owes, marked to market. That is the starting point. That is the stumbling point. That chasm needs bridging up front.

The perennial challenge is getting that consolidated balance sheet of net worth together. It is usually a challenge because invariably the wealthy client is served by a slew of service providers, undoubtedly first rate but all working in their own silos. There is no internal or external resource aggregating the entire portfolio. Simply adding up reports from various counterparties will also not do the trick due to different reporting methodologies, dates and formats.

In the absence of a consolidated bird's-eye view of the net wealth, all decisions by the wealthy client are largely akin to taking a stab in the dark.

Regardless of whether the wealth is old or new, the wealth adviser is usually faced with typical situations where the investment portfolio seems to be all over the place – literally and figuratively. While there is always room for improvement on structuring or in pruning certain orphan assets or ditching a few counterparty relationships, the starting point is always about first securing an accurate, consolidated inventory of the wealth.

Wealth advisers wish to begin the advisory relationship by getting a better handle on the types of investments: whether they are liquid or illiquid, their geographical dispersion, the currencies involved and whether they are in personal or corporate names. Wealthy clients usually have a lot to say but are not necessarily accomplished in sharing an up-to-date summarised dashboard to back up their assertions. It takes a major chunk of the pre-engagement timeframe to fill that hole. Legal structuring, choosing domiciles, estate planning, etc all remain hostage to the inaugural task of consolidating the inventory and calculating the net wealth.

3. So, what is the wealthy client going to do about it?

The purpose of this chapter is to help wealthy clients identify the steps they alone can take or dictate that assist in yielding for them a truly internal and comprehensive dashboard, providing evidence for their consolidated balance sheet. It might only be for their eyes or for clarity, but it is becoming increasingly important for wealthy clients to truly understand the depth and breadth of their global investment portfolio and how that translates into net assets, sliced and diced not merely by currency and geography but also by legal titles, access or liquidity profile.

In the market, there are multi-family offices and custodians who promise to collate all and provide that elusive one-pager dashboard for the wealthy client. Without calling out the obvious shortcomings of most of those offerings, it is but evident that at times the wealthy client would choose to split the reporting into

4. silos such that different bankers or service providers only get to see a partial picture. While the wealthy client may have their reasoning for putting a spoke in the wheel themselves, with privacy being the primary or possibly only motivator, it does not take away from the overwhelming need that the wealthy client has to be able to quantify their wealth at any point in time.

Wealthy clients continue to be troubled by the frenzied pace with which their wealth is being impacted by taxation, regulations, market movements, political climate or even Tweets etc. It is therefore imperative for them to have a good handle on their exact net wealth.

Getting to the consolidated balance sheet of the wealthy is a two-step process that originates at the wealthy client's end; the rest can take care of itself.

The first step is the internal realisation that there is definitely a need to collate and quantify the investments that have mushroomed and that outsourced models do not necessarily work towards providing a truly effective consolidated overview. A talk with their family business or wealth adviser or a family business practitioner will validate that realisation.

The second step is hiring a specialist and the ideal specialist to help with internally consolidating that balance sheet is a chief financial officer (CFO) at the holding company, family office or personal level. This is a big leap of faith for many wealthy clients. The perception is that the CFO is ideally suited for operational level activities and clients fear that at the family office or personal level he or she might end up being a glorified personal assistant. That fear is unfounded and, were that the case, good luck trying to find a CFO worth their salt who will accept an offer where it does not entail good utilisation of their skillset. While onboarding a CFO at that personal level may be a challenge, it is not impossible. CFOs are no longer a luxury but a necessity. Demand is up for CFOs in this non-traditional domain.

The wealth adviser or family business practitioner can certainly come in handy in that recruitment and onboarding process. However, for the sake of this chapter, let us assume that the challenge is successfully tackled.

Those were the only two steps that the wealthy client need take.

4. The ball is now in the CFO's court

Once on board, the CFO can proceed with the quest to organise the consolidated balance sheet for their wealthy principal. Depending on volume or complexity, the task may take some time, but a year to 18 months is certainly not an unrealistic timescale.

Let us spend a short amount of time detailing why the CFO is ideally suited to this quest.

- To manage finances, you need spotless back office operations. You need a specialist. You need a professional. You need a jack-of-all-trades who is also a master of all tricks.
- Given the typical CFO's educational and work experience background and their extensive interaction with bankers, lawyers, regulators and other stakeholders, the case is clearly made for a seasoned and versatile CFO to take charge. Family offices worldwide are clearly accepting that premise.
- CFOs are usually the first C-title outside the family hierarchy to be hired – even before a chief investment officer (CIO). It is an inevitable recognition of the value that a CFO can lend to a family investment office.
- A CFO – whether through education or previous posts – generally comes armed with experience of: other industries, the latest financial products, treasury, taxation and governance issues, budgeting and cost minimisation tactics, internal controls and system implementation. This expertise – if it can be combined with a sense of loyalty to the family and an absolute regard to confidentiality – is what wealthy clients dream of and pray for – and will pay for.
- Family businesses with affluence and a sense of corporate governance are gradually seeing the benefits that trusted CFOs can bring to family financial affairs. CFOs can streamline the finances, provide transparency for all family members who are beneficiaries, review investment decisions on their behalf, manage cash flow mismatches and exposures, and at the same time act as custodian, conscience, strategist, adviser and educator.
- These CFOs also act as risk managers by helping the family understand the risks and complexities of the business, investment decisions and related activities. In finance, risk is the probability that an investment's actual return will be different from expected. This includes the possibility of losing some or all of the original investment. The CFOs' added value is that they bring risk management – embedding risk tolerance in the investment framework or the ability to price that risk into the cash flows, P&L and the family mindset.
- Working with wealthy clients, there is generally zero tolerance for surprises. Why? Because surprises are usually the tip of the iceberg. Therefore a CFO's role in such situations is to ensure

that the books and records are true and fair, reflect completely the financial affairs and health of the principal's investments, assets and liabilities and provide an honest reflection of the state of affairs. So, if impairment has happened and a haircut is prudent or a write-off is inevitable, it is the CFO's responsibility to challenge the valuation and provide the value at risk, so to speak!

- In an unfortunate situation, CFOs can be asked to be 'creative'. Ideally, the CFO stands up and reminds everyone that they are not a novelist or a painter. However, when asked to be a 'solutions provider', the CFO is usually able to manage the business and financial implications of past or proposed decisions and help steady the boat.
- Investment decision making might be person-centric, but the CFO is expected to chip in with an honest, professional assessment devoid of influence. This independent opinion (with the customary and necessary deference) becomes a legitimate and useful resource to the wealthy client. This is what a fair, corporate-structure-oriented principal or family office requires and what the CFO is best suited to deliver. Fortunately, family offices everywhere are beginning to recognise this.
- As with most things, specialisation is the buzzword. When it comes to having somebody on board to manage the finances, collaborate in strategic decision making and consider the implications of it all on wealth preservation and generation, CFOs tick all the boxes.

5. The CFO's toolkit

An effective dashboard consolidates wealth from multiple inputs into an easy aggregated display that is inclusive and responds immediately to user engagement. The complexity today of a wealthy client's portfolio rivals that of the medium-sized companies of yesteryear, so tackling the same cannot be done without institutionalising and professionalising the approach to it. The CFO would understand that from the very onset and ably tackle it.

Many people have assumed aggregating the assets and liabilities on an MS Excel spreadsheet provides the ultimate consolidated dashboard. Nothing could be farther from truth. Furthermore, the wealthy client of today is not amused by receiving a statement of account every quarter with a quarter lag on valuation. The old way of doing things does not cut it any more. The CFO would, again, understand that from the very onset and ably tackle it.

We can now move on to setting out the steps that a CFO will ordinarily need to take to accomplish the task of internally generating that comprehensive consolidated balance sheet for their wealthy principal.

In its simplest form, it is another two-step process: inventory and valuation. Inventory would be the task of ensuring all assets and liabilities are recorded and accounted for. Valuation would be the task of ensuring the most representative current re-saleable or divestment value is provided for each such asset or liability.

6. Inventory

The first step is to decide a cut-off date. This will usually be the calendar or fiscal year end but the cut-off date here essentially refers to how many years in the past one wishes to go to set as year zero. This is especially crucial where legacy investments have been around for a few decades without ever having been properly accounted for. For that date onwards, the first port of call would be the varied bankers and service providers to obtain statements of account, detailing all that is in their custody for the wealthy client. It would be useful to create either digital folders or binder files for each investment, warehousing all legal documentations relating to each asset or liability. Whether it's a limited partner (LP) position in a private equity fund, a penthouse in a distant land, a special purpose vehicle (SPV) in some offshore jurisdiction, the discretionary portfolio mandate for a specific strategy, a credit line against personal guarantee or asset-backed collateral – all needs to be catalogued.

Once the entire list is drawn up, conversations with the wealthy client may reveal investments off the books that need to be roped in. This sounds incredulous but it can indeed happen, as principals sometimes make investments on the go, using personal accounts or cheque books that never get custodised with a central or mainstream service provider. A few conversations may help jog their memory. Therefore, it is not just about collecting the knowns but also collating the unknowns or invisibles and bringing them back on the tally board.

As the inventory-taking is underway, it would be useful for the CFO to pull up as many bank statements as possible, dating as far back as possible. Sizeable debits or a random credit can all point to missing investments that might otherwise slip through during the aggregation exercise.

While compiling the inventory, it is also important to keep an eye on where and with whom the particular asset is custodised, if subscription documents or share certificates evidencing ownership are available, if they are collateralised or have other encumbrances attached thereto, etc. Sometimes it might be unclear whether the asset falls within a family ownership or a purely personal stake; payments might have gone from a personal account for a family asset and vice versa. It is important to establish the money trail and then secure a clear understanding of where the asset is to be parked and who is to own the liability, if any, associated with it.

For all investments with a staggered investment mechanism, such as private equity investments, it is advisable to obtain a control sheet detailing the date of investment and details of all capital calls and distributions. Columnar segregation evidencing which of the distributions are recallable is crucial in order to understand how much of a commitment is truly outstanding on such positions. On the consolidated balance sheet, the contingent liabilities emanating from outstanding commitments on such investments may form a significant chunk that can influence liquidity and future investment decision making.

It will also be useful at this stage to cross-reference the capital calls with the PPM, term sheets or other representation to ensure that payments are only being made up to the predetermined and agreed investment period.

While certain investments will be marked down to zero due to lack of performance, it is important to keep them on the list. They may have associated liability or, if nothing else, serve as a reminder of a zombie investment out there. The wealthy client might want to secure shares or work towards divesting or doing a secondary, even if at nil consideration, or a clean exit. Removing such items from the consolidated reporting framework would drop them off the radar, which is not helpful.

It might seem moot but it is important to reconcile numbers, such that a sum due to/from the wealthy client is recorded as due from/to the shareholder. That is best practice accounting, even if from an optical aspect it is merely moving stuff from one pocket to another.

It's not just about assets. All liabilities, contingent or otherwise, need to be noted down and factored in, and sensitivity analysis performed to clearly understand what will trigger margin calls and how to respond to them.

7. Valuation

Once a consolidated list of assets and liabilities is worked out, it is equally imperative to secure the most up-to-date and recent valuation to understand the unrealised gain/loss thereto. This unrealised amount will be a crucial number to factor in to all analysis, on an ongoing basis.

It will be important to review the methodology adopted by custodians, asset managers or bankers with whom the assets and liabilities (essentially the investment portfolio) are placed. These are the institutions or people that will be providing the valuations, and the CFO must contact them and understand the basis, formula and regularity of the valuations that they undertake. For larger real estate or significant operational assets, it might be useful to engage valuation agents or to benchmark against other public or comparable transactions to see if the internal estimates are within the same range.

The ultimate validation would be to engage an auditor. Sometimes auditors are confused or hesitant when requested by an individual rather than a corporation. It is equally likely that the principal will not want auditors involved and the CFO should understand and respect that. However, it is an option that should definitely be put forward for their consideration.

Regardless of whether auditors are engaged, the CFO should prepare a set of financial statements, encompassing all jurisdictions and currencies, as the consolidated balance sheet for the principal.

The ideal reporting timeline is to conduct monthly net wealth reporting. Daily sensitivity analysis in the range of 10–20% flash crash for public equities is a useful tool. Reporting this helps determine the impact on margin calls that might be triggered due to downward pressures in the market and is thus a worthwhile component in dashboard analysis.

Wealth gets skewed when long duration assets are funded with short duration liabilities. That is the typical asset liability maturity mismatch and is measured in terms of duration gap. It is crucial to measure and monitor this, otherwise it could lead to bankruptcy, wealth dissipation or other liquidity challenges.

The CFO will need to have a handy cash-flow forecast available for all assets and investments in the portfolio and repayment schedule for all onboarded debts. The cash-flow forecast, gleaned from regular conversations with asset managers, will allow for better management of the outflows and utilisation of the inflows.

8. Conclusion

This chapter has looked at the initial steps that need to be taken when the wealthy client wants to know the exact quantum of their wealth. The journey starts by hiring a CFO, consolidating the inventory of assets and liabilities, and preparing a dashboard that is all about constant aggregation, monitoring and valuation.

Intuitive, technology-driven timely reporting at the consolidated level of the net wealth of the wealthy client is no longer a dream. Wealthy clients have been clamouring for it for a while. Hiring an in-house CFO gets the ball rolling and then it becomes an ongoing process, as the investment portfolio is not static and market movements, regulatory changes, etc mean the 'total wealth' number changes regularly. The consolidated balance sheet can never really be put on autopilot. The role of the CFO will ensure that the dashboard is regularly curated to be reflective of market movements, where the needle moves significantly where significant wealth is concerned.

Purchase of substantial properties

Jeremy McGivern
Mercury Homesearch

1. Introduction

If you are advising a client who wishes to acquire a substantial property you have two basic goals:

- to buy the best property possible within the budget; and
- to acquire it on the most favourable terms possible.

Unfortunately, this is not as simple as it sounds. Research by Savills has shown that between 2005 and 2013 the top decile of properties in prime central London (PCL) increased by 190% while the bottom decile only increased by 63%.

This is the equivalent of you and a friend both buying a property for £3 million and one of you having a property worth £8.7 million while the other has a property worth £4.89 million.

Irrespective of whether you are buying a home or an investment, which would you prefer?

Now, you would not have achieved that 190% increase in every area and price range within PCL, but within every area and price range there will be properties that outperform and underperform. This is true for any location.

Unfortunately, while some buyers may understand that certain properties outperform, they don't really understand why, which properties will do better and by how much.

This is partly due to complacency – we all grew up in a property, so people mistakenly think that it is as simple as looking on the internet until you find a few properties you like and, then, buying one.

The apparent simplicity masks a more complex situation, which is why the masses are totally unaware of the seven most expensive mistakes property buyers make.

Indeed, every week I see poor or average properties being bought when I could literally have shown the buyers a better property – often just around the corner – which could have been acquired for the same price or less.

So, would it be a bad idea to discover what the seven most expensive mistakes buyers make are, so that your client can avoid them?

2. The question I am asked the most

"Is now a good time to buy?" Obviously, I don't know when you happen to be reading this, so you would need to contact me to give you a sensible answer. However, what I am about to tell you is information that is wilfully ignored by mainstream economists, city analysts and consequently the mainstream press. Peter Thiel, one of the co-founders of PayPal, is famous for asking the question: "What important truth do you know that most others disagree with you on?"

Well this is mine.

In the UK, US and many other property markets based on the Anglo-Saxon model, there is a property cycle that repeats like clockwork. Indeed, in the UK and US it has only failed twice – during the two World Wars.

This has been well documented and, if you understand the cycle, you can work out when is a good time to buy and when you should wait. I expect right now that you are rolling your eyes and thinking "This can't be possible. If it was that obvious why doesn't everyone know about it?"

Don't worry, you are not alone. But amazingly this information has been available for centuries. Indeed, David Ricardo wrote about the Law of Economic Rent in the early 19th century. Unfortunately, I don't have the space to go into any great detail here. Suffice to say that you might want to read studies and books by Fred Harrison, as just one example of someone who has undertaken this research.

When Tony Blair became prime minister in 1998, Fred wrote a letter to him predicting that the property market would crash in 2008. He got the date right to within a month. That is how powerful this information is and it is not just a recent phenomenon – the cycle has repeated like clockwork for centuries.

In short though, you want to ignore much of what you read about the property market in the press, even if the article quotes highly respected figures, because it is invariably too general to be of any real use.

For example, data and reports on the prime central London market are not very helpful as there are dozens and dozens of markets in PCL. What happens in the £2 million market in Belgravia will be different to what is happening in the £10 million market in Belgravia, which in turn will be different to what is happening in the £10 million market in Kensington and so on and so on.

Likewise, what is happening to prices for apartments could also be very different to what is happening in the house market even within the same area and price range. Indeed, there can be massive price variations within individual streets and even buildings. This is true for cities around the world.

But the information or views expressed in the press are often just downright wrong. Probably the most famous example from the last cycle was by one of the Bank of England's 'wise men' who in 2003 said that house prices were so overvalued that they would drop by up to "30% over the next four years". This prediction was plastered over all the newspapers because it came from a highly respected and 'reliable' source.

As it happened, prices nearly doubled between 2003 and 2007. Yet this was someone that most people listened to because he had a better understanding of economics than everyone else and access to better data, being one of the Bank of England's 'wise men'. Hmmmm ...

I can provide dozens of similar examples. History has proven, decade after decade and century after century, that you do not want to take action when the masses are jumping in – it doesn't matter if it's Tulipmania, the South Sea Bubble, Dotcoms, cryptocurrencies or property. Warren Buffett's quote "be fearful when others are greedy and greedy when others are fearful" is absolutely right.[1]

Yet most buyers sit on the sidelines when it is a fantastic time to buy because they are waiting for 'certainty'. They want to feel safe and so buy when everyone else does. Ironically, they rely on the papers to tell them it's safe which is invariably the wrong time – cast your minds back to 2006 and 2007 when the last of the bears capitulated and the experts were telling us that "it was different this time!", "prices do only go up!" and "we had a new paradigm".

In other words, we went from fear to irrational exuberance and animal spirits. Please do not make the same mistake.

So, you must take a different approach to the masses if you want to be successful. Be greedy when others are fearful. Likewise, the masses tend to wade into the market in a panic and buy indiscriminately. Hopefully the figures at the start of this chapter by Savills show you why you mustn't do this. You must be more astute in advising your client.

---

1 www.investopedia.com/articles/investing/012116/warren-buffett-be-fearful-when-others-are-greedy.asp.

So what do you need to do? Well, the good news is that there are a few simple steps you need to follow to ensure that you find the best homes or investments and then acquire them on the most favourable terms possible.

Please do not be fooled by the simplicity of some of these tactics. I have been advising the world's most successful families, businesspeople and entrepreneurs on their property acquisitions for over 18 years. What I am about to reveal has been tested and proven to work.

Ironically, most people probably dismiss these proven methods because they seem too simple. Please don't make the same mistake.

3. The easiest way to negotiate a price reduction

What I am about to tell you is not glamorous or exciting, which is why most buyers fail to undertake this most basic and important step. However, if you implement what I am about to show you, the results will be exceptional and the good news is that you can delegate most of the work.

Quite simply, you must be prepared. I warned you this wasn't exciting but it is massively important. Fortunately for you, most buyers do not treat the purchase of a home as a business transaction. Consequently, they are ill prepared. You must not make the same mistake.

Why? So that your client is in a position to act swiftly when you find your perfect home or fantastic investment. If not, then it is likely that you will suffer the frustration of losing it to another buyer. I have also often been able to secure advantageous terms for our clients or had offers accepted which were not the highest put forward, simply because we made sure we were able to act more quickly than anyone else.

One classic example was a building we acquired for a member in Kensington in 2009. The property comprised three flats, which the owners had planned to convert back to a house. The attraction of the building was that it included the original artist's studio with fantastic light and double height rooms, that is, 8m-high ceilings.

However, we had discovered that the owners had got themselves into serious financial trouble and needed to sell quickly. We were able to secure the property at a very favourable price simply because we had ensured that our clients were fully prepared for such an eventuality and could exchange contracts in three days.

Likewise, imagine you were selling a property and you had two offers: one from a person who had been a bit indecisive and who could not provide the name of their solicitor or show proof of funds; the other from someone who included their solicitor's details in the offer letter, together with a letter confirming the funds were available and a clear timeframe within which the transaction would be completed.

Would it be absurd to suggest that you would be more inclined to agree terms with the latter?

And you can put your client in a strong position with some very basic preparation:

3.1 Have the finances in place

However you plan to finance the acquisition, you have to ensure your financier is aware of your plans so that he or she can move quickly when asked.

If you require a mortgage or financing, it is essential that this is agreed in principle before you start looking and that you have a good, experienced broker or banker who can organise swift approval of the mortgage when it is required.

3.2 Seek tax advice

This is absolutely essential. Tax rules keep changing, so it is vital that you have a team of advisers who can formulate the most tax-efficient way for you to acquire your property in any given jurisdiction.

I have heard horror stories where buyers have bought a property and then looked into the tax issues. In the worst instances they have ended up paying double the cost of the house because they have used funds that were in fact liable to double taxation and then bought in an inefficient manner (in terms of tax).

I cannot stress this point enough, because even if buying a home, the long-term returns can be severely affected by not having the right advice from the start.

You must have this organised prior to making an offer and you must also advise your financier or mortgage broker if you are not buying in your own name as it could well affect the financing. If you don't then there will be delays which may cause you to lose the property. In the UK, the vendor can pull out of the agreement at any time, especially if the transaction is taking too long.

Why take this risk? Prepare for Stamp Duty Land Tax and other purchase taxes.

3.3 Instruct a solicitor

It is essential that you use a solicitor who specialises in property transactions in the city in which you are buying. You would not rely on a criminal expert to work on a corporate case, so do not instruct a solicitor who is not a property specialist.

They do not have to be based in the city in which you are buying but they must be experienced in handling transactions in that city otherwise unnecessary delays can occur. For example, if the solicitor is not used to dealing with Grosvenor Estate leases in London, then it can create huge delays and complications.

They must be available to act as soon as you are ready to make a purchase. Therefore, you should have instructed a solicitor to act for you before you even start looking for a property. There are anti-money laundering laws which require solicitors to check identifications and the source of funds before a transaction can proceed. This will be more complicated if a specialist structure is being used.

3.4 Be available

You may need to view properties at short notice. Obviously, this may not always be possible, but if you have people whose opinion you trust, ask them to view properties for you.

If you are well prepared this will be the basic foundation for your success. If you are not, I can guarantee you will:

- Miss the best opportunities. Our best acquisitions have always been made when we have been able to move swiftly and pre-empt other buyers.
- Have to offer more to make your bid more attractive than that of another buyer who can move more quickly than you.
- Lose the property even if you have agreed a price and been sent the contract. The delays caused by your lack of preparation will mean the seller will lose confidence in your ability to complete the purchase. They will allow other potential buyers to acquire the property. You will have wasted a lot of time, energy and money.

Important note: Property transactions are often complicated and can take time. In the UK, there is no legally binding agreement until you have exchanged contracts. Agreeing on the price is *not* the end of the negotiation and is *not* legally binding.

Frankly, there is a lot more you need to do on this subject, but this should stand you in good stead.

4. How can you find the best opportunities?

If someone is buying a property for less than £1 million then you can probably get away with relying on the websites. However, if your client is acquiring a property for over £1 million you really need to have a better strategy. And the higher the budget, the more important this becomes.

What do you think 90+% of buyers do? They rely on websites and email, hoping that technology will make life easier. And indeed it is easier, but is it effective? If everyone else is using the websites and simply emailing the agents do you really expect to gain an advantage and have first refusal on the best properties?

So, you need to do something different. You need to actually speak to the estate agents on a regular basis. Why? Because it will make you stand out, you will build a relationship and therefore be the person they call about properties before they become widely available.

But remember, you need to be very clear on what the agent's role is because it can vary from country to country. In some, they will act for both the buyer and seller. In others, like the UK, estate agents should really be called sales agents.

This puts buyers at a disadvantage:

- Estate agents are employed by owners. They are legally obliged to sell their clients' properties for the highest price possible and on the most favourable terms possible.
- You are not the priority. Each agent can have over one hundred buyers registered with him/her. As friendly as the agents may be, they are not concerned who buys the property as long as a full price is achieved for their client, the seller.
- Their focus is not to find you your perfect home, but to sell any one of their clients' properties to any one of the 'applicants' (estate agent jargon for buyers) on their books.

This does not mean that you should avoid the agents but you have to be very clear on their role in the transaction and their motivations because this will be critical when it comes to the negotiations, and I will comment on that later.

Nevertheless, the agents will probably be your main source of properties. But, you cannot rely on them to contact you – most are simply not that organised or you will simply be added to an email list with hundreds of other buyers.

You need to ensure that you are at the top of their list of 'preferred buyers', so that you are the first to hear about the best opportunities when they become available. Therefore you need to:

- Register with every estate agent in your target area. In the UK, the agents can normally only show you the properties on which they have been directly instructed. Therefore, you need to be registered with every suitable agent to ensure that you do not miss out on the best opportunities. At the time of writing there are 223 estate agencies in prime central London. If you only register with 10 agents you are immediately reducing the probability and likelihood of success.
- Do not rely on the internet. Everyone is using it and the best properties often sell before going onto the internet or are never openly marketed. Indeed Savills has reported in the past that 46% of properties on its books at £2+ million are *only* available privately, and Knight Frank has reported that more than 30% of sales of £2+ million homes and 52% of the £5+ million are off-market properties.
- To be the first to see the best properties, you must call the agents at least once a week and do not rely on email, which is impersonal and will be deleted and forgotten.
- Provide a clear list of criteria for the estate agents and they will see that you are serious and focused on the search. The clearer the requirements, the less of your time will be wasted.
- Let the agents know you are organised and can move quickly. Ultimately they want any sale to go through fast, so that they can earn their commission. Show them that you are prepared.
- View properties whenever possible or have a representative view them on your behalf. Meeting the agents is vital for being front of mind.

5. Brief tips on viewing properties

I find this an extraordinary fact, but according to research carried out by the *Daily Telegraph* the average property buyer spends just 96 minutes in total viewing potential properties before they buy.

This is 46 minutes less than people typically spend choosing a holiday or buying a computer. Does this strike you as an intelligent approach to acquiring a multi-million-pound asset?

Consequently, you need to have a standard plan for each viewing, so that you consider all the possible issues. This is especially important because it is very easy to be attracted to a property because of the stunning façade or beautiful artwork and furnishings inside, which can distract you from issues which are not immediately noticeable but could be hugely problematic.

A classic example of this is aeroplane noise; parts of Chelsea are directly under the flight path to Heathrow, which will obviously have repercussions if you are a light sleeper and the building does not allow air conditioning and/or double glazing.

You need to have a list of questions that you ask at every viewing and you must take notes. If nothing else, this will give you a great reference point for when you need to calculate the fair value of a property, because you will need this information to help make an accurate judgement. Here are a few tips.

5.1 Do not dismiss a property before you have viewed it

Initially it is worth seeing as many properties as possible to get a feel for what is available and to make sure you haven't inadvertently discounted a potential style of property. You will also quickly learn how to read between the lines of the agents' details.

5.2 Check the curtains

This sounds ridiculous, but I am serious. Many rooms are made to look dark and dreary by oversized curtains. Sometimes you can uncover a gem simply by pulling back the curtains to reveal more light.

5.3 Don't judge a book by its contents

Don't be swayed by the 'developer's finish', artwork that won't be included in the sale, the smell of scented candles or the fresh bread that they just happen to be baking .... You have to look at the 'bones' of the property.

Conversely, you must also look past the hideous garden, peeling paint and curious furniture to see if the property suits your needs. A property can often seem smaller than it is simply because of the number of people or the amount of furniture in it. Try to imagine what it will be like once you have decorated and furnished the property to your tastes.

Most buyers are not able to do this. As just one example of this, we acquired a fantastic house for a client that had been on the market for about nine months. It had been slightly overpriced at £5.25 million. Over the nine-month period the price was reduced to £4.5 million, but still no one was buying despite the fact that the price was very reasonable – £4.75 million would have been fair value in our opinion – and prices were increasing rapidly at the time.

As it happened, we agreed to represent a client whose requirements were a close match for the house. Understandably, the client questioned why what seemed to be such a good house at such a reasonable price was not selling.

Our view was, first, potential buyers were being put off simply by the fact that no one else was bidding. The perception was that there must be something intrinsically wrong with the house, which was the same question our client was posing.

But, this is a classic example of herd mentality. Just because no one else was buying it doesn't mean there was something wrong. You have to do your own research. Likewise, you do not want to rush into buying just because everyone else is – you must do your own research (how many people would have avoided Bernie Madoff if they had commissioned their own due diligence?).

Secondly, some of the decor was rather garish; the agents had advised the seller to repaint the house and remove the floor-to-ceiling lime green suede in the master bedroom – but he was unwilling to do so.

It was clear to us that these two circumstances combined were putting off buyers. Consequently, we negotiated a further discount and then spent a minimal amount rectifying the decor.

6. The most expensive mistake you can make and how to avoid it

I am often asked what is the biggest discount I have negotiated on a property. Unfortunately, this misses the point completely. The size of the discount is only relevant if the property is fairly valued. Negotiating a discount of 20% is no good if the property was 50% overvalued in the first place.

As an example, I was negotiating on a property that was on the market at £6 million. If I had not known the real value and if I had believed that a 25% discount (ie, a purchase price of £4.5 million) represented a brilliant piece of negotiating, then my client would have overpaid by roughly £1 million.

Obviously, this is an extreme example, but if you want to make an astute acquisition, accurate information is essential. If you have a good feel for values then you will spot the bargains and be able to move before anyone else. You will also avoid unwittingly overpaying.

Unbelievably, people spend very little time doing the necessary research or calculations. Consequently, buyers needlessly waste hundreds of thousands of pounds – and often considerably more – when some good research was all that was required.

I am not suggesting that the price you calculate will be the price that you pay. What you want, though, is to be able to make an informed decision.

Although we advise our clients on price, we also back up our valuations with accurate information. We have a huge database of recently sold properties that includes floorplans and detailed information on each property.

Unfortunately, accurate comparable data is not easy for the average buyer to obtain. The data is invariably incomplete and therefore dangerously misleading. Remember the estate agent is paid by the seller to obtain the best terms possible. Therefore, he or she is likely to give you comparators that enhance *their* position. *These may not be the best comparators!*

So, when you collate the data you must compare like for like. It sounds obvious, but this is not always easy as prices can vary massively in the same street for one reason or another. Indeed, they can vary in the same building.

Therefore, you must be very careful in what you use for comparators. Double check all information and find as many comparators as possible. Only once you have a good idea of what similar properties have sold for can you start making an informed decision on what you should be offering to acquire the property.

6.1 Points to consider when making your valuation

- How does the price compare per square foot to similar homes in the area? This should only be used as a rough guide as there are many other factors to take into consideration.
- How long is the lease in comparison to the comparators you are using?
- Is the condition better?
- Is there parking?
- How strong is the market? Is the market racing up or is it stabilising before further falls? You cannot tell for certain, but you need to assess the state of the market.
- How many similar properties are available? Is there an oversupply?
- How many comparators do you have? If you only have one or two, you need to be very careful. It is possible that that purchaser paid a huge premium and so the price may not be a true indication of fair value. Conversely, the buyer may have negotiated an extremely good price, so you may be put off

making an offer because the property you like seems overpriced in comparison when in fact it may still be a good buy.

The most important information is often related to the owners of the property themselves. Some useful questions to ask the agents and the owners include:

- How long has the property been on the market?
- How many viewings have you done in that time?
- How many offers have you had?
- Why do you think you have not had any offers?
- How did you calculate the asking price?
- What price do you think they would accept?
- Why are they selling? Where are they moving to and have they found somewhere to buy?

The better the relationship you have with the agent, the more information you will uncover and they may let slip a vital detail. This could make all the difference in the negotiation.

7. Six ways to negotiate significant price reductions

It is mildly absurd to discuss negotiation strategy and tactics in as brief a space as I have here. After all, there have been numerous books – both good and bad – written on the subject down the years. So, unfortunately, I can't give you two or three fail-proof secrets which will work in every situation. Such 'tricks' simply don't exist and anyone who tells you otherwise is probably a con artist.

However, it has been scientifically proven that humans react to stimuli in certain ways and if you understand how to use this to your advantage then you will be far more successful in negotiations – be they in business, property or with your children!

Here are six essential tips to help you achieve the best price possible.

7.1 Work out your walk-away price and terms before you start the negotiation

Most buyers only have an arbitrary idea of what this figure is. More often than not, they just start with an offer below the asking price and wait to see how the seller responds.

But how do you expect to be successful when you don't have a very clear vision of the price and terms you want to achieve? How can you build a negotiation strategy without this in mind? So you need to spend time establishing what is fair value and what the maximum price you are willing to pay is. This figure should not change unless you discover more information during the negotiation which has a material effect on your calculations.

It is very important to portray throughout the negotiation that you are not afraid to walk away from the property.

7.2 You will not succeed with logic

The default position for the naive negotiator is to look at comparable properties and bombard the seller with logical arguments as to why the property is worth what you think it is using pound per square foot comparisons and other such indicators. Unfortunately, we humans are influenced far more by our emotions than by logic.

Therefore, it is imperative that you build rapport with everyone involved in the negotiation, including the estate agent. This does not mean that you have to become their best friend, but it has been proven that people are 31% more likely to do business with you and agree to your requests if they like you. The best way to create rapport is to ask lots of questions and actively listen to the answers so that you understand what they really want. The main motivator is rarely the highest price.

A useful exercise is to envisage yourself in the seller's shoes to get an idea of what they are feeling and thinking. I know this sounds mildly odd and a bit 'airy fairy' but you will be surprised by the insights it will give you.

Important note: this is not part of aiming for a win–win outcome. Such negotiating goals may work when looking at something simple like sharing an apple, but life tends to be more complicated. If you aim for win–win, you will probably concede too much (conversely, you don't want to batter the other side into submission as I will explain later).

7.3 You want them to reduce their price before you even make an offer

But you will have more success with this if you let them think that they are in control. Most negotiators start with something like: "The price is too high, all the other properties in the street have sold for £x per square foot, so I am offering £x per square foot too which equals £y". Instead, you might want to say: "Sorry I'm confused. Please could you help me – how did you reach this valuation?" The agent will often admit that their valuation was lower than the guide price or that the owner will accept considerably less than you initially thought.

The point is you are putting the onus on them to think about the price. You have reversed the responsibility while making them think they are in control.

7.4 Beware anchors

By starting with a high price, good negotiators set or anchor expectations higher than they should be. Many buyers are often reluctant to put in offers that are considered 'low' and very often creep up in the negotiations until they overpay. Be very clear on what the property is worth to you and then use an appropriately low anchor to reset expectations if the seller is playing hardball.

If it's a weak market, make it clear what they will lose if they don't reach an agreement with you, eg, they may have to wait several months if not longer for another offer and the market may well be lower. Do they want to undersell their house in six months' time because they didn't deal with you now? What is the opportunity cost for them of not transacting quickly? By the way, this isn't just financial, so highlight the emotional cost to them which will be far more persuasive.

7.5 If you have to offer first you can give them a range

For example, "Well an investor would offer £4 million–£4.25 million, so my offer is £4 million". However, only use this approach if you have a very clear understanding of valuations and obviously the range you give is lower than what you will be willing to pay. Just as the seller has tried to anchor you with a high asking price, you need to change that dynamic.

They probably won't accept this range, but you will have planted your own anchor. So, later in the negotiation, if they feel they have got you to pay more than you wanted, then *the other side will feel that they have won* even if the opposite is true. This is important as nothing is legally binding until you have exchanged contracts, which can take time. Are the sellers more likely to follow through with the sale if they think they have been battered into accepting a poor price?

7.6 Massaging the sellers' and estate agent's ego

This is far more important than you would imagine, so it is imperative that you don't let yours get in the way. Ultimatums do work in certain situations but more often than not, you will achieve much better results by letting the sellers think they have won.

8. Conclusion

The ideas above are just a few tactics you want to use and this is really not even the tip of the iceberg. Every negotiation is different and there are dozens and dozens of strategies, tactics and techniques you will need to use together if you want to negotiate the lowest price and best terms possible.

One final point. The way property is bought and sold will vary from country to country. However, it is vital to remember that the negotiation doesn't end when you have agreed the price. It only ends once you have taken over legal ownership of the property.

There are all sorts of things that can go wrong between agreeing the price and this happening. For example, in the UK it can take several weeks if not months between agreeing a price and taking legal ownership. Nothing is legally binding and either side can pull out of the transaction without any penalty. So, it is important that you monitor the solicitors and surveyors and maintain good communication with everyone else involved.

Irrespective of whether you are buying a home or an investment property, if you're not prepared and don't approach the opportunity with deliberate detachment, it is very easy to throw away hundreds of thousands, if not millions, of pounds. You can make a poor purchase, pay too much or waste money by paying tax unnecessarily. In the worst cases you can do all of these – and many people do.

Fortunately, most of the steps you need to take to avoid these mistakes are relatively simple. For many they appear too simple or boring to make a difference, which is why most buyers fail to follow them. Consequently, they make average or poor acquisitions and fail to put adequate structures in place to protect their wealth.

Admittedly, you'll need to spend some time and energy following these steps, but over the entire process they are guaranteed to save you time, stress and money.

You have the choice – follow the boring, disciplined approach that *works* or try the haphazard approach adopted by most buyers and hope you get lucky. Which will you take?

Risk assessment and strategic insurance planning

Linda Bourn
Crystal, Alliant Private Client

1. Introduction

Managing risk is an essential part of advising wealthy clients. Most people become familiar with the meaning of risk based upon what they have experienced personally or have seen in the news. Lately there has been a diversity of risks reported in the news that have impacted people globally. The COVID-19 pandemic has created a new normal for how we need to manage health risks by adhering to practices set forth by governments, their health protection agencies and leading epidemiologists.[1] Climate change has created billion dollar natural disasters (eg, wildfires in Australia and the United States, floods in Venice, Italy[2]) and data breaches have exposed the personal information of millions of people (eg, Equifax 2017, Facebook 2019, Marriott International 2019[3]).

The diversity of risks, which arise on a regular basis, creates the need for wealthy clients to evaluate their own risk profile and plan for unforeseen events.

This chapter discusses the importance of personal risk management, where core components include: assessing risk by family risk mapping, risk mitigation, strategic insurance planning and discussing risk during annual meetings to keep pace with changing risk profiles (see Figure 1).

It will provide advisers with an annual risk assessment process that can be applied to the diversity of risk exposures faced by wealthy clients.

1 World Health Organization (WHO), COVID-19 Strategy Update, 14 April 2020.

2 Amy Gunia, "Bushfires Are Raging Outside Every Major City in Australia. They're Going to Get Worse", *TIME*, December 2019; National Oceanic and Atmospheric Administration (NOAA), *Billion-Dollar Weather and Climate Disasters Mapping – United States 2016–2019*; Erica J Lyman, "After Record Floods, Venice Assesses the Damager and Braces for More Climate-Related Disasters", *Fortune*, 14 November 2019.

3 Jonathan Berr, "Equifax Breach Exposed Data for 143 Million Consumers", *CBS News*, 7 September 2017; Kenneth Kiesnoski, "5 of the Biggest Data Breaches Ever", *CNBC Personal Finance*, 30 July 2019.

2. Personal risk management

When assessing risk it is helpful for families to see the big picture. Over the years of working with global families, a couple of common questions have consistently surfaced: What's the best way to understand our risks? Can you help us take the first step? A risk assessment begins with an annual process that helps the family see their holdings through a risk management lens.

Having an established assessment process will benefit the family greatly. The clear process can create annual goals, map family risks, review risk mitigation measures, assess insurance strategy and monitor the programme annually to address necessary changes. This annual approach can help the family maintain smart risk and insurance management solutions that are tailored specifically for their unique risks, which may change over time.

Figure 1. Key steps

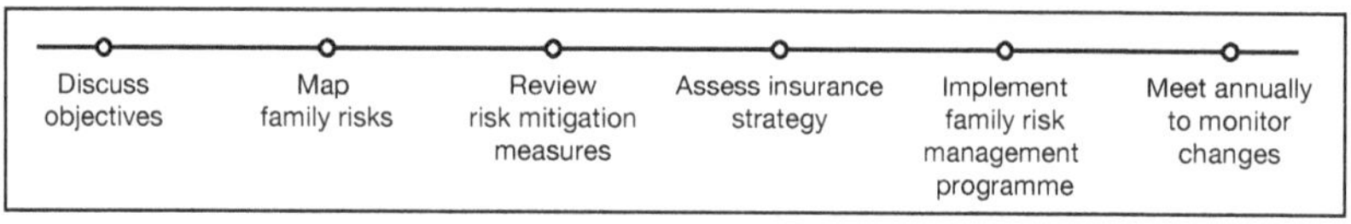

Source: Crystal, Alliant Private Client

3. The family risk map

A risk map is a way to simplify the concept of risk and to build awareness of the various exposures associated with the family holdings.

Many families and their advisers have developed what they refer to as their 'organisational chart', which describes their holdings by category, as well as entities, and illustrates how they connect to each other. While it expresses what is owned, it does not map the risk associated with ownership.

In order to map out that risk, Table 1 can be used to paint the larger family risk profile. The map includes categories, risk exposures of the specific holding and some key questions to ask which can help provide clarity on the category.

Figure 2 is a sample family risk map which demonstrates the categories that generate risks (property, digital, roles and travel – located in the left column). The map highlights what is owned and includes some high-level questions to help support the risk assessment discussion with the family and their advisers. In practice, this map would reflect a family's specific holdings and risk exposures.

Table 1. Risk exposures

Category description	Risk exposures	Key questions to consider
• Property holdings • Digital risk profile • Roles • Travel planning	Unique risk exposures that apply to each category	These questions can help understand the risk profile of each category and holding

Source: Crystal, Alliant Private Client

Figure 2. Family risk map

	Description	Risk exposures	Key questions
Property	• Real estate • Art collections • Unique assets, aviation, yachts, farm, ranch	• Gulf/coastal flooding zones • Hurricane/typhoon regions • Wildfire areas • Aircraft hull & liability exposure • Yacht physical damage & protection & indemnity liability • Farm/ranch property & liability	• What is planned over next 12 months? (purchases, renovations, loaning artwork, transferring property ownership to LLC, Trust) • Describe the management of aviation and yacht. Who advises you on care and maintenance of these assets? How are pilots and crew hired and managed? • What mitigation measures are in place for properties in natural disaster areas? • What is the scope of operations of the farm or ranch? • How is insurance managed for these assets?
Digital	• Devices • Home networks	• Personal data breach • Cyber financial loss/extortion • Ransomware • System attack-unauthorised access	• How are you limiting exposure to cyber crime? • Is your social media presence creating risk or proactively managed to limit risk? • Are mobile device settings securing your devices and protecting data if your device is lost or stolen?
Roles	• Public profile • Boards • Trustee • Employer	• Personal liability • Director's & officer's liability • Professional liability • Employment practices liability	• Do you have a process for managing the hiring and termination of domestic staff?
Travel	• Adventure travel • Remote locations • International locations	• Country/city specific risks (natural disasters, crime, protests) • Security of accommodations	• Do you have an adequate emergency medical and security response plan? • How are you staying aware of what is happening where you travel?

Source: Crystal, Alliant Private Client

4. Risk mitigation measures

There can be a host of risk mitigation measures to consider, depending on the asset to protect. As billion dollar natural disasters have been consistently occurring globally, the graphic below can be used to help limit the impact that natural disasters have upon a client's property. Figure 3 highlights risk mitigation services for various assets and also helps to address speciality areas, including fine art.

Figure 3. Risk mitigation services

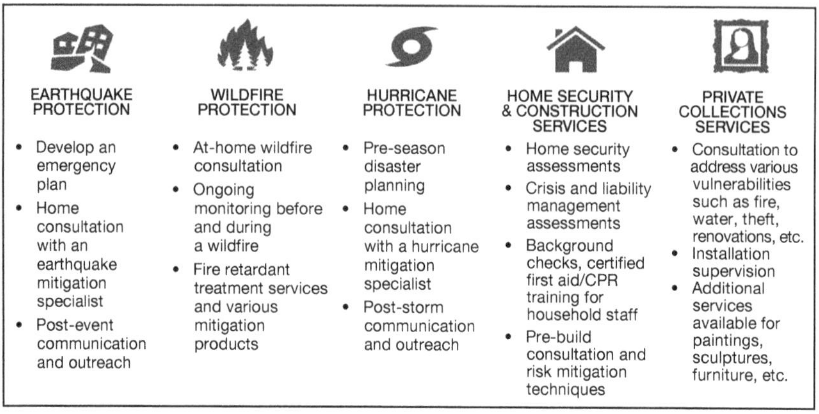

Source: Crystal, Alliant Private Client

Figure 4. Insurance review process

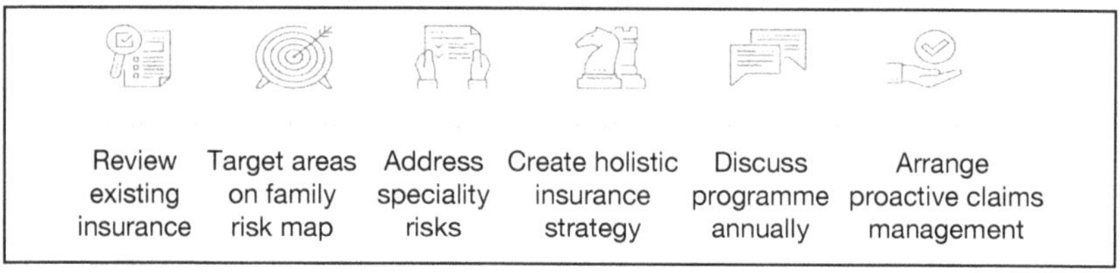

Source: Crystal, Alliant Private Client

5. Reviewing insurance

A family risk map reflects the unique risk areas. Once exposures are identified, insurance should be used as a strategic tool to mitigate those risks. The structure of an insurance programme should be strategic and tailored to respond to the family's specific risks and liabilities. Because wealthy clients have complex needs, families benefit from having a holistic strategy for insurance rather than just transactional support (ie, buying insurance to support acquisitions of property). Therefore, insurance should be a core component of wealth preservation planning.

An insurance review process (see Figure 4) should include reviewing existing insurance, confirming that policies address risks unique to the family risk map and, if needed, negotiating new policies each year to help keep pace with any new risks or changes that occur annually.

Some of the common examples of insurance that respond to family wealth risk maps are indicated in Table 2.

Table 2. Common insurance types

Insurance type	Description
Personal	Home, auto, art collections, personal liability
Natural disasters	Wildfire, flood, earthquake, windstorm-hurricanes/typhoons
Domestic staff	Workers' compensation, employment practices liability
Special risk	Kidnap, ransom, extortion
Unique assets	Aircraft, yacht (requires risk and insurance knowledge to evaluate the type of asset, risk exposures and specialised insurance)

Source: Crystal, Alliant Private Client

6. Review ownership entities as reflected within an insurance structure

Wealthy clients often have a higher number of ownership entities, such as LLCs and trusts, or other entities established for various purposes, such as shared assets, domestic staff and transfer of wealth to the next generation, and unique assets like art, aviation and yachts.

Ownership entities should be reflected within an insurance programme for the asset they own. For example, if a home is owned by an LLC that entity should be properly reflected for coverage under the insurance policy for the home.

Figure 5. Holistic risk assessment process

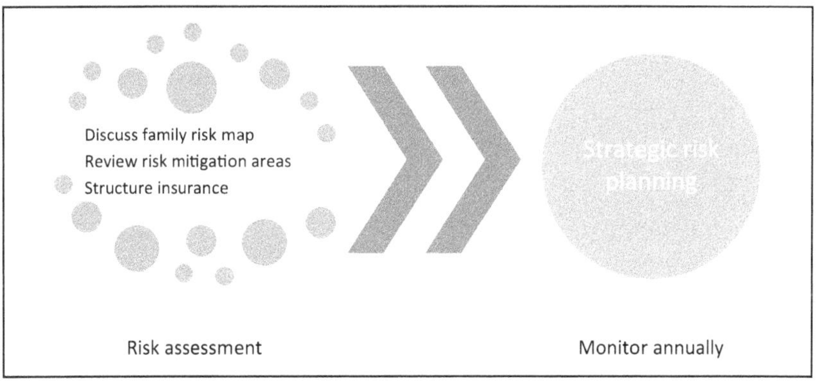

Source: Crystal, Alliant Private Client

7. A strategic personal risk management programme

The holistic risk assessment process (see Figure 5) should result in all of the pieces coming together. The annual process should help families understand their risks and put a strategic plan in place which can then be monitored annually.

8. Annual client and adviser meeting

Annual client meetings should incorporate a discussion surrounding managing risk for global clients. By bringing together an interdisciplinary team and thoroughly reviewing risk, as well as discussing insurance planning needs, one can ensure the changes are tracked and the family's wealth is protected.

The objectives of an annual meeting, aside from reviewing all the details of the family risk map, insurance and changes, are listed below.

- Assess the characteristics and behaviours that define the family's unique risk map;
- Turn heightened risk awareness stemming from current events into an opportunity to educate the family about risks of all types; and
- Utilise an interdisciplinary approach and collective knowledge when managing risk for the family. A legal adviser to the family may view a liability situation differently from the perspective of a tax adviser.

9. Summary

Assessing risk should be a part of your annual planning process. Family risk mapping, risk mitigation and strategic insurance planning are all important areas to discuss during your client meetings. The benefit of a holistic assessment is the family being risk aware so that measures can be taken through proper mitigation or insurance to protect family assets.

Evaluating general risks: the prepared mind

John Deverell
www.thepreparedmind.net

1. Introduction

It is a truism to say that everyone faces risks. As with most things, it is important to find an appropriate balance – in this case between complacency and stress-inducing worry. Most of us will recall the children's story of Henny Penny, also known as Chicken Licken, a folk tale with a point. The chicken thinks the sky is about to collapse. As a result of this story the expression 'the sky is falling' has become a stock phrase for a hysterical and usually mistaken belief that disaster is imminent. Conversely, to continue the avian analogy, it is no good to emulate the ostrich with its head in the sand, hoping – like Charles Dickens's Mr Micawber – that troubles will go away and that 'something will turn up'.

The reality is that most things that go wrong are preceded by some indication, or early warning, of difficult times ahead. They might therefore be described as 'predictable surprises'. At the time of the 2003 Iraq war, US Defense Secretary Mr Donald Rumsfeld was ridiculed by many for talking about "known unknowns" but his expression captured the notion.

And in his best-selling book *The Black Swan*, Nassim Taleb describes the phenomenon of unlikely events that have an extreme impact. 'Black swans' will appear in our lives at some time or another.

A comprehensive risk assessment process provides a systematic basis to prioritise and prepare accordingly, reducing the likelihood and the impact of events that might otherwise evolve into personal or family crises.

However, the risk assessment process is not without its own dangers. This might sound paradoxical – after all, how can a risk assessment itself be risky? That depends on how it is conducted and, having gone through the process, how it is then used.

First, the risk assessment must be 'dynamic', that is to say that it needs to be updated as situations change. But all too often the risk assessment sits on the shelf until the next formal review period.

And in itself, while useful as a foundation, a risk assessment is no good unless taken forward as the basis for a contingency plan.

Secondly, the impact of a risk materialising is often expressed solely in financial terms, but that fails to take account of the personal dimension. For example, insurance might compensate for the loss of financial value, but – as we are frequently reminded – 'money is not everything'.

Thirdly, while risk registers typically include a column for 'likelihood' and another column for 'impact', they usually – and I believe wrongly – omit to have a column for risk velocity. While many risks are comparatively 'slow burn', things can go wrong very quickly where there are reputational implications. That needs to be noted accordingly.

And, finally, the fact that a risk assessment has been completed can breed complacency – which is tantamount to an invitation to be blind-sided by an adverse event when one's back is turned.

2. Political risks

Having covered these generalities, I will deal with two particular risks: political and reputational. When conversations turn to those items, many families tend to put them fairly low down their list of concerns – most of the time.

Political risks can apply to investments in particular countries. They might also be relevant if a younger family member plans to travel to an unstable country, perhaps on a gap year, to enjoy an adventurous holiday before starting university. Worst case, that person might have to change their travel plans, leave quickly or find another way out if flights are grounded. Indeed, that has been one of many adverse features connected with the COVID-19 crisis.

And more stable countries are not without political risk either: for example, there are concerns from time to time that elections might bring in governments actively hostile to personal wealth. For example, the possibility of the UK Labour party led by Mr Jeremy Corbyn being elected in 2019 was sufficiently worrying for a significant number of British residents to shift assets offshore – including consideration of moving residences out of the country altogether.

In such cases the 'risk velocity' is relatively low, given that there is plenty of warning of political intent through manifestos and the like.

3. Reputational risks

As for reputational risk: this includes any action, event or situation that could adversely affect a family's, an individual's or a business's reputation. Views differ as to whether this is a category of risk in its own right or whether it is a result of some other risk materialising. But increasingly it is perceived as a specific risk that needs to be considered as such.

In any event, reputational risk has a markedly different velocity to most other risks. As Warren Buffett said: "It takes 20 years to build a good reputation and five minutes to ruin it".[1] That is especially the case in this era of social media. And, having been lost, a good reputation is hard to retrieve. As Benjamin Franklin, one of the USA's founding fathers, opined: "Glass, china and reputation are easily cracked and never well-mended".

I remember discussing reputational risk with the CEO of a family office whose most significant holding was a large slice of city property. The family had held much the same property portfolio for several hundred years. The family's name was well known but its members kept a low profile. They did not indulge in extravagant lifestyles and had always steered clear of scandal. The CEO told me: "The family regards their low profile as their best defence". On that basis he had deduced that the family's reputational risk was almost negligible. In response I pointed out that reputational damage could arise from many causes – some of them not the fault of the family. An example could be collateral risk arising from the activities of another player in the property sector. I mentioned that reputational damage could even result from falsehoods that, if not proactively countered, could harm social standing and business interests.

As a result, the family accepted a plan that I wrote to enable an appropriate and timely response to mitigate reputational damage - if and when required.

4. The implications of political and reputational risk

One way to test the extent to which a family and its office have considered the implications of political and reputational risks is to run a workshop based on possible scenarios. This is a well-honed training tool employed by the army and academia – and which I have used many times in support of commercial and family enterprises. Such workshops are easy to organise and don't need to last for more than a couple of hours. The scenarios should be written by someone who will not be a 'player' but who will help facilitate the discussions. Someone with appropriate experience from outside the family and who has an understanding – on a non-disclosure agreement basis – of the family office's interests and procedures is ideal for the role.

---

1 www.forbes.com/sites/jamesberman/2014/04/20/the-three-essential-warren-buffett-quotes-to-live-by/#305b1da96543.

Objectives of such a workshop include anticipating worst-case possibilities and preparing accordingly, thus reducing the likelihood and impact of adverse events. Such preparation is not necessarily or always expensive, since it often only requires thinking through the identified possibilities and what will need to be done in good time in order to address them.

Workshops thus provide the opportunity to understand the reputational impact of identified adverse events and the principles that govern media engagement, as well as the more practical or tangible side of what may need to be done.

In the remainder of this chapter, in very short workshop style, we will walk through a fictitious incident based on a compilation of real-time events that happen to have been relevant to a particular family. Through this scenario we pose some questions relevant to you, if you were managing this hypothetical situation.

So, let us now assume as follows:

4.1 Scenario – background

You are a member of the office that looks after the business affairs of the Inglenook family. Thomas Inglenook (a fictional name) founded the business in 1974. It manufactures domestic control systems and has made the family wealthy. Last year Thomas put in place ambitious plans for expanding the business. These include building a new factory in Eastern Europe where costs remain relatively low.

The plans are under review by the local planning authorities, as are the construction and labour permits needed to start work. The facility is due for completion by the end of this year.

In the meantime the business is renting a temporary factory in the area and production has been underway for several months.

Unfortunately, ill health has recently obliged Thomas to hand the reins to his son Rob without having had time to implement his plans fully.

Rob Inglenook's style is different to his father's. He is relatively 'hands-off'. He expects you and your colleagues in the family office to run the day-to-day affairs of the business and to deal with most contingencies.

4.2 Update

The family office has just learned that the owner of its temporary factory has been arrested. Information is scant and rumour-driven. The suggestions range from embezzling funds from government contracts, to paying bribes to local officials and to overlooking health and safety failings in his other factories. There is nothing to suggest that the factory owner's crimes are linked to his involvement with the Inglenook family business.

Note that local prosecutors have the power to question anyone and seize any evidence that they may feel is relevant to the case.

Each question listed below constitutes an invitation to discussion. There are no 'right' or 'wrong' answers and anyone on the family office team may speak during this workshop. From experience I anticipate that many relevant points will emerge.

- How should the family office navigate through the situation now facing it? In particular:
  - What questions should be asked and what tasks need to be undertaken?
  - What tools should the family office have in place for dealing with the situation?
  - What might need to be done to protect the family's interests elsewhere in the light of possible developments?
- On media issues:
  - How might the family office come up with a media strategy and what might the strategy look like?
  - What role might social media play in this situation, both proactive and reactive?
- Might the family office itself – or even the family – be legally impacted now or later?
- Is there a possible concern about the loss of confidential and proprietary information? If so, is there anything to be done?

The ensuing discussion is likely to bring out the following points, amongst others (covered here in brief outline).

- It is important to have timely compliance and legal advice on hand – with access to local lawyers of proven standing.
- Computers and files may be seized and employees taken away for questioning. The office should have the capability to respond very quickly, having already ensured full knowledge of local law and precedents. And in the event that files and computers have been taken, back-up data must be available in order to continue operations.
- There is particular value in having a retained and experienced communications adviser who can brief British and local media as well as input to social media – if appropriate (sometimes of course it is better to say nothing, and this is where good and timely judgement is important).
- There is a clear need for good due diligence and background check processes to be in place for vetting prospective employees, suppliers and enablers at home and abroad.

- Insurance is essential – but it will only cover so much.
- It is important to have a crisis plan in place, covering reputational as well as operational contingencies.
- Businesses will never grow and prosper if they don't take risks. But risks and their consequences must be fully explored before taking them on.
- Major crises are usually caused by coincidences of several contributing factors, of which the activities of the family business may be only one. If the family is operating in two or more countries experiencing political tensions, it needs to be aware that it may incur collateral damage.
- 'Bad news' or 'problems' are a feature from time to time in all enterprises. There is a danger that those who run the family office may not be made aware of the warning signals for various reasons. Therefore, a constant effort is required to ensure that information flows upwards to decision makers and in good time. And, those decision makers need to be inquisitive at all times. They can never afford to be 'asleep at the wheel'.
- And, to ensure that critical information flows to the top, the family office must instil a culture where senior people are seen to be taking full responsibility for the actions of their subordinates and where subordinates know to seek out the guidance of senior people on serious issues.
- Risks involving money are a legal and financial issue. Risks involving reputation are a moral issue. The penalty for the latter is always greater.
- A spirit of openness and honesty will always enhance reputation. Any suspicions that facts are being hidden will do the opposite.
- It is vital to be prepared to engage with the media at the earliest opportunity. The vacuum created by the failure to communicate will quickly be filled with rumour, misrepresentation, gossip and poison. The family's standing and wider interests could be adversely affected as a result.

5. Conclusion

Having a plan and a dynamic risk assessment in place – and frequently considering 'what if' type questions amongst those running the family office – will make for effective risk management. And that in turn means that risks are less likely to develop into crises. To use a simple analogy: to be able to give first aid is important, but it is not a substitute for looking after your family's and your colleagues' health – and helping others to do the same – in the first place.

Reputation management

Charlie Bain
Digitalis

1. Introduction

Just last week the telephone on my desk rang and it was a contact with some disturbing news. He was an independent consultant and leader in his field, and he'd discovered a blog site constructed on the internet in his name. The site had his photograph and biographical information on. There was an opinion piece, written in his style. Everything about it looked like it was his. Except it wasn't. The opinion piece was highly inflammatory and contentious. He'd been told that at least two potential clients had steered clear of him after reading the blog and he reckoned he'd lost business as a result.

Earlier that week a global businessman rang saying someone had defaced his Wikipedia page and posted up inaccurate material. It took a phone call to his office from a journalist for him to realise the posting had been made and for him to categorically deny it was true. Someone had maliciously tried to manipulate his reputation. As I write, the *Financial Times* has just written a large article about how Facebook are battling to close down thousands of fake accounts. The 2019 UK General Election has just concluded and one of the biggest debates centred around what pictures and words put out by political activists were fake or real. In May 2019, a video of Nancy Pelosi, the Democratic speaker of the House of Representatives, purported to show her slurring her words and apparently drunk. But this was entirely untrue, the footage had been simply manipulated and slowed down to make her appear that way. YouTube took down the video.

I could go on and on with examples I have seen over the last couple of years where the internet has been used as a tool to mould a reputation or influence a perception. In all the cases, ultimately the truth came to light. However, whether the information was true or not is, to a certain extent, irrelevant. What was important and terrifying was the uncertainty created around their existence and how that affected the reputations, albeit temporarily, of the victims. The other unavoidable fact is the ease with which a reputation can be attacked in the digital world and the sheer speed of the assault.

For some of the wealthy and successful clients and families I advise, their online reputations are becoming more and more important by the day. Picking up these attacks, analysing them and working on a strategy to counter them has spawned a new era in the skill that is reputation management. The internet has become a battle ground for narrative and counter-narrative where opinion drowns out fact and a reputation built up over many years can be ruined in a matter of seconds. It has turned the reputation management game on its head and called on new skills and quick, sound judgement. Managing a reputation, therefore, has become harder than it ever was before.

In this chapter we will look at the history of reputation management, an industry that barely existed until the late 1970s in its current guise, and the rise of digital and social media that is contributing to our growing digital footprints. We will also examine the recent trend of fake news and explore the rise of deepfake videos and audio, which I firmly believe could be the most worrying new kid on the block. For the high net worth individual, family office or company CEO, it is critical to be aware of the issues because at some stage everyone will become affected.

2. What is reputation management?

Perhaps it is best to start with why people would need a reputation manager at all and above all what it is. The first thing to say is that it's very different from public relations (PR). PR is – stripped back – generating good publicity about a person, company or product. Reputation management is more strategic and often involves not saying or publicising anything.

Having a good reputation, almost all PR professionals will agree, does not involve spin or manipulation. Your reputation is defined by what you do. If a company or individual conducts themselves improperly then, in this age of demand for transparency and digital recording, it is likely to get found out. It was Socrates who came up with the now infamous quote: "Regard your good name as the richest jewel you can possibly be possessed of. The way to gain a good reputation is to endeavour to be what you desire to appear".

3. Why is reputation management important?

The starting point for anyone has to be to endeavour to do the right thing and act properly. And whether that's a large family, corporate or start-up business, that has to come from the very top.

When I started out in journalism in the mid-1990s, I asked a more experienced colleague what was the one story which all journalists knew but could not publish. He said it was the fact that the famous British TV presenter Jimmy Savile was a paedophile. Countless newspapers had tried to run the story around that time, but Savile was so adept at denying it that they could never publish on legal grounds. He turned to his work raising money for sick children and persuaded the media that the rumours were nothing more than a joke – just because he had a popular TV programme where he worked with children. The result was that he received a knighthood and, when he died in 2011 aged 84, he passed away with his reputation intact. But to my point about your reputation being defined by what you do, he was later exposed for his horrific crimes. He could not gloss over or hide his awful actions and eventually the truth outed.

Other people have committed far less serious acts and been held to account by the media to find their reputations ruined. Some have conducted themselves with honour and tried to do the right thing but, somehow, they have made one ill-thought-through comment and the whole house of cards has come tumbling down. This is often when reputation management advice is utterly critical. In a communications crisis the subject of the scrutiny should never, in my view, take the decision on their own communications response by themselves. In fact, the one person who shouldn't devise the communications strategy is that person. In the eye of the storm they can't see the wood for the trees and often make mistakes. People often think they are saying the right or correct thing when in fact it is what they want to be the right or correct thing and the two are very different.

4. The rise of the reputation management sector

This is why the reputation management sector was born. Nick Davies, in his 2009 book *Flat Earth News*, charts the start of the modern PR era as being in the mid-1980s in the UK in particular. He said that when he started out in journalism in the 1970s, it was rare to encounter a public relations executive. Indeed, other business journalists who worked around that time remember being able to telephone a FTSE chairman or CEO, even at home, and enjoy unfettered access to company leaders without having a PR executive 'getting in the way'. Davies believes that one of the drivers of the new PR sector in the 1980s was the wave of redundancies in print journalism during that decade, meaning many journalists crossed the divide over to PR. By 2009, he said the UK had more PR professionals than it did journalists, and that has grown even more today. He also quotes a statistic to illustrate this rise: in 1979, 28% of the top 50 companies in *The Times* 1,000 list used PR agencies but just five years later 90% of them were doing so.

Back in the 1980s, most PR professionals in the City of London were focusing on the relatively mundane process of 'financial calendar' work. This essentially involved informing the correct person at the appropriate news organisation about the latest quarterly results of a listed company, issuing press releases, making sure the messaging was clear and answering questions from journalists who needed help. It was a heady era of City excess – sharp suits, fast cars and pay packets which spawned the City 'yuppie', a new breed of ostentatious, upwardly mobile, Square Mile professionals with mobile phones in their hands. Listed companies realised that paying a good PR consultant could help your share price. So the PR professionals made money and everyone was a winner. The rise of big-selling tabloids like *The Sun* also spawned a new type of relationship between PR and journalism at this end of the spectrum. *The Sun* wanted scoops and big interviews with celebrities and the celebrities wanted exposure so they would become better-known.

So PRs and tabloid journalists were forever doing deals which would benefit both of them. This cosy relationship lasted for some time and in those days it was relatively easy for a PR professional – or by this stage the new breed of reputation manager – to keep control of a reputation. A newspaper came out once a day. There was an evening paper in most towns. And there were generally three mainstream news programmes, which went out at 1pm, 6pm and 9pm. If you could control what those channels and news outlets were saying, everyone could sleep well at night knowing nothing major was going to disturb them until the next morning.

All that changed, in my view, in the 1990s with – in the UK – Sky News and the arrival of global 24-hour news channels.

These broadcasters demanded a non-stop stream of news to fill their programmes. The smallest story was picked open and expanded. Even more worrying, the channels were so hell bent on breaking the story first they would flash it up on their screens without knowing the full facts.

What happened next triggered a new need for anyone managing a reputation to be on constant alert. Comment started to drown out fact. As the story broke and the journalists would run off to collect the facts, the news channels would wheel out experts to fill airtime.

These 'talking heads' would discuss what *might* have happened rather than what *had* happened. Speculation was rife, conspiracy theories would abound and by the time the real facts had been discovered and combined the actual story was wildly different. Sound familiar? Yes, 24-hour news was really the start of the social media revolution and this kind of comment is the norm for all of us today. But when social media did explode on the scene it would change everything.

It is astonishing to think that Facebook is barely 12 years old in its current, mainstream guise. At the time of writing, it has over 2.3 billion users, which is over a quarter of the world's population. Instagram was launched some 10 years ago. Twitter was presented to the world in 2006 and took a while to gain popularity but by 2012 it had 100 million users posting 340 million Tweets a day.

I remember that around the time Twitter was new and exciting I wrote to some of my clients warning them to be careful. It may be *de rigeur* to use this shiny new tool to communicate, but it could come back to bite you. It also became apparent that anyone, literally anyone, could now have a voice or an opinion on you as an individual or company. The man on the street normally wrote a letter to a newspaper if he wanted to be heard widely. Now he could just Tweet if he was unhappy. Going back to my earlier point, however, if a company or an executive was conducting themselves appropriately, he or she had nothing to worry about. What was more concerning was what my clients might actually Tweet themselves. What they probably didn't understand was that they were creating a digital breadcrumb trail of views and opinions which may in a few years' time cause them problems. They were starting a digital journey and because it was so new, we didn't know much about it.

Fast forward a decade and sharing our business or personal lives via social media – Facebook, Instagram, Twitter – is now an unstoppable train. It is entirely normal and, in some cases, necessary. While we and our friends or colleagues project every aspect of our lives online, an uncontrolled narrative is created. As more and more historical archives about our lives get digitalised, so the picture grows. Before we know it, there is a wealth of information about us in the digital stratosphere, some we may be aware of because we posted it ourselves, but most often not. It has really redefined how we approach reputation management.

Writing in the *The International Family Offices Journal* in 2019, I recounted a story about how I had met a senior member of a private family business who told me how he was the opposite of the new breed of social media 'sharers'. He had never used social media, never registered an account, never posted a picture. This person was in his 50s and was convinced that there was nothing online about him. However, to his surprise and dismay, when he 'deep' Googled himself he found articles and records detailing his business dealings 20 years ago readily available on the internet. How could this be? It is very simple. The world has moved firmly into the digital age and paper archives are now gradually moving online. Day by day, databases are being created for people to access information instantly, which fits neatly with the modern-day craving of receiving information immediately. Take Companies House in the UK, for instance. That used to be a paid-for service. Now it is free for all to access and with that comes the potential for people to find ages, in some cases home addresses, of shareholders and directors of companies.

5. The communications crisis

One of the biggest areas in which private families and businesspeople run into trouble is during a communications crisis – when a company or individual is catapulted into the limelight. This may be of their own making: the company they run has hit financial trouble; they have let corporate governance slip and an error has been made public; they have said something in an open forum which has been reported and sensationalised. Or it may be of someone else's making: a disgruntled ex-employee has suddenly posted an allegation on social media or given a story about a family to a newspaper or TV station.

Very quickly – and I cannot stress this enough – the situation can get out of hand. I work with some of the best communications advisers around and every one of them will say that if you don't get to hear about and then get on top of a communications crisis within 10 minutes of it breaking, you run the risk of losing control. Citizen journalists and hostile stakeholders can quickly gain a voice. Opinion is manifold. Most of all, amid the feeding frenzy around a family or business's misfortune, people push the boundaries and nothing is off limits in this new age of digital data availability.

A family business which has had an extremely and deliberately low profile for decades can very quickly be profiled. Hostile third parties, criminals or cyber hackers and journalists can skilfully and efficiently navigate through the wealth of information online – a precious digital library at their fingertips.

The historical, irrelevant comments made in an interview by the CEO suddenly become very relevant indeed. A run-of-the-mill

Twitter posting from two years ago is suddenly picked through for nuance. Worst of all, you unexpectedly and bafflingly find the CEO's daughter or son's Facebook picture of the family holiday on their personal yacht in Ibiza featured in Mail Online. A perfectly engineered story about them – with their help – is constructed in seconds.

Another factor which has emerged in the last few years is the increasingly personal attacks on senior businesspeople. There are two reasons for this in my view. The first is an increasingly anti-wealth agenda which has formulated itself mainly since the 2008/9 financial crisis. Just one example of this is the way traditional tax havens have become the focus of activist anger. The second reason is because there is simply more information about them online in order to conduct those attacks. Twenty years ago, it would have taken a journalist days, or even weeks, to find someone who would be prepared to talk about a business or a senior business leader. Nowadays they can probably find what they are looking for in seconds. Either because the information is readily available online, in other words 'ready-made' for them. Or because to find someone who might know that individual is now so much easier due to the interconnected world of social media.

6. Protecting your client's reputation in the digital age

So, what is the best course of action to insulate and protect your client from a quick-fire reputational crisis in the digital age? How can a family business limit the damage to a reputation or insulate itself from inconvenient or sensationalist reporting, be it via citizen bloggers or trusted media?

One of the first steps is knowing what's out there about your client. We often talk about the Google first page being a global business card and that is true. What is on that first page of Google will be seen globally in an instant. With the advent of the smart phone, people are scrolling up and down page one of Google more and making instant decisions as to whether they want to do business with people. Interestingly, time and again, the research shows that only a small percentage of searchers venture on to page two. But that is only a tiny proportion of the story. A bit like the senior member of a private family in his 50s mentioned above, it's what you don't know is out there which will amaze you. Most of this information is contained in an area called the deep web. This is not to be confused with the dark web where a lot of illegal activity takes place and frankly is tiny. The deep web, according to commonly used estimates, contains around

96% of what is out there about us and it is publicly available. The remaining 4% is indexed by search engines.

Scouring the deep web and finding what is out there about your client is a critical first step in preparing for a crisis. This includes examining social media, public records, databases. You name it, if it's out there you need to know about it.

The next step is to analyse that for digital and reputational risk. Is your client happy that their home address is online? Or the floor plans of their house from the estate agent's website when they bought it? Or the interview they did with a student newspaper 30 years ago? Or the Tweet they made in 2013? What would happen if that was discovered and used against them in the present day?

Social media postings are often a vulnerability. I hate to apportion blame on the next generation for this – because genuinely they are not always the culprits – but often it is the 18–35 generation who have posted something online which, if found, could affect the reputation of a family business. Often this business has an impeccable reputation which has been built up over many, many years. And that one posting could ruin that reputation in seconds.

I always think it's a mistake to ban the next generation from social media and it is rarely the answer. For many, it is part of their everyday lives and a ban just alienates them from their peer group and makes their social lives awkward. Likewise, I would never advise a senior business person to stop giving interviews to a newspaper or live the life of a digital hermit. But being aware of how information can be used against you does change a mindset – albeit very gradually. The internet can be a force for good but it can also be a dangerous place. In some cases, understanding the threats just makes people think twice before posting online.

Privacy settings on social media are also key. I personally am seeing a big shift in this area. People generally are becoming more private and using privacy settings more. But that is not always the case. We are also seeing some generations moving more to what we call 'closed social'. Communicating via WhatsApp, Telegram or Signal or other chat apps on the market. That's fine, but the risk of information ending up online publicly is still the same: anyone can maliciously take a WhatsApp posting and make it publicly available. Especially in chat 'groups' where people are not good friends with people in that group.

There are often a number of legal routes that can be used to remove information, especially if it's defamatory or plain incorrect. But what if it isn't? Communications planning is always sensible.

If the information contained in your client's digital footprint can't be removed what are you going to say when it is discovered and sensationalised, for instance by a hostile blogger? Spending some time thinking about that again will stand you in good stead.

Above all, however, it is imperative to be continually aware and possess the technological weapons and intelligence to manage your client's digital footprint as it evolves and as unforeseen digital vulnerabilities appear with the growth of their family or business. This is largely down to digital monitoring. You need to know if their name is mentioned, the minute it hits the internet.

The reason for this is because we are increasingly living in a world where it is becoming difficult to separate fact from fiction.

For much of the 20th century, magazines, newspapers and television broadcasters checked and managed the flow of information to the public. These were professional institutions with rigorous standards and trained journalists.

Social media gave anyone a voice and its prevalence is huge. We live in a world where there are 1 billion Facebook postings a day and 500 hours of video uploaded to YouTube every minute. This allows anyone reading or watching social media to access vast amounts of opinion. But the big question is whether those unprofessional 'citizen journalists', who can launch their own accounts in seconds, are telling the truth.

7. Fake news?

When Donald Trump popularised the phrase 'fake news' in many of his broadcasts and broadsides he was globalising an emerging phenomenon. Yet in politics, propaganda or disinformation is as old as politics itself. It has gone on for centuries.

What was new about fake news is that it was essentially driven by short soundbites on social media or tantalising video clips. It preyed on the vulnerability of our short attention spans, especially those of the young. We are now bombarded by so much information that we prefer bitesize bits of news and analysis and we are likely to digest sometimes hundreds of these a day. If a short video clip of a CEO or politician or high profile person is sent to us we are likely to view it if it's brief. We may immediately spot it as fake or a joke, but it will still sit in the memory. Or we may believe it. Before we know it, it becomes fact. That's why fake news is so insidious. It disorientates us.

Which brings us to the other new phenomenon which is emerging at an alarming speed – the rise of the deepfake. Some of us will remember the emergence, in the 1990s, of Photoshop, which made it easy for anyone to doctor a photograph. The technology that powers deepfakes is known as Generative Adversarial Networks (GANs), which some people have traced back to being invented in 2014. It essentially consists of two rival computer networks which synthesise and assess new video content based on original content.

According to the *Sunday Times*, the first known episode of a deepfake being used inappropriately was in November 2017 when a user on the online forum Reddit uploaded pornographic videos with the digitally transformed faces of some female celebrities.[1] Reddit took down the post but since then deepfake technology has advanced in major ways.

There are a number of honourable applications for deepfakes. For instance, they could be used to restore speech to people who have lost the use of their voice through illness or an accident. They are used in Hollywood movies as well. However, deepfakes can facilitate a wide range of damaging actions. Crucially, they can enable anyone to create false evidence of someone doing or saying something they never did.

High profile public figures, such as politicians, are likely to exploit this, in a phenomenon dubbed the 'Liar's Dividend'. This is when genuine footage of controversial content is released, but the subject claims it is a deepfake. Even if the video is later proven to be true, the damage of their claim will have already been done, as individuals who support the subject are likely to trust both the subject and their pre-held beliefs.

Furthermore, according to a researcher from the Transatlantic Commission on Election Integrity, once a political narrative has been shifted, it is almost impossible to bring it back to its original trajectory.[2]

The *Financial Times* reported this year that a huge marketplace has opened up online offering deepfakes to customers.[3] In Japan, for instance, a small start-up offers deepfakes at US$2 per hour of processing time. Therefore anyone could go online and buy one

---

1 *The Sunday Times*, Danny Fortson, 22 December 2019, www.thetimes.co.uk/article/the-rise-of-deepfakes-what-are-they-and-how-can-we-know-whats-real-x03jp3rqr.

2 *The Guardian*, Simon Parkin, 22 June 2019, https://guardian.com/technology/ng-interactive/2019/jun/22/the-rise-of-the-deepfake-and-the-threat-to-democracy.

3 *The Financial Times*, Siddharth Venkataramakrishnan, 24 October 2019, "Can You Believe your Eyes? How Deepfakes are Coming for Politics", www.ft.com/content/4bf4277c-f527-11e9-a79c-bc9acae3b654.

and that will only increase. I can imagine a day when an easy downloadable app can create a deepfake for anyone within seconds.

At the moment, the main worries around these digital forgeries are confined to politics but I believe it is going to become a real problem for families and ultra-high net worth individuals as well.

Robert Chesney and Danielle Citron, writing in *Foreign Affairs* magazine in January 2019, made a very interesting point about deepfakes. They talk about how a "picture may be worth a thousand words, but there is nothing that persuades quite like an audio or video recording of an event".[4] They are absolutely correct. Video these days piques our interest more than anything else. And it is hard for us to compute that an actual video can be majorly doctored. In their article, Chesney and Citron run through various scenarios where a deepfake can be devastating and trigger untold chaos and unrest. They ask readers to imagine a video depicting the Israeli prime minister in private conversation with a colleague, seemingly revealing a plan to carry out a series of political assassinations in Tehran. Or an audio clip of Iranian officials planning a covert operation to kill Sunni leaders in a particular province of Iraq. Or a video showing an American general in Afghanistan burning a Koran.

In 2018, Ali Bongo, the president of Gabon in West Africa, hadn't appeared in public for many months after reportedly suffering a stroke. It therefore came as a surprise when a seemingly official video appeared online on New Year's Day 2019 in which he gave his traditional address to the Gabonese people. He looked a bit disoriented and his eyes didn't move properly.

Bongo's rivals declared the video to be a fake. A week later army officers launched an abortive coup.

Bongo wasn't dead. And the video wasn't a deepfake. But the opposition were right about one thing – creating uncertainty around the health of a president was easy.

The example at the beginning of the chapter about Nancy Pelosi is now described as a so-called 'shallow-fake'. A slight manipulation of a video but not a total one.

Apply this to the family office or corporate world. Fraudulent clips of a business leader could literally highlight a half truth about a company which could send it out of business. Fake video of central bankers could send markets into freefall. Trusted news organisations

---

4 Robert Chesney and Danielle Citron, *Foreign Affairs*, January 2019, "Deepfakes and the New Disinformation War: The Coming of Age of Post-Truth Geopolitics", www.foreignaffairs.com/articles/world/2018-12-11/deepfakes-and-new-disinformation-war.

might scramble to verify a video is true and reveal it is or isn't, but often it's too late. We live in a world where people react immediately.

A private family may have a video made about them so journalists swarm to the family home to check if it's true. By the time they've confirmed it is not true the very fact the video has been made is a story in itself. So a low-profile family who did nothing to get news coverage suddenly become the centre of scrutiny.

The destructive nature of deepfakes is also stretching unsurprisingly into fraud. And it's not just video fakes but audio fakes too.

Cyber fraudsters trying to trick senior executives into wiring money is nothing new and normally happens over email. However, in September 2019, *The Wall Street Journal* wrote about the first reported instance of an audio deepfake fraud.[5] The publication reported that an energy company's chief executive was tricked via telephone into wiring US$220,000 to a Hungarian supplier because he believed his boss was instructing him to do so. But the energy company's insurance firm told the journal that a clever fraudster was using deepfake software to mimic the voice of the executive. The software was able to imitate the voice, accent and even the tone of the boss.

What intrigues me about deepfake audio scams, and I'm sure there are many that go unreported, is how the fraudsters get the victim's voice in the first place. I can guarantee in most scams the victim has given a publicly available interview and – yes, you've guessed it – it is part of his or her readily available digital footprint online.

8. Be prepared

This takes us back to the whole purpose of modern-day reputation management. It is now a matter of knowing the unknown, of being the first to uncover and react to digital threats and, above all in the lightening-quick world of reputational ruin, being prepared.

A reputational crisis happens quickly and, a bit like a fire, spreads if you haven't prepared properly and so know what to do. And the landscape is evolving by the day. The sorry rise of deepfakes tells us that despite burgeoning efforts to get to grips with this new phenomenon, the ability to produce fake content is evolving far faster than our ability to combat it. It is a deeply worrying thing to say that you should know your digital profile as well as you know yourself or your business, but it has never been so true.

---

5 *The Wall Street Journal*, Catherine Stupp, www.wsj.com/articles/fraudsters-use-ai-to-mimic-ceos-voice-in-unusual-cybercrime-case-11567157402.

Protection from marital claims

Amy Radnor
Rose Spencer-Longhurst
Farrer & Co

1. Context

In the wider context of wealth protection, divorce and family breakdown is a time of particular vulnerability for individuals, trustees and family offices. Few people welcome the prospect of losing assets on divorce, but the approach of the English court renders divorcing and dividing assets in this jurisdiction much riskier, more uncertain and more expensive than would be the case in most other jurisdictions.[1]

England has a well-deserved reputation as the most generous jurisdiction in the world for the weaker financial party. Several factors play a role in this, but some of the most important are:

- the absence of any matrimonial property regime;
- the very wide discretion given to judges to order the outcome they consider 'fair'; and
- the elastic concept of 'need'.

Many other jurisdictions, including many European jurisdictions, operate what is known as a 'matrimonial property regime'. At the time of their marriage, couples choose what property regime they wish to apply to them and their assets, and that regime in turn dictates how these same assets would be divided on divorce. If couples do not choose a regime, a default regime will be applied to them instead. A very typical property regime would be that all property accrued *during* a marriage as a result of the parties' own endeavours (ie, income from employment, savings from income, joint gifts) would be matrimonial and shared equally on divorce. The assets which each party owned *prior* to the marriage and any inheritances or sole gifts received *during* the marriage would be non-matrimonial and would not be shared.

---

1 'Marriage' in this chapter includes civil partnerships, and 'divorce' includes civil partnership dissolution. References to the English courts in this chapter include the courts of Wales.

The advantage of this approach is that both spouses know at the start of the marriage what the outcome would be on divorce. If the marriage does end in divorce, the lawyers involved can advise their clients with some certainty what the final outcome will be. Inherited, gifted and pre-acquired assets can all be excluded from division on divorce (assuming of course that the correct property regime was selected at the time of the marriage).

There is a significant disadvantage too in this approach. In a case where all the assets have been inherited by one spouse, or were acquired by them prior to the marriage, there may be no matrimonial property at all to be divided. Perhaps neither party has worked, and they have instead lived throughout their marriage on the income generated from those inherited or pre-acquired assets. On divorce, the weaker financial party (usually, but not always, the wife) may be left in a situation of real financial hardship, even after a long marriage with children, because none of those assets can or will be shared. The weaker financial party may be unable to house themselves or have insufficient money to live on. The financial security of the other spouse, retaining all of their inherited/pre-acquired assets, will be very different.

The English courts, in contrast, do not apply a matrimonial property regime. All the assets which either party owns or has available to them at the time of the divorce (and potentially assets which they disposed of in the run up to the divorce) are valued and included in the 'marital pot' as available for division. Inherited, gifted and pre-acquired assets will not automatically be shared equally, but nor are they are automatically excluded.

English judges have a very wide discretion to decide an outcome which is fair in all the circumstances of each particular case. They will consider the totality of the assets and how to meet both parties' needs for housing and income. Section 25 of the Matrimonial Causes Act 1973 sets out the checklist which the court must consider in assessing what is fair, and although "contribution" (ie, who brought what to the marriage) is a factor, so too are many other factors including the length of the marriage, the needs of children and the ability of either spouse to support themselves. Each outcome is bespoke and fact-specific and although there are trends and authorities from case law, there is much less certainty as to outcome and lawyers can usually only give their clients a 'bracket' of potential awards. This inevitably gives rise to more litigation.

A wealthy individual divorcing in England can have no certainty that assets he or she brought to the marriage, or assets inherited by them during the marriage, will be protected. The overriding consideration for the English court is 'need', that is, what do both parties need to house themselves and live on. 'Need' is a famously elastic concept and varies depending on the subjective views of the individual judge as well as the length of the marriage, standard of living during it and a host of other factors. Awards are regularly made in the English courts which require significant payments to be made by one spouse, from their inherited or pre-acquired assets, in order to meet the needs of the other.

In response, individuals, families and their advisers have developed mechanisms aimed at protecting assets on divorce. This chapter discusses two of the most frequent and most effective, namely prenuptial and postnuptial agreements (PNAs) and trusts.

2. PNAs

At their base, PNAs are contracts. They are signed either before a marriage (in the case of prenuptial agreements) or after marriage (in the case of postnuptial agreements). Other than timing, there is no difference between the two.

What is being agreed in the contract is the financial provision to be made on divorce – the parties agree essentially to 'override' the court's jurisdiction and substitute their own outcome.

The most important element of a contract is its enforceability. PNAs are technically *not* enforceable in England and there is no legislation governing their use. That gap has been filled by case law, most notably the landmark 2010 decision of the Supreme Court in *Radmacher v Granatino* [2010] UKSC 42. That case involved a German wife and a French husband. The wife belonged to an extremely wealthy family – she had been gifted significant family assets already and was gifted more during the marriage. Prior to the marriage the couple entered into a German prenuptial agreement, signed in front of a German notary who had given some legal advice, jointly, to the couple.

The prenuptial agreement provided for the husband, who was a high earner at the time of the marriage, to receive nothing from his wife on divorce and vice versa. When the couple came to divorce eight years later, having had two children, the husband was no longer earning at a high level and sought significant financial provision from his wife, notwithstanding the terms of the PNA.

The Supreme Court's decision in this case changed the law for practitioners and gave couples much more confidence to enter into PNAs on the basis they would be upheld.

Although it is still the case that PNAs are not automatically enforceable by law in England, as they are in many other European and worldwide jurisdictions, the Supreme Court judgment (at para 75) was clear that:

the court should give effect to a nuptial agreement that is freely entered into by each party with a full appreciation of its implications unless in the circumstances prevailing it would not be fair to hold the parties to their agreement.

The principles practitioners have distilled to meet this fairness test are:

- both parties should have independent legal advice;
- there should be sufficient financial disclosure for the weaker financial party to understand what they are giving up a claim to;
- there must be no duress or undue pressure and sufficient time before the wedding to allow for proper reflection; and
- the result of the PNA should not leave either party, or a minor child, in a situation of real need.

Any PNA prepared by specialist practitioners will meet the first three requirements. Mr Granatino did not of course have independent legal advice or full financial disclosure and the Supreme Court did not find that an obstacle to upholding the PNA. It is good practice, however, to ensure these requirements are met.

Dealing with need and fairness is the most challenging aspect of any PNA. The tension for practitioners is to meet the needs of the weaker financial party, but to a lesser extent than the court would in the absence of a PNA.

A PNA which provides for the weaker financial party to receive nothing will usually be a valueless document because it will not meet their needs and they will not be held to it as a result. It is worth noting in this context that although Ms Radmacher won her case she still had to make some financial provision for Mr Granatino, in the form of substantial child maintenance and allowing him the exclusive and rent-free occupation of two houses belonging to her until their children were adults.

The court will judge a PNA on whether it is fair at the time of the divorce, rather than at the time of the wedding or at the time it was signed. At the time Mr Granatino and Ms Radmacher entered into their PNA, Mr Granatino was earning at a high level as a banker with JP Morgan; by the time of their divorce he had left the City and was a PhD student. Fairness is also considered in the context of the same Section 25 factors discussed above, so the length of the marriage, standard of living, needs of any minor children and earning capacity, among others.

As is evident, couples may not know what the future holds or what their future standard of living will be. Inherited assets may not yet have been passed down. A PNA may set out provision for the weaker financial party which seems, in the context of how the newly engaged couple is living, to be entirely reasonable (perhaps a deposit for a small flat). If the couple come to divorce in, say, 20 years' time, after significant assets have been handed down, their lifestyles and needs may have become very different. The weaker financial party's needs may well not be met by the deposit for a small flat which may have seemed appropriate at the time of their marriage.

Couples entering into PNAs in England cannot have the confidence of couples in the US and many European jurisdictions that their PNA will be enforced automatically on divorce. They should, however, work on the basis that their PNA will be upheld, provided the formalities are complied with and the effect is not to leave one party or any children of the marriage in real financial need. Couples with significant inherited or pre-acquired assets on one or both sides are free to come up with their own creative solutions (a former spouse being given a house to occupy for their lifetime, for instance, rather than a lump sum outright which can only be raised by selling inherited assets).

The position is far from perfect but there is much greater certainty now than existed prior to 2010. Many practitioners believe it is inevitable that Parliament will at some stage legislate in this area and in the meantime more and more couples are choosing PNAs to protect their current and future wealth.

3. Trusts

Families and individuals can also use trust structures as a means of protecting assets from a spouse in the event of marital breakdown. However, the English court, with its broad discretionary stance on the division of wealth on divorce, has applied a creative and purposive approach to ensure that the existence of a trust will not interfere with the guiding principle of fairness on the basis that:

... if justice is to be achieved between spouses at divorce the court must be equipped, in a society where the forms of wealth-holding are diverse

and often sophisticated, to penetrate outer forms and get to the heart of ownership[2]

Advisers therefore need to be alive to the limitations of reliance on trust structures for effective asset protection.

3.1 Trust assets as available resources

A trust may be impacted by financial proceedings where it is treated as a resource available to one or both of the parties.

When considering an appropriate division of matrimonial assets, the English court must consider all of the circumstances of the case, including the financial resources of each of the parties to the marriage – both now and in the foreseeable future. The court will take into account the parties' income, earning capacities, property and "other financial resources"[3] – and it is clear that "other financial resources" can include a beneficial interest under a trust.[4]

In circumstances where trustees have previously granted requests for distributions from a trust routinely, the court may well regard the assets of the trust as assets available to that spouse and take them into account on divorce. In these circumstances, a beneficiary spouse may find that the English court makes orders against them in financial proceedings that they are unable to meet without the assistance of the trustees.

The test applied by the courts was set out in *Charman v Charman*[5] as "whether, if the husband were to request it to advance the whole (or part) of the capital of trust to him, the trustees would be likely to do so". In applying this test, the court will look at the history of the trustees' conduct and the realities of the situation[6] and it will perform a broad review of the available evidence[7]. The court will take into account, for example:

- The history of distributions from the trust and whether these have always been made on request or sometimes refused. If all previous requests to distribute funds have routinely been acceded to the court may assume that this will continue – or even that the trustees may become more generous to the

---

2 *Thomas v Thomas* [1995] 2FLR 668.
3 Matrimonial Causes Act 1973, Section 25(2)(a).
4 *Thomas v Thomas* [1995] 2FLR 668.
5 [2005] EWCA Civ 1606.
6 *Thomas v Thomas* [1995] 2FLR 668.
7 *Charman v Charman* [2005] EWCA Civ 1606.

spouse beneficiary following a divorce if that spouse's needs are greater as a result of a divorce;

- The circumstances in which the trust came into existence (particularly if these point to an intention to put assets out of legal reach of a spouse in financial remedy proceedings)[8] and any specific purpose, for example, funding education costs. Any letter of wishes by the settlor of a trust (and evidence as to whether trustees have acted in accordance with such) will also be relevant;
- The interests of other trust beneficiaries. If there are multiple beneficiaries under a discretionary trust it may be more difficult for the court to find that one will be preferred by the trustees over the others. The position may be more straightforward if there is just one beneficiary;
- The way in which trustees have engaged with financial remedy proceedings including the extent to which they have provided disclosure. This can create a dilemma for trustees: failure to cooperate with requests from the court or other spouse for evidence may lead to adverse inferences being drawn as regards the extent of their independence – and yet trustees may consider the provision of certain information to be inappropriate;
- The nature of the trust assets and how liquid these are. The court may consider it unlikely that trustees will agree to short-or medium-term capital distributions where, for example, assets are illiquid and have been invested to provide income.

In *Daga v Bangur*,[9] for example, the court found that trust funds were not an available resource in reliance upon which any award could be made. The judge took into account strong and clear letters of wishes and that there had never been distributions from the trusts.

It may be difficult to predict how the court will apply the *Charman* test. However, advisers should, in the context of trust planning, be mindful that the ways in which a trust is established and run may be of great significance (and the subject of close scrutiny) in financial remedy proceedings. The courts cannot order trustees to make specific provision for a beneficiary of a trust and it is acknowledged

---

8 *AAZ v BBZ* [2016] EWHC 3234 (Fam).
9 *Daga v Bangur* [2018] EWFC 91.

that they should not put improper pressure on trustees in this regard. However, they can give judicious encouragement to trustees by making orders against the beneficiary in proceedings that in effect encourage them to act in a particular way.

3.2 Variation of 'nuptial settlements'

The integrity of a trust might also be threatened by financial remedy proceedings on divorce to the extent that it is capable of variation as a nuptial settlement. From the court's perspective, varying a nuptial settlement can be an effective way of obtaining financial relief for one (or both) parties.

The English court has power to vary a nuptial settlement on divorce[10] and thus allow a spouse to invade it. The court may make "an order varying for the benefit of the parties to the marriage and of the children of the family or either or any of them any ante-nuptial or post-nuptial settlement (including such a settlement made by will or codicil) made on the parties to the marriage".

A trust can only be varied if it is found to be 'nuptial' in character and therefore the question of whether or not a trust is nuptial will be key.

Unfortunately for advisers, there is no statutory definition of a nuptial settlement, which can cause uncertainty. However, it is clear that there must be a 'nuptial' element. The meaning of this was set out in *DR v GR*[11] as "any arrangement which makes some form of continuing provision for both or either of the parties to a marriage". Thus the definition is broad with the effect that the court's power to vary a nuptial settlement on divorce is wide-reaching.

In *BJ v MJ*,[12] for example, a husband set up two trusts after the marriage, both of which owned shares in the same company. The first trust included the wife and children in the class of beneficiaries and was clearly a postnuptial settlement but the parties and their children were specifically excluded as beneficiaries from the second trust. Nevertheless, the court found that the second trust was an integral part of the overall scheme of arrangements by the husband. The trusts were viewed as a whole on the basis that the value of the company could be extracted via either trust and they (and the company owned by them) were together found to be a postnuptial

---

10 Matrimonial Causes Act 1973, Section 24(i)(c).
11 [2013] EWHC 1196 (Fam).
12 [2011] EWHC 2708 (Fam).

settlement capable of variation. In *Chai v Peng*[13] the court found that the provision of accommodation (via a notional licence to occupy) was capable of variation so as to provide accommodation for the wife post-divorce.

There are limits, though, to what will be recognised as a nuptial settlement and in *Quan v Bray*[14] the court made clear that a trust must make some form of continuing provision for both or either of the parties to a marriage in order to constitute a nuptial settlement capable of variation – so that a trust established for the benefit of a wildlife charity, to further the cause of the Chinese tiger, was not capable of variation.

Where there is a nuptial settlement, the court's powers of variation are very broad. The Court of Appeal provided guidance as to how such powers should be exercised in *Ben Hashem*.[15] This makes clear that, for example, the court's discretion to vary is unfettered, the court must have regard to all circumstances of the case, the objective is to achieve a result fair to both sides and the court ought to be very slow to deprive innocent third parties of their rights under a trust.

In some cases it may not be clear whether a trust would be deemed by the English court to be a nuptial settlement and, if so, what the implications of this might be for the parties involved. Advisers should, though, be clear to their clients that, if found to be nuptial, a trust will be variable in the context of financial proceedings on divorce and this could mean, for example, that capital is taken out of the trust or that other property held within a trust is redistributed.

Advisers of spouses seeking to benefit from the court's broad powers to vary a trust will also need to be mindful of enforcement limitations – particularly where trusts are located offshore – and, where there are different orders that a court could make, enforcement considerations may be determinative. Variation orders made in the context of financial remedy proceedings in England will only be effective if they are enforceable and this may be difficult if the jurisdiction of the trust in question has 'firewall' legislation in place. Many jurisdictions (Jersey and Guernsey, for example) have introduced 'firewall' legislation to try and restrict the enforcement of judgments of foreign courts in relation to their

---

13 [2017] EWHC 792 (Fam).
14 [2017] EWCA Civ 405.
15 [2008] EWHC 2380.

trusts. The legislation is designed to protect trustees by ensuring that any questions concerning the trust are to be determined according to local law without reference to foreign law.

If a party is seeking to vary a trust that is outside the English court's jurisdiction, local law advice in the jurisdiction where the trust is based – and a joined-up approach as regards the court order sought in England and offshore – will be key.

4. Advising the wealthy

We have set out some of the main mechanisms for the protection of assets on divorce in England. As can be seen it is imperative that you seek specialist advice on behalf of your client at the earliest opportunity.

Choice of residence

Nicola Saccardo
Maisto e Associati

1. Introduction

Although wealthy clients have always shown a higher inclination towards international mobility than other taxpayers,[1] in recent years we have been witnessing a steady increase in this phenomenon. In fact, in a globalised world, it is becoming even more crucial for wealthy clients to choose the country in which to place their residence. Surveys confirm that, when choosing their residence, wealthy clients tend to adopt a holistic approach, taking into account several factors relating to business and professional opportunities, quality of life and quality of services.

The intensification of the mobility of wealthy clients has been confirmed by recently published statistics,[2] according to which approximately 108,000 wealthy clients migrated to another jurisdiction in 2018, compared to 95,000 in 2017, 82,000 in 2016 and 65,000 in 2015.

The data suggests that in 2018 the most attractive countries for the relocation of wealthy clients were Australia, the US and Canada, which recorded respectively a net inflow of wealthy clients of around 12,000, 10,000 and 4,000.[3] This information on wealthy client inflow highlights a stable trend across the last four-year period. Indeed, since 2015 Australia has been the country with the highest wealthy client net inflow, followed by the US and Canada. The most significant factors encouraging wealthy clients to move to Australia include its high level of services, top-quality healthcare and education, growing economy, language (ie, English-speaking),

1 OECD, *Engaging with High Net Worth Individuals on Tax Compliance: Joint Study of the Forum on Tax Administration and Working Party No. 8 on Tax Avoidance and Evasion*, May 2009.

2 New World Wealth (NWW), *Research and Markets*, 2018. This report covers individuals who have overall net assets of at least US$1 million.

3 NWW, *Research and Markets*.

wide availability of space and good quality environment, as well as the absence of inheritance taxes.

Conversely, in 2018 the countries with the largest loss of wealthy clients were China, which recorded a net outflow of 15,000 wealthy clients, followed by Russia, which suffered a loss of 7,000 wealthy clients, India with a loss of 5,000, Turkey with a loss of 4,000 and France and the UK with a loss of 3,000 wealthy clients each. It is noteworthy that the number of wealthy clients migrating from India and China was broadly counterbalanced by the new wealthy clients that the same countries produced. On the other hand, the data shows a loss of appeal in jurisdictions such as the UK and France which have traditionally been attractive for wealthy individuals.[4] Indeed, while over 80,000 wealthy clients have moved to the UK since 1990, over the past two years the UK has lost approximately 7,000 wealthy clients (ie, 4,000 in 2017 and 3,000 in 2018). The potential reasons explaining this trend include the political instability connected with Brexit and the 2017 changes to the resident non-domiciled regime, whereby such a regime became unavailable after 15 years of UK residence. The high level of taxation seems to have been the trigger for the outflow of wealthy clients from France.

The intensification of the mobility of wealthy clients led to several countries introducing new regimes meant to attract wealthy clients, thus creating competition among jurisdictions. In particular, Europe has witnessed a proliferation of favourable tax schemes in recent years, aimed at attracting wealthy individuals as well as highly skilled professionals. While some countries, such as the UK, Switzerland, Malta and Ireland, have been accustomed to this practice for many years, other countries, such as France, Spain and Portugal, have only begun to experience this phenomenon since the early 2000s (and these three particular jurisdictions amended their regimes in just the last two years). Moreover, at the end of 2016 Italy introduced a lump sum tax regime for wealthy individuals moving to Italy. Subject to the condition that the individual has been a non-resident for at least nine of the last 10 years, the regime applies a €100,000 flat rate annual tax on foreign-sourced income and gains and exempts foreign assets from any wealth tax and inheritance and gift taxes. The Italian regime, albeit introduced recently, has reportedly been highly successful. However, detailed reliable statistics on its success are not yet available. The number of jurisdictions implementing further favourable tax

---

4 NWW, *Research and Markets*.

schemes is likely to grow. For example, Greece has recently introduced a tax regime that is similar to the Italian lump sum regime.

2. Criteria for choosing a country of residence

As mentioned, wealthy clients consider a variety of factors when deciding on a new location. Even if economic factors, such as the level of taxation and business opportunities, remain fundamental, social, political and environmental factors are important too. They seek, for themselves and for their family, a good balance between economic efficiency and lifestyle choices. Furthermore, empirical evidence shows that the factors attracting wealthy clients to certain jurisdictions are the same factors that encourage these wealthy individuals to leave their home countries.

In particular, the main driving criteria influencing the choice of residence amongst wealthy clients include the following:

- *Quality of life and high standard of services.* According to a survey by *The Economist,*[5] improvement in quality of life is the most widespread reason pushing wealthy clients to relocate abroad. In fact, 75% of the wealthy clients that participated in the survey cited this as the main driver for deciding to leave. The same survey demonstrates that quality of life is also a crucial criterion in selecting the new country of residence. In particular, 73% of the respondents who moved or planned to move declared that the expectation of finding a better quality of life was a very important factor that they had taken into account. A high standard of services is also an important criterion for choosing a place of residence.
- *Personal safety.* Data highlights that there is a strong correlation between the level of safety of a country – especially women and children's safety – and the inflow of wealthy clients. In that regard, Australia, which has recorded the highest inflow rate of wealthy clients over the last few years, is also a top-ranking country in a list of safest places in the world[6] and in 2019 was ranked as the safest country in the world in annual ratings of women's safety.[7] This correlation between the safety

---

5 Aviva Freudmann, "The Wealthy Migrants", *The Economist,* 8 October 2015, https://eiuperspectives.economist.com/financial-services/wealthy-migrant/white-paper/wealthy-migrant.

6 *Global Peace Index 2019,* http://visionofhumanity.org/app/uploads/2019/06/GPI-2019web003.pdf.

7 NWW, *Research and Markets.*

of a country and its appeal for wealthy people is supported by the survey conducted by *The Economist*,[8] which found the expectation of obtaining a safer physical environment was the second factor pushing wealthy clients to move outside of their country (64% of the people interviewed declared that the lack of safety was the main reason why they moved outside the country).
- *Education opportunities for children.*
- *Work and business opportunities.* Business reasons and professional opportunities tend to rank higher than other factors for triggering the relocation of wealthy clients to another country. In particular, according to *The Economist*'s survey,[9] 81% of respondents who relocated to another country stated that business opportunities in the country of destination were a significant factor to consider upon relocation.
- *Favourable tax treatment.* According to a survey conducted by Citi Private Bank and Knight Frank in 2008,[10] 29% of the wealthy clients interviewed declared that taxation was the most important factor influencing the location of their residence.
- *Political stability.*
- *Protection of wealth and property rights.*
- *Top-standard healthcare system.*

3. The emigration/immigration checklist

When a wealthy client moves from one jurisdiction to another, a number of legal and tax issues have to be addressed. This paragraph aims at setting out some of the main legal and tax issues that need to be addressed, in the state of departure and/or in the state of arrival, with a particular focus on the tax issues.[11] The list is general (ie, not related to specific jurisdictions) and not exhaustive.

3.1 Tax issues

First, it needs to be ascertained whether the wealthy client effectively loses the tax residence status of the state of departure.

8 Freudmann, "The Wealthy Migrants".
9 Freudmann, "The Wealthy Migrants".
10 Knight Frank/Citi Private Bank, *Wealth Report 2009*, https://content.knightfrank.com/research/83/documents/en/2009-2.pdf.
11 This paragraph is based on the checklist reported in N Saccardo, "The Immigration/Emigration Checklist", *STEP Journal*, July 2018, p41.

Different countries apply different criteria for determining whether an individual remains resident or not for tax purposes in their territory. For example, in the UK, under the so-called Statutory Residence Test, the residence of individuals for income tax purposes is based on the number of days that they spend in the UK during any given tax year. The number of days that an individual can spend in the UK without qualifying as a UK tax resident depends on the number of ties that he or she has with the country (for example, whether he or she has a home in the UK, whether his or her spouse and/or minor children are resident in the UK, etc). Other countries apply more general criteria that require a case-by-case analysis of all relevant facts and circumstances. For example, in Italy, individuals are considered to be non-resident if their habitual abode and their main centre of business and personal interests are outside Italy and if they are not registered as resident for the majority of the tax year. While the last of these criteria is merely formal, the others require a careful analysis of all the facts and circumstances, as, in effect, their ties with Italy need to be weighed up against their ties with the state of arrival. If a client's state of departure applies general criteria, such as in Italy, his or her personal circumstances must be carefully reviewed to make sure that he or she actually loses tax residence in the state of departure and accurate evidence must be gathered for possible future reference.

While worldwide income taxation is usually based on tax residence, worldwide exposure to other taxes may be based on other criteria or on a different notion of residence. For example, in the UK, exposure to inheritance tax on worldwide assets is triggered by a domicile (or a deemed domicile; see below) in the UK. An individual may well be non-resident in the UK for UK income tax purposes but still be domiciled in the UK and, therefore, exposed to UK inheritance tax on all of his or her estate. In Italy, an individual is resident for inheritance and gift tax purposes – and therefore subject to such tax in relation to all his assets – if his or her habitual abode is in Italy. The individual should check which conditions need to be met, after the transfer, in order to cease exposure to such other taxes.

Certain countries feature deemed residence (or domicile) rules for individuals who move abroad. Sometimes these rules apply only if the individual moves to a low tax jurisdiction. For example, French nationals that move to Monaco are deemed to be resident in France. Italian nationals that move to certain low tax jurisdictions (such as Switzerland or Monaco) are deemed to be resident in Italy unless proof of the contrary is provided. Similar rules provide for extended liability for a certain period after the individual has moved abroad (eg, German extended liability rules apply for a 10-year period for nationals ceasing to be resident in Germany and moving to a low tax jurisdiction). Another example is the UK, where an individual is deemed to be domiciled in the UK for all tax purposes if he has been resident in the UK for income tax purposes for 15 of the previous 20 tax years. Because of this rule, an individual is exposed to UK inheritance tax on all his or her assets for a certain number of years after losing UK income tax residence. The impact of these deeming rules should be checked and it may be worth planning in order to protect the individual from potential adverse consequences in the country of departure (for example, an insurance policy against the risk of exposure to UK inheritance tax in the period of UK-deemed domicile).

The timing of the loss of income tax residence and that of the acquisition of income tax residence in the state of arrival may not necessarily match. These mismatches in the timing of loss versus acquisition of tax residence must be determined and taken care of. They may lead to double taxation or sometimes double non-taxation. The mismatch may be due to the fact that the state of departure and the state of arrival have different tax years or due to the different split-year rules. For example, in the UK, the income tax year for individuals runs from 6 April to 5 April of the following year; in Australia it runs from 1 July to 30 June of the following year, while in the states of continental Europe (such as Italy, Spain and France) it corresponds to the calendar year. An individual who moves his or her tax residence from the UK to Italy at the end of the UK tax year may be considered a dual resident of the UK and of Italy in the period from 1 January to 5 April of that year. This may have material adverse consequences as any income or gains realised in such timeframe may be exposed to double taxation if the transfer is not carefully planned. On the other hand, such mismatches may also result in periods of non-residence in both the state of departure and the state of arrival. For example, an individual transferring to Italy from Australia after the end of the Australian tax year may be considered non-resident in Australia from the day of transfer to 31 December of such year and also non-resident in Italy in the same period. This is because Italy has no split-year residence rules and an individual is either resident or non-resident for a whole tax year. The individual should check whether such mismatches may arise and should carefully plan his or her transfer in light of them. If the mismatch triggers a period of dual residence, relief from double taxation may be obtained through treaty or domestic provisions in either of the two states. If there is a period of dual non-residence, it may be useful for the individual, from a tax perspective, to use such period in order to trigger the realisation of income or gains.

In certain countries, it is the residence of persons other than the individual that triggers worldwide tax exposure. For example, in France and Germany, the entire estate of an individual is exposed to inheritance tax if the heir is a resident of such countries regardless of the residence of the deceased at the time of demise. In these cases, it is worth checking whether there is an inheritance tax treaty between the state of arrival and the country of residence of the heir that may limit such exposure to inheritance tax.

The loss of tax residence in the state of departure may trigger certain adverse tax consequences that an individual should take into account. The most notable example is the exit tax that is levied by certain countries. For example, individuals who lose French tax residence and who hold certain substantial shareholdings (eg, a shareholding entitling the shareholder to receive at least 50% of the company's profits) may be exposed to an exit tax on the unrealised gain relating to such shareholding. If an individual was benefitting from a deferral of the payment of certain taxes in the state of departure, the loss of tax residence in such a state may trigger the termination of the deferral regime. Furthermore, in some jurisdictions the loss of tax residence may imply the clawback of prior deductions or the obligation to settle all outstanding tax liabilities.

It is worth checking whether a strategy to accelerate or defer income, gains, losses or gifts should be pursued. The individual should also be aware of differences in the tax treatment of income, gains or gifts in the state of departure as compared with the state of arrival (this is the case, in particular, if the individual is planning to benefit from a favourable regime in the state of arrival). For instance, if the state of arrival provides for a taxation of capital gains that is generally more favourable than the taxation in the state of departure, it may be advantageous to delay the realisation of any gains until he or she has lost tax residence in the state of departure. A case-by-case analysis must be made. Indeed, for example, even if taxation in the state of arrival on capital gains were to be more favourable, it could be more advantageous for the individual to realise a gain while he or she is a tax resident in the state of departure if such gain could be offset against capital losses realised during the same year or by capital losses carried forward from previous years that the individual would no longer be able to use after departure. One could also consider accelerating a capital loss in the state of departure if, for example, it could be used to offset a capital gain therein and could not be used after departure (eg, due to a step down to fair market values in the state of departure).

Moreover, timing mismatches in the determination of the date of a taxable event must be monitored. Indeed, the state of departure and the state of arrival may apply different criteria in determining in which tax year a certain income or gain has been realised and so should be subject to tax. Mismatches in such criteria, if not properly managed, may lead to cases of double taxation. Assume that the state of departure considers that a gain on an asset is taxable in the year when the asset is sold while the state of arrival considers a gain as taxable in the year in which the proceeds are cashed. If the individual sells the asset while a tax resident of the state of departure but receives the payment of the proceeds while a tax resident in the state of arrival (this is the case, for example, where the individual has agreed to receive the payment in instalments), he or she may be subject to tax in both states.

The loss of the individual's tax residence in the state of departure may also impact on the tax residence of companies or other entities, if the management and control of such entities is viewed as being transferred abroad and, therefore, the entity loses tax residence in the state of departure. This may have adverse income tax consequences if the state of departure levies an exit tax on entities. Likewise, it is important to check whether the entities may become tax resident in the state of arrival of the individual and, if so, what the consequences would be.

Other areas of analysis may include reviewing the future expected income, gains and assets in the state of departure in order to identify strategies to minimise local source/*situs* taxation after the change to non-resident status and advising on potential temporary non-residence rules that may apply if the individual moves back within a certain timeframe (such as those that exist in the UK).

From the perspective of taxation in the state of arrival, one has to determine the tax basis of assets owned by the individual, in particular whether the acquisition of residence triggers a step up of the tax basis up to the fair market value of the assets upon the change of residence and whether and to what extent such step up depends on the levy of an exit tax by the state of departure. In the absence of a step up, it must be checked whether the tax basis as determined in the state of departure would be recognised in the state of arrival or whether it is possible to obtain a step up of the tax basis in the state of arrival by entering, prior to the change of residence, into a transaction that is tax neutral in the state of departure.

If the individual moves to a jurisdiction offering a favourable tax regime (such as a lump sum tax regime), it should be checked whether the application of the regime may have consequences in terms of treaty protection in the countries where the individual is likely to generate income or hold assets. In this respect, there may be specific treaty provisions that exclude the application of the treaty if a person is subject to a favourable regime in one of the contracting states. For example, under Article 4(5) of the income tax treaty between Switzerland and the US, individuals who are residents of Switzerland under the lump sum tax regime are not treated as residents of Switzerland for the purposes of the treaty and, therefore, are denied treaty benefits.

It is also important to check whether the state of arrival has relevant anti-avoidance provisions (eg, controlled foreign companies legislation), to review the existing ownership structures to understand whether they should be amended upon the change of residence, and to assess to what extent the legislation of the state of arrival will allow tax benefits to be achieved by using, for instance, trusts, insurance policies, usufruct and other estate planning tools.

Finally, it is imperative to check whether the transfer of residence of the individual to the state of arrival may trigger rules regarding the importation of valuable assets. Such circumstance may have adverse indirect tax consequences. It may be the case, for example, that the transfer of the habitual abode of the individual to the state of arrival may trigger the importation of assets such as works of art, yachts and jets. Specific exemptions for privately used assets may apply.

3.2 Other issues

In addition to tax issues, other areas of work, when advising a wealthy client moving to another jurisdiction, include the following:

- Checking the entry visa requirements;
- Checking whether the individual needs to carry out certain formalities upon the transfer of residence from one country to another (eg, de-registrations or registrations);
- Checking the social security ramifications from the transfer;
- Checking whether the transfer may impact on the applicable law to the succession of the individual, which would be the consequences of such change and whether a choice of law, the

execution of a will or the execution of succession agreements are available/recommended;

- Checking whether the transfer may impact on the applicable law to the matrimonial regime with the spouse, which would be the consequences of such change and whether a choice of law or the execution of a postnuptial agreement are available/ recommended;
- Checking whether works of art are to be imported into the state of arrival and, if so, checking whether they will become subject to any limits, laid down by the State of arrival, as to their export or disposal (for example, ban on export or right of first refusal); and
- Checking the conditions for obtaining permanent residence or nationality in the state of arrival.

4. Concluding remarks

As discussed in the introduction, we are witnessing an increasing mobility among the very wealthy. This has triggered competition, with states offering favourable tax regimes to attract wealthy clients to their jurisdiction (such regimes possibly further increasing the mobility of wealthy clients). It is worth trying to foresee what these trends may lead to. It is expected that jurisdictions suffering from a significant outflow of wealthy clients might wish to introduce provisions aimed at preventing or limiting such outflow or at least the negative financial consequences from such outflow. Such provisions may include exit taxes, rules meant to make the loss of residence more difficult (such as deemed residence rules), exchange controls meant to prevent the outflow of assets so that the state of departure may still levy tax as the source state, or even taxation based on criteria other than residence (eg, citizenship). The application of some of these rules may be problematic in the light of the existing tax treaty network. However, this may simply lead to these states negotiating amendments to their tax treaties (see, for instance, the recent decision of Finland to renegotiate the income tax treaty with Portugal in order to be able to levy taxes on Finnish pensions paid to individuals who benefit from the Portuguese 10-year exemption on foreign income), or lead them to interpret existing tax treaties as not applying to individuals who are residents of a foreign country and subject therein to a favourable tax regime.

Managing taxes

Jeremy Arnold
Withersworldwide

This chapter covers how a wealthy client should manage their tax affairs. It covers the common characteristics of a wealthy client from a tax perspective, what are likely to be the key tax issues affecting such clients and how tax matters should be managed from the perspective of the wealthy client.

1. Jurisdictions

Of course, tax is highly jurisdictional in the sense that each country will have its own tax rules and also in the case of some countries there may be national or federal taxes and state taxes. But it is likely that the wealthy client will also have a need for international and cross-border tax advice. That is because wealthy clients will be more likely to change their tax residence at various points in their lives, they may have family members who live in different tax jurisdictions and they are likely to have investments and personal real estate which are located outside their home tax jurisdiction. This means that advice will need to be taken outside the home jurisdiction and the application or otherwise of double tax treaties is likely to be relevant. There are also now supranational taxes that may need consideration through the OECD base erosion and profit shifting (BEPS) initiative. The wealthy client may also own luxury assets such as art, aircraft and yachts which by their nature move around and therefore are likely to have their own special tax treatment.

2. Structures

A wealthy client is also likely to have structures in place so that tax advice needs to be business focused rather than being just personal. These structures may relate to the onward transfer of wealth such as trusts, foundations and companies, or structures may be in place to reduce ongoing taxes. Investments are likely to be made through structuring vehicles where a thorough understanding of the tax treatment of such structures is required. For the wealthy client, structures need to be designed so that they are flexible and adaptive. This is especially important for the wealthy client who moves between jurisdictions and members of the wealthy client's family who do the same. There has to be a thorough understanding of how any structure will be taxed when the owner or person who created the structure moves between jurisdictions. Of course this may in itself open up tax planning possibilities.

3. Income tax

The taxes a wealthy client will need to consider will be numerous. The most immediate taxes will be income taxes, whether that is a tax paid on earnings, dividends, rent, interest, royalties or other types of income. In some jurisdictions capital gains taxes will need to be considered. Commonly, rates of tax on capital gains will be lower than on income and therefore there is often an incentive to generate profits through capital gains as opposed to income. In many jurisdictions anti-avoidance provisions have been introduced to prevent this happening, particularly on carry-type remuneration structures.

4. Estate and gift taxes

Perhaps the most important tax wealthy clients need to consider, and in particular where they wish to hand on assets to the next generation, is the application of estate and gift taxes. While some jurisdictions (such as Australia or Canada) have no estate and gift taxes, others (such as the United States and the UK) have high rates of estate and gift tax, which can have a very material impact on the amount passed on to the next generation and the degree to which a family can keep its wealth intact. A key point here is the ability or otherwise that the wealthy client has to make gifts to the next generation during his or her lifetime which are tax free when made and not includable in the taxable estate on death. For example, the UK has a regime where certain gifts made within seven years of death are free from inheritance tax.

5. Transfer taxes

Transfer taxes, particularly on the acquisition of property, are likely to be relevant, as are consumption taxes such as VAT. In the EU, VAT is a material and important tax with rates as high as 20% or more and is particularly relevant to wealthy clients who have high rates of consumption, including the purchase, use and enjoyment of luxury assets such as aircraft, yachts and art.

6. Tax relief

The wealthy client will also need to consider the application of reliefs and exemptions to all these taxes. The section below looks at how the wealthy client should approach or not approach tax avoidance and tax 'shelters' but the best way to avoid tax is to make use of tax exemptions and reliefs where specific legislation is in place to grant those exemptions and reliefs. In some jurisdictions the rules around the granting of reliefs and exemptions can be complex and difficult and therefore the application of the relevant relief should not be assumed or taken for granted. For example, in the UK how a business holding is structured may limit inheritance tax reliefs. Charitable reliefs may be particularly relevant and important to the wealthy client.

Even if the country of the home jurisdiction in which the wealthy client lives does not impose taxes on a certain type of transaction or asset, taxes may well apply in the other jurisdiction in which the asset is held. There may be special taxes which apply where non-residents acquire assets in certain jurisdictions. For example, if someone living outside the UK buys property in the UK they will need to consider the application of Stamp Duty Land Tax on the property acquisition, income tax on rent, the availability of capital allowances, VAT, capital gains tax on a future sale (or income tax in the case of a development) and also inheritance tax in the event of the death of the owner or where a lifetime gift is made. Similarly the acquisition of real estate in the United States will require consideration of income tax, capital gains tax and estate tax at a state and federal level. Also the Foreign Investment in Real Property Tax (FIRPTA) may apply in the case of non-residents.

7. Multi-jurisdictional impact

Because the application of taxes to a wealthy client is likely to be determined most by the jurisdiction in which they are tax resident and in which they live, there needs to be an awareness of how much tax is paid in the home jurisdiction compared with how much tax might be paid if the client were resident in another jurisdiction. The wealthy client tends to be highly mobile and in many cases will not have a job tie to their home jurisdiction. There is an adage that clients should not change where they live and where their economic and family ties are so as to reduce the tax burden. Many wealthy clients will not do this but some will and they will want to know what to do if tax rates increase to what they consider to be an unacceptable level in their home jurisdiction. The wealthy client will want to be aware and be appraised of what different tax jurisdictions have to offer and particularly those that seek to attract people to move to the jurisdiction. In Europe, jurisdictions such as Italy and Portugal have introduced tax regimes with particular incentives to attract wealthy foreigners and jurisdictions such as Switzerland have a regime which is more established. The UK has a particular regime dating back to the 18th century which taxes people who are not domiciled in the UK on a more favourable basis than those who are resident and domiciled in the UK. Sometimes, but rarely, a wealthy client may not be resident in any jurisdiction. Such a status is likely to be treated sceptically by taxing authorities and cause practical problems in banking and other financial relationships. Because wealthy clients are highly mobile and so are their family members, they need to have an appreciation of tax residence rules. It is important to avoid inadvertently becoming resident in another jurisdiction or becoming resident in a tax jurisdiction before intending to do so. Most sophisticated countries will have codified tax residence rules which will have day count tests which determine an individual's tax residence. That day count may vary according to the links the individual has with the jurisdiction in terms of work, property and family, etc. Wealthy individuals need to be aware of these rules and the people who advise them need to be aware of them as well. It is also important to keep in mind when a period of residence will commence for tax purposes, such as whether that is on the date someone first arrives or at the start of the relevant tax year in which residence commences. The other side of the coin is for wealthy clients to understand when they might cease to be tax resident in a tax jurisdiction and how long certain taxes in the jurisdiction will apply to them, particularly if they return to that jurisdiction after a certain period of time. The United States taxes individuals according to citizenship and residence so that individuals may need to give up US citizenship to cease being subject to US taxes.

8. Tax mitigation

Wealthy clients will often focus on how they can mitigate taxes whether those taxes relate to employment or in respect of investment-related returns.

Generally speaking, the ability of wealthy clients to mitigate employment taxes is increasingly limited in most high tax jurisdictions. There may be some scope for investment-related returns related to employment to be treated as capital gains (with a generally lower rate of tax) – such as on carry-based returns related to private equity, on employment-related co-investment or on employee-related share options – but the scope for that is increasingly restricted. Similarly, those with high earnings may want those earnings to accrue in another jurisdiction in which tax rates are lower or they may wish the tax point on those earnings to be deferred. Again, that is increasingly difficult as tax authorities in high tax jurisdictions have clamped down on such arrangements. Business structures such as companies may reduce taxes on earnings to lower corporation tax rates but this is increasingly seen as an abuse of the tax system. Pension planning can of course be important to the wealthy client and cannot be ignored. However, increasingly pension reliefs and exemptions are limited in their scope and benefits capped. Certain investments may attract relief from income tax when made (as governments wish to encourage investment in higher risk businesses or in deprived geographic areas) but again these can be restricted in high tax jurisdictions.

There may be more scope to mitigate taxes on investment-related returns, either by way of reducing tax rates or by deferring taxes to a later point in time when tax rates may be lower, or indeed by accelerating a tax charge where tax rates might increase. It might be possible to defer a tax charge to a point in time where the tax residence of the individual may have changed. Of course jurisdictions may impose tax exit charges where an individual ceases to be tax resident (such as in Canada or the USA) or have exit taxes that apply to certain investments. Taxes may apply for a certain period of time after a person has ceased to be resident or may crystallise if there is a return to the jurisdiction within a certain period of time.

Individuals who invest into foreign jurisdictions may not be taxable on the capital profits realised in that jurisdiction, although this is increasingly not possible in relation to real estate. Gains realised by non-residents on UK real estate are fully taxable in the UK whereas before 2015 they were not. To the extent that income profits arise through trading or rental activities, it has been common to reduce those taxable profits by interest and other deductions which are taxable in lower tax jurisdictions. However, this base erosion is a particular focus of the OECD BEPS initiative and the scope to do this is becoming much more limited.

It may be possible for investment taxes to be deferred through the use of regulated funds and certain insurance-type products. The key thing is to avoid taxes being paid each time an investment is purchased or sold if the client does not require the proceeds of sale to be paid out. Of course, this adds to the compounding effects of investment returns but there may be an added management cost and there may be less flexibility over the choice of investments. It might be possible to set up a closely held corporate vehicle so that investment profits are subject to lower rates of corporation taxes until those profits are extracted and subject to likely higher rates of personal tax.

The mitigation of estate and inheritance taxes is likely to be of particular concern to the wealthy client where they apply. As noted above, these taxes are likely to be mitigated by reducing the size of the taxable estate on death. Where the tax regime permits, this can be achieved through lifetime gifts and there may be sophisticated planning techniques to reduce the value of the taxable estate on death. Tax exemptions and reliefs are likely to be highly relevant, particularly where an estate tax charge can be deferred through the use of a spousal exemption. The use of trusts may facilitate the making of lifetime gifts where significant tax charges don't apply when they are created. In the UK the use of trusts has been severely constrained since 2008. The structure of the will of a wealthy client will be critical to the taxation of the estate on death and also for the surviving family members.

As mentioned above, the common feature of the wealthy client is that they are highly mobile, either through accident or design, and the same applies to family members. Often this will open up tax mitigation strategies and opportunities, some of which can be very long lasting.

9. Tax shelters

Of course, wealthy clients tend to be those who are approached to invest in 'tax shelter' products. Those products may reduce rates of tax, defer taxes or eliminate taxes through the use of real or manufactured tax losses. There is an obvious appeal in such products to the wealthy client where in absolute terms the amount of taxes being paid may be very significant indeed. Again, in most high tax jurisdictions, governments, tax authorities and the courts have attacked the artificiality of such arrangements and either through legislation or the courts have outlawed such arrangements. Furthermore, some jurisdictions such as the UK have introduced general anti-avoidance legislation, following the example of jurisdictions such as Australia and Ireland. The acceptability of wealthy clients entering into such arrangements from a societal point of view is much more limited and can result in adverse media comments. For those who head up or own successful public companies the adverse publicity which comes with the association with tax avoidance may be particularly damaging on a customer base. The public's perception of what activities amount to acceptable planning rather than unacceptable tax avoidance or evasion is extremely narrow and politicians see political capital to be made by attacking tax avoidance and conveniently choose not to differentiate between tax planning or acceptable avoidance and unacceptable evasion. In some countries, such as the UK, there is intense media interest in the tax affairs of wealthy people, particularly where wealthy people choose to move from the UK to another jurisdiction or choose to relocate their business. This means that wealthy people in the UK, with a public profile, may need to be able to turn to a reputational management lawyer at short notice if the media are in danger of misrepresenting what they have done or indeed their motives for doing so. It is very easy for the media to misrepresent or not understand tax matters.

10. Penalties

Wealthy clients need to be appraised of the consequences of being non-compliant with their taxes. In high tax jurisdictions the penalties for non-compliance are often severe and may result in criminal prosecution. This means that for the wealthy client tax compliance is of increasing importance due to the penalties and potential adverse publicity in not being compliant. A wealthy client is likely to be best served by spending money on tax compliance as opposed to spending money on tax avoidance strategies that may not work, particularly when those strategies are contrived.

Although the use of 'tax shelters' and artificial arrangements should be avoided by the wealthy client, that does not mean that the wealthy client should not plan carefully to mitigate taxes within the tax rules which exist. As mentioned above, often the tax which may concern a wealthy client most is estate or inheritance tax. This can be a difficult discussion to have with the client, who has to deal with their own mortality. The most effective way to deal with estate taxes is to give property away. The wealthy client has to consider the best way to do that and typically it will involve the use of a structure such as a trust, a company or a partnership. In common law jurisdictions, trusts are likely to be the vehicle of choice to pass assets down and in a way which will mitigate inheritance and gift taxes. There has been an increased tendency for wealthy individuals to make known that they do not wish to benefit the next generation and instead leave their money to charity but it would be fair to say that that is the exception rather than the rule. Most wealthy clients will wish to pass on their assets to the next generation and in a controlled manner. It is important that the wealthy client has a suitable will in place and this will often need to cater for his or her assets being held in multiple jurisdictions. Also, a properly prepared will is likely to allow some opportunity for post death tax planning and most often this will be possible if a will is drafted in a flexible way.

11. Charitable exemptions

The wealthy client may wish to give a portion of their wealth to charity either during their lifetime or on death. Most sophisticated tax jurisdictions have meaningful charitable exemptions for charitable gifts and wealthy clients will wish to avail themselves of those exemptions. Charities which attract tax reliefs and exemptions are likely to be highly regulated both from a tax and governance perspective in terms of how the charity is run, how its funds are expended and how its activities are reported. Often the wealthy client will have an overlap between charitable and non-charitable activities and where that happens care will need to be taken to manage conflicts of interest and the inadvertent provision of benefits. Charitable giving is also a mechanism where wealthy families will introduce the next generation to the better management of wealth.

12. Family office or outsource

The way a wealthy client manages and takes tax advice requires careful consideration. Typically the issue will be around the degree to which tax management and strategy is dealt with in-house through a family office or by suitably qualified professionals either in-house or on an entirely outsourced basis. Tax management will tend to cover the tax compliance function, comprising the preparation and delivery of returns and the payment of taxes. In the context of a wealthy client who has a family office in multiple jurisdictions and where the interests are international both in respect of structures, investments and family members, the compliance function itself may be highly complex and involve a number of in-house professionals. Tax compliance is about collating and providing information to tax authorities. Therefore, having people in-house who collate that information and submit the information to the relevant tax authority may well be more accurate and more efficient.

It may also be less intrusive to a family if its own employees carry out these functions. Of course the challenges, if such functions are carried out in-house, are well known. There is a need to recruit and retain staff who are well qualified and who can be trusted to carry out the professional functions they have. It will be important, where there is a function that involves a number of people, that suitable and robust governance structures are in place given the significance and importance of the tax compliance function. The tax compliance function might report into an oversight committee and it will tend to link up closely with any internal accounting and finance function. An important element to tax compliance is the management of the associated risk that goes with it. As discussed above, the penalties which often now apply to tax compliance failures are severe and therefore the risk of failures in the function need to be recognised and mitigated. A sophisticated family office structure may have an internal risk function that has oversight of the tax compliance function. Again, in a sophisticated family office setup the tax compliance and risk function may have oversight of the way internal structures are managed and ensure that management takes place where it is meant to and by the right individuals so as not to prejudice the tax effectiveness of the underlying structures. Whether or not tax strategy can be provided in-house or externally will depend on the financial resources of the client and whether an individual who is in-house has the relevant experience as a tax professional to provide strategic advice. Most commonly, input from an external lawyer or accountant will be required to help formulate tax strategy.

13. Information disclosures

A key consideration for wealthy clients, closely linked to the management of taxes, is the disclosure of information to relevant tax authorities by third parties. This follows the global reporting obligations imposed under the Foreign Account Tax Compliance Act and, more recently and on a much more widespread basis, under the Common Reporting Standard. These reporting regimes further enhance automatic reporting regimes under double tax treaties. There is now an acceptance by almost all wealthy clients that it is no longer possible to hide investments or assets from tax authorities. Some wealthy individuals and families may feel they have good reasons to do so if they are susceptible to kidnap or other similar types of criminal act where they are already complying with their own tax reporting and tax payment obligations. As more and more financial information passes from one government authority to another, the greater the chance that that information will be lost or possibly sold as a result of criminal activity. The key thing for the wealthy client and their advisers is to understand what information is being disclosed and to which tax authority. This is especially the case where structures are put in place which involve legal entities such as trusts and companies and the various office holders in those structures. Indeed, when a structure is set up, any tax analysis should include details about what disclosure will be made and to whom. The degree of disclosure which is required might be a relevant factor in determining the jurisdiction in which to make an investment or establish a structure. Wealthy clients may wish to establish structures in jurisdictions which have lower or no taxes on the structures themselves even if the client may be subject to full taxes in his or her home jurisdiction. Quite often where families have members in many different jurisdictions it may be more efficient for the family assets to be located in a low tax jurisdiction. Those jurisdictions which are British Crown Dependencies or British Overseas Territories are likely to be low tax jurisdictions and are likely to result in cross-border reporting. Those jurisdictions have also introduced economic 'substance rules' to avoid being 'black listed' by the EU. Again, wealthy clients and their advisers need to be aware of these rules, determine whether the rules apply and, if they do, make sure they are not breached.

It is quite possible that under these disclosure regimes a tax authority will receive information of which it was not already aware, so the wealthy client may need to be ready and prepared for enquiries which arise. Therefore, there is an increasing need for the wealthy client to keep good and sufficient records so these enquiries can be dealt with as expeditiously and cheaply as possible.

14. Tax advice

When the wealthy client seeks external tax advice it is important that they get the best advice possible. It is not only a question of getting the best strategic and planning advice but also the best compliance advice, given the comments above. It is most common for compliance advice and services to be provided by the accountancy profession and fiduciary services. It is not uncommon for accountants to provide strategic and planning advice as well. In some jurisdictions, planning and interpretation of tax laws is the exclusive preserve of the legal profession but in others, such as the UK, there is less of a distinction between tax lawyers and accountants. A point which needs to be borne in mind in common law jurisdictions such as the UK and the US is that legal privilege will only attach to legal advice given by a qualified lawyer, and when and where legal privilege does or does not apply is a highly complex area of the law. Nonetheless, in the context of tax litigation, legal professional privilege can be highly valuable. Where tax advice is required across jurisdictions, the wealthy client needs to be mindful of those jurisdictions, such as the EU, where professionals are required to report suspicious activity pursuant to money laundering laws and regulations, which will include suspicions of tax evasion, and where 'tipping off' is also an offence. Some wealthy clients may decide to get tax advice from a number of professionals so that no professional knows the overall picture of the client's affairs. This is not to be recommended because of the knock-on effect that of one piece of advice could have on a structure or circumstance of which the tax adviser is unaware. Of course, if the client has a family office it may be that the office is sophisticated enough such that external tax advice can be obtained on specific matters, and the family office of the client will be aware of whether the advice given on that particular piece of advice might impact some other matter to do with the client.

15. Conclusion

As can be seen from the above, the wealthy client is likely to need sophisticated and multi-jurisdictional advice. Often the challenge is that the wealthy client who was once or is still a successful entrepreneur wants tax to be simple and straightforward but sadly that isn't the case and, despite calls for tax simplification, tax law becomes ever more complicated and voluminous in terms of the number of laws and regulations which exist. The challenge for those people who advise the wealthy client is to get the advice right and also to be able to explain that advice to the client in a way that can be understood. Often the right answer may not be immediately apparent or the client is faced with options and choices. The skilled tax adviser will be able to exercise judgement in helping the client reach the right decision. That is a difficult skill and one which comes with experience as well as technical knowledge.

Reviewing the trust agreement

Gail E Cohen
Gerard F Joyce
Fiduciary Trust Company International

1. Introduction

The need to review a trust agreement arises in many different contexts. A named successor trustee reviews the agreement prior to accepting its responsibilities; a review may be warranted to determine if the trust continues to meet the needs of the creator; and a beneficiary of a trust may review the agreement to assure that the trustees are adequately fulfilling their duties to the beneficiary. How one reviews the trust agreement – and what one is looking for – depends on the reason for the review. This chapter contains general guidelines for anyone who reviews a trust agreement – regardless of the reason for the review – and it touches on the provisions that should be included in all trust agreements.

The permutations of intent, beneficiaries and assets are endless, but in order to assure that the trust is effectively drafted, the reviewer should have answers to the following questions: (1) Who is the trust agreement intended to benefit and, if for multiple beneficiaries, do they have potential or actual conflicting needs? (2) What is the time horizon for the trust? (3) What are the trust assets – initially and into the future?

This chapter will discuss the elements necessary to appropriately review all trusts, regardless of the trust's jurisdiction. From time to time, however, provisions applicable solely to US-centric trusts will be specifically mentioned as well as provisions that are specific to cross-border trusts.[1]

1 A cross-border trust in this chapter will usually be one created by a non-US client for the benefit of one or more US persons (and possibly for a combination of both US and non-US beneficiaries). This planning has become extremely common because of two big trends within wealthy families: (1) their children attend US university and stay in the US, particularly if they meet a US person whom they marry or live with in the US; and (2) the family business (or a substantial investment) branches out to the US, given the opportunities within the US economy.

2. Identifying parties to the trust

A trust agreement creates a third-party beneficiary contract; that is, two or more parties entering into a contract for the benefit of a third party. The person or persons who create the trust and who transfer assets to the trust are referred to as 'grantors', 'donors', 'creators' or 'trustors'. The counterparty to the trust is typically known as a 'trustee'. The persons for whose benefit the trust is created are known as 'beneficiaries' and may be either current beneficiaries or beneficiaries who will receive a future benefit. The beneficiaries who are to receive future benefits are known as 'remainder beneficiaries'. Often, the same individual or individuals may have multiple roles. For example, a grantor of a trust may also be a trustee and a beneficiary.

The identity of the remainder beneficiaries may impact the manner in which the trustee administers the trust. For example, if a current beneficiary has multiple trusts, and those trusts have different remainder beneficiaries, determining which trust should pay for an extraordinary expense becomes complicated. Making a distribution from one trust rather than another may create tension where the family cannot agree on which trust should pay for a certain expense or undertaking (such as education or major medical expenses). This may become especially contentious if the remainder beneficiaries are children of blended families.

Trust agreements should clearly identify individuals or corporations who are parties to the agreement. The names should be spelled correctly and there should be enough identifying information to assure no mistakes are made in carrying out the intentions of the grantor. For example, if a specific charitable organisation is a beneficiary, the exact name and address of that charity should be verified with the institution, keeping in mind that many charities have operations in different geographic locations and the creator may have wished to benefit a specific location. The correct legal entity name and address of a corporate trustee should be verified with the trust institution to assure that the proper organisation is acting; a provision should be included in the trust that the named corporate trustee includes any successors to that trustee, to take into account company acquisitions and mergers.

3. Trust dispositive provisions – understand the grantor's intent

A review of a trust's dispositive provisions requires, first and foremost, understanding what the grantor's wishes are in creating the trust. An understanding of those wishes drives the conclusions one reaches as to whether the dispositive provisions accurately reflect the grantor's wishes. If, for example, the grantor wishes to benefit the siblings, parents and children, but the trust provisions reflect only the children as beneficiaries, the document does not accurately express the wishes.

Often a trust instrument will be drafted or presented in isolation. This is typical for tax-driven trusts or trusts designed for a specific purpose, such as a family 'education' trust. Even for such targeted trusts, it is important to understand how the trust fits into the family's overall planning.

It is also important to understand how the trust fits in as a percentage of the overall wealth available to the beneficiaries. A smaller trust may have to be carefully crafted to ensure that it lasts for the long term if the intention is to assure that there is a modest income plus emergency funds available for the beneficiaries.

Many trust agreements contain tax-driven provisions. For example, in the UK a will may create a 'nil-band' trust. In the US, trusts may take advantage of both the credit amount (similar to the nil band) and the marital deduction. These provisions are highly technical and they are typically drafted as a formula so that changes in the law will allow for these dispositions to self-adjust.

In the US, one would review the formula to determine if the document attempts to first carve out the credit amount and then leave the rest of the property as the marital amount, or vice versa. The drafting will impact the income tax implications of the disposition. For individuals whose estates fall below the current credit threshold (which, in relation to the federal estate exemption for 2020, is US$11.58 million), the 'residuary' should be the credit amount to avoid the realisation of gain in funding the trust.[2]

If a marital share is to be held in trust for a surviving spouse, the IRC requires very specific provisions in a document to allow a trust to qualify for the marital deduction.[3] Basically, there are three types of trusts that will qualify. Each of these trusts must be for the surviving spouse's sole benefit during the spouse's lifetime. In all events, the surviving spouse must be entitled to receive this benefit as of the date of death of a spouse, with the IRC allowing up to a six-month

2 See the Internal Revenue Code §2010. A decedent does not owe an estate tax if their credit amount does not exceed the exemption amount.

3 See the Internal Revenue Code §2056.

waiting period of survival.[4] The three trusts are as follows: (1) an 'estate' trust, which allows for discretionary distributions of income to the spouse, but requires that at the spouse's death the trust pours into the spouse's estate; (2) a 'general power of appointment' trust that requires all income to be distributed to the surviving spouse during lifetime, but the spouse must possess a general power of appointment over the trust; and (3) a 'QTIP' trust, that requires all income be payable to the surviving spouse during his or her lifetime, directs distribution of the trust at the surviving spouse's death and requires that the personal representative of the deceased's first spouse make an election on the estate tax return to qualify it for the marital deduction. This third type of trust – the QTIP trust – is the type of trust overwhelmingly used by current practitioners because the first spouse to die can designate the remainder beneficiaries who will inherit after the death of the surviving spouse.

In reviewing a trust agreement, one should assure that any tax payments are directed to be paid from the correct source. There are a variety of options for paying taxes. For example, if the decedent has property that is taxable but that does not pass under the trust agreement or will, should taxes be paid from that other property? Or should taxes be paid from the property passing under the trust? Or should there be a hybrid approach? The determination of where taxes are paid can have an enormous impact on the value of an inheritance, yet often drafting attorneys do not discuss this with their clients.[5]

When a trust agreement makes a charitable bequest, the drafter should consider whether the bequest should be made outright to a surviving spouse with the request that the spouse make the charitable gift. This is a tax efficient method of making gifts – there is no estate tax on the gift to the spouse, yet the spouse may also be entitled to an income tax deduction in the year the surviving spouse makes the gift. This may not work for all situations, especially clients whose spouses would not make the requested gifts, since there can be no obligation on the spouse to make the gift.

---

4 See *Estate of Heim v C.I.R.*, 914 F.2d 1322 (9th Circuit 1990), in which the Court of Appeals affirmed the Tax Court's decision that a provision leaving a gift to the surviving spouse if she should "predecease me or fail to survive distribution" disqualified the gift from being entitled to a marital deduction because the distribution could have exceeded the six-month period allowed by the Internal Revenue Code.

5 See *In re Estate of Kuralt*, 315 Mont 177, 68 P3d 662, 2003 MT 92 [2003]. The Court held that the daughters of Charles Kuralt must pay US$350,000 in estate taxes on a property in Montana that was bequeathed to his mistress in a handwritten codicil.

In the US, there are additional taxes payable when a gift is made to a member of a class of individuals who are two or more generations younger than the creator; this is known as the 'generation-skipping transfer tax'. A trust agreement should attempt to shelter the current exemption from that tax (which, in relation to the federal estate exemption for 2020, is US$11.58 million per person). Trusts that are intended to shelter assets from this tax are usually drafted as long-term or 'dynasty' trusts. Since non-US grantors' assets are not subject to this tax, cross-border trusts are often drafted in this manner as well. Because these trusts can last for such a long time, they put a premium on the trusts' governance. Specifically, these governance issues will include who should act as trustee, as well as how a trustee is appointed and removed.

4. Understanding the assets funding the trust

The type of assets that fund trusts will have a critical impact on how the trust should be drafted. For example, a trust holding shares in a closely held company must be coordinated with the other related shareholders to ensure that the company's governance is bolstered and not splintered as a result. Consideration should be given to using non-voting shares to avoid nuisance litigation by a minority shareholder, particularly where the beneficiaries' views of the company differ from the other shareholders. Issues can arise with respect to the company's dividend policy or strategic decisions such as whether to make an acquisition or to sell to an acquirer.

In reviewing a trust instrument, it is critical to know the nature and size of the assets expected to be held and administered by the trustee. As mentioned above, holding a closely held business interest requires a different skillset versus holding an investment portfolio. And, if the trustee is holding only a minority interest in a closely held business, the responsibilities are even less complicated than when holding a controlling or swing vote interest. The trust should reflect the nature of the assets held and it should enable the trustee to deal effectively with the trust assets.

For so-called 'unique assets', such as business interests and tangibles such as paintings, as well as residences and office buildings, the first question is whether it is intended for the trustee to actually manage the asset. Often, the asset is placed in trust for wealth protection reasons, including tax minimisation, and not because the trustee has the requisite skills needed to manage that particular kind of asset. In these cases, a 'directed trust'[6] will often be a useful solution. A directed trust permits a trustee to hold an asset and see to its overall administration while assigning the management of the asset to an 'investment adviser'. The investment adviser will have the sole responsibility for the management of the trust asset. In drafting to name an investment adviser for the directed trust, many practitioners will expressly provide that the investment adviser is a fiduciary. The reason for this is that otherwise there will be no person responsible for management of the trust asset who is a fiduciary. As a result, many corporate trustees and grantors want to assure that the investment adviser has trustee accountability to ensure that the trust asset is properly managed.

5. Flexibility

As mentioned above, trusts are drafted to last for many years, often into perpetuity. As a result, when reviewing a trust, one should look for flexibility in the drafting of the document. Without flexibility, a trust will become difficult – if not impossible – to administer in the future since no one can predict what the future will bring. This applies not only to the future circumstances of the beneficiaries, but also to future financial instruments and other investments, future tax laws, future substantive laws and future trustee circumstances.

Flexible provisions must be included in several areas of the trust: in the dispositive provisions to take into account future beneficiary circumstances; in the powers clauses, to take into account future investment strategies; in the governing law provisions, to take into account changes in the current jurisdiction's laws and changes in tax laws; and in the trustee appointment provisions.

For example, a trust should allow the trustee to invade principal for the current beneficiary to allow for appropriate distributions based on total return of the portfolio. These distributions should be broad based, consistent with any tax issues that might arise.[7] Additionally, beneficiaries should be granted powers of

---

6 See Delaware Code §3313 for Delaware's directed trustee statute. There are 30 states that have directed trust statutes, but all directed trust statutes are not created equally, so it is important to understand what duties, rights and limitations each statute affords to a directed trustee.

7 See the Internal Revenue Code §2041. When a beneficiary is also a trustee, the trust should limit that beneficiary/trustee's distribution discretion to an "ascertainable standard". An ascertainable standard is the power to invade the principal for health, education, support or maintenance. The exercise of discretion using this standard prevents a beneficiary/trustee incurring gift tax consequences when making a

appointment to allow changing the governing provisions and the future beneficiaries, if this is consistent with the grantor's wishes. Putting limits on these powers of appointment may be appropriate. For example, a beneficiary may have the power to appoint to his or her spouse at death, but the grantor may wish to limit the power to be exercisable only in trust for the spouse, with remainder to the grantor's descendants.

At times, a trust document will exercise a power of appointment that was created in another trust. In that case, in reviewing the exercise, it is necessary to review the document that created the power to assure that all formalities of the exercise are observed. A review should also ascertain that the appointees of the power are all permissible appointees and that the exercise does not violate the rule against perpetuities. Often, the assets subject to the power are limited by the rule against perpetuities applicable to the trust that created the power.

For trustees, it will be important to assure that the trustee has the power to resign. Additionally, a mechanism for removal and replacement of a trustee should be included in the trust agreement.[8] The agreement should also include a methodology for selecting successor trustees if an individual dies or becomes incompetent. Some professional trustees will charge a commission upon the termination of their role; the trust agreement should expressly provide that no 'termination commission' should be payable to the trustee upon the removal or resignation of the trustee. Review any trustee liability limitations or indemnifications to assure that they do not violate public policy.[9]

Some important fiduciary powers to include in a trust agreement are:

- ability to abandon worthless property;
- ability to terminate small trusts – and provide a guideline as to what is 'small';

---

distribution. Also see the Internal Revenue Code §672. For an independent trustee, a broader discretionary standard (such as "comfort", "best interests" or "happiness") will allow the independent trustee more flexibility in making distributions.

8 A protector is often included as another party to a trust agreement. Grantors impose varying duties on protectors, but typically a protector may have the ability to change trustees or assist the trustee in executing its duties.

9 See, for example, New York's Estates, Powers and Trusts Law §11-1.7, which states that it is contrary to public policy to attempt to exonerate certain fiduciaries from liability for not exercising reasonable care, diligence and prudence. See, also, Uniform Trust Code §1008 deeming unenforceable a term of a trust relieving a trustee of liability for breach of trust under certain circumstances.

- discretion to allocate receipts and disbursements between income and principal;
- ability to lend money from the trust and to pledge trust assets as collateral for a loan;
- ability to employ agents and advisers;
- discretion to change trust *situs* and governing law – both the administrative and substantive law;
- discretion to merge similar trusts;
- (for a corporate trustee) authority to invest in registered and unregistered funds, including affiliated funds, for which the trustee receives compensation; and
- ability to borrow – including to borrow from itself if the trustee is a lender.

While a trustee may have many of these powers because the trust's governing law automatically grants them to a trustee, it is nevertheless helpful to include them in the trust agreement since the governing law may change in the future to a new jurisdiction that does not contain these provisions.

6. Governing law

Governing law and taxes are often intertwined considerations since the choice of law may itself have tax implications. The choice of one jurisdiction's governing law and creating a nexus to that jurisdiction may result in subjecting property to that jurisdiction's taxes; conversely, the choice of a particular jurisdiction and creating the appropriate nexus may eliminate a tax that might otherwise be payable. For example, the mere choice of a non-US trustee with authority over one or more substantial trust decisions (ie, investments, distributions, etc) will cause the trust to be foreign for US income tax purposes, thereby avoiding US taxation except for income deemed 'connected' to the US.[10]

The choice of governing law has additional implications. In cross-border trust planning, that choice can be used to override the forced heirship rules or other local property laws that could otherwise apply to the property. Creating the appropriate nexus to allow for the choice of a jurisdiction's governing law varies from one jurisdiction to another. Often the law is tied to the trustee's location – while not always the case, the trustee or trustees may be

10 The Internal Revenue Code §7701(a)(30)(E)(ii).

located in the place of the governing law. This is particularly true where corporate trustees are involved as they will want to assure that they are fully conversant with the law applying to the trust administration. Trustees can otherwise be subject to criticism for not understanding the requirements or features of the governing trust law, so choosing the local law is often the prudent course.

Often the governing law will be chosen for one of its special features such as enhanced asset protection or a so-called 'directed trustee' provision. There is great competition among the jurisdictions (Delaware, South Dakota, Alaska, Nevada and New Hampshire to name several just in the US) to ensure that they adopt the latest and best variation of these modern trust features. Where a family chooses to use the law of one of these jurisdictions, they will be advised to choose a corporate trustee from this jurisdiction in order to assure that there is a recognised legal nexus.

Just as important as the choice of a particular jurisdiction's governing law is granting the power to change the governing law. It is also wise to consider having the trust instrument provide which law to govern (a) the interpretation and validity, and (b) trust administration matters (fees, allocation of principal and income). The same law can govern both sets of legal issues, but one should understand that the mere act of moving the trust to a new jurisdiction by choosing a new trust may allow for or trigger the application of the law of the place of administration.[11]

Closely related to governing law are the so-called decanting statutes whereby trusts can be relocated from one jurisdiction to another. Modifying, 'fixing' or decanting trusts has become a cottage industry within the trusts and estates world as attorneys are 'decanting' trusts to jurisdictions such as Delaware and then making changes to a variety of trust provisions, such as extending the term of the trust,[12] deleting beneficiaries, granting powers of appointment and other such changes. Decanting and trust modifications have

11 The legal position in Delaware illustrates this concept well. Here, there are two statutes that work in tandem. The first, Delaware Code §3340, essentially provides that a trust is deemed to be administered in Delaware if it has a Delaware trustee. The second, Delaware Code §3332(b), states that the laws of the State of Delaware govern the administration of a trust *while it is administered in Delaware* unless the governing instrument expressly provides that the laws of another jurisdiction govern it and further provides that the laws governing administration shall not change on account of a change in the place of administration of the trust (emphasis added).

12 But not extending the perpetuities period of course.

become so[13] prevalent that the use of Non-Judicial Settlement Agreements (NJSAs) is commonplace and truly call into question whether any trust provision cannot be amended. One wonders if eventually trusts may be drafted to forbid the use of an NJSA to modify certain trust provisions.

7. Income taxes

Well-designed trusts are tax efficient – meaning that they do not create unintended tax consequences and they take advantage of applicable exemptions and planning opportunities that various tax laws permit. Again, this is an area where a team approach to professional advice is critical. Once the client's plan is outlined, the structure should be drawn up and then evaluated from a tax perspective; with cross-border trust planning, the evaluation should include both US and home country perspectives. It is important that the two major tax regimes in each jurisdiction should be evaluated: both income taxes (especially capital gains, if any) and transfer taxes on estates, inheritances and gifts.

Most cross-border trusts created by non-US persons for the benefit of one or more US persons are designed to avoid the US estate tax that would otherwise come into play if the beneficiary were to have instead received an outright bequest. As a result, a trust agreement should ensure that the trust does not terminate during the beneficiaries' lifetimes, nor should it grant a beneficiary a general power of appointment which would make any property subject to it includible in the US beneficiary's estate for US estate tax purposes. As a result, any trust that has principal termination provisions (even staged provisions, say one-third at age 35, half at age 40 and the balance at age 45) should be modified before it becomes irrevocable to avoid increasing the size of the US beneficiary's estate.

Awareness of local legal and tax rules is critical as even the most plain-vanilla trust instrument (from a US-standpoint) can have disastrous home country consequences. For example, most US planners would think little could go wrong by simply creating a revocable trust and funding it during a grantor's lifetime. This is because the revocable trust is treated as being owned by the grantor and therefore largely ignored for US tax purposes during the grantor's lifetime. However, a US-style revocable trust for a person living in the UK and which names UK resident trustees could immediately

13 Adding beneficiaries under a modification may be problematic if not prohibited. See, eg, Delaware Code §3342.

trigger a 20% UK inheritance tax. As a result, it is always important to ensure that the document has been designed and approved by tax counsel in each relevant jurisdiction.

In reviewing trusts to determine how they will be treated for income tax purposes, we will look at: (a) the residence/citizenship of the trustee; (b) the governing law (likely giving a US court primary jurisdiction over the trust and trustees); and (c) whether there is an 'automatic flee clause' that triggers the movement of the trust *situs* upon specified circumstances (ie, a change in government, etc).

It is helpful to include statements about intended tax consequences, such as "I intend for this trust to be a grantor trust for US income tax purposes during my lifetime". These types of provisions can be very helpful where the draftsman has been either imprecise or even made a drafting error, as a clear statement of intent may allow for a clarification or modification without triggering negative consequences.[14]

A discussion of the benefits of powers of appointment for flexibility purposes was discussed above. Powers of appointment are important tax tools for cross-border trusts, as well. For inbound US trust planning where substantial wealth is passing from a non-US person to a US person, the estate planning immediately becomes multi-generational. That is because in addition to the transfer from the grantor to the children's generation, there will be a subsequent transfer upon the passing of a child. If the trust assets constitute the bulk of the wealth in the family, then the trust created by the grantor effectively serves as the child's will in that it directs what happens to the trust assets upon the child's death.

As a result, what appears to be the parent's trust also doubles as the child's because most of the 'child's wealth' is in the trust. If the major purpose of the trust is to protect against tax at the child's death, the child should have the power to dispose of that property in a manner similar to the manner in which the child could have disposed of it had the child received the property outright. Drafters will often have the grantor give the child a 'power of appointment' to enable the child to determine who gets the property upon his or her passing. The power can allow for a broad or wide class of recipients (including non-family members) or it can be limited to a class of people. For US beneficiaries it is important not to grant a

14 In the case of an inadvertent creation of a US or a foreign trust under the Section 7701(30) rules, it would be very helpful to have a clear statement of intent or even a savings clause to avoid inadvertently changing the US income tax status of the trust.

so-called 'general power of appointment', which would cause the property subject to the power of appointment to be included in the beneficiary's estate for US estate tax purposes. It is also a good idea to specify the manner by which a power of appointment can be exercised so that there is no inadvertent exercise of the power causing the property to pass other than how the beneficiary intended.

8. Definitions

Definitions of terms used in a trust agreement can typically be found hiding in the back of a trust agreement. These definitions comprise a critical part of the manner in which trusts operate, and they should not be ignored simply because they fall towards the end of the document.

One of the most critical definitions is that of 'descendants' or 'issue'. Modern reproductive methods have evolved so quickly that there is no simple method of defining who is a person's 'child'. Grantors should be given the opportunity to reflect on issues such as *in vitro* fertilisation, either post-mortem or during lifetime. For example, if their son predeceases but the surviving spouse has a child from his sperm after his death, should that child be considered the grantor's 'grandchild' for purposes of the trust agreement?

Clarifying adoptions is another important part of defining 'issue' and 'descendants'. A grantor may be comfortable that a child who is adopted by their child should be considered a grandchild for inheritance purposes. However, if a child adopts their spouse or partner, should that spouse or partner be considered a grandchild for inheritance purposes? Many grantors would like to avoid that result. One way to accomplish that is to put an age limit on the adoption – so, for example, a child adopted under the age of 18 may be considered a 'child' for inheritance purposes, but not a child adopted over the age of 18.

In many trusts, a definition of 'spouse' is appropriate. Many grantors feel that a marriage valid in the jurisdiction the marriage is entered into is valid for purposes of the trust, regardless of the law governing the trust agreement at the time the determination of 'spouse' is made. Additionally, many grantors include 'partners' as 'spouses' and define who might be someone's 'partner' for purposes of the trust agreement.

It is advisable to include a definition of the term *'per stirpes'*. That term is used to describe the shares that a descendant may inherit, based on the relationship that descendant has with the grantor. So, for example, if a person's trust leaves property at the person's death to 'my issue, *per stirpes*', and that person has three children all of whom survived, each child would inherit one-third of that property. If, on the other hand, only two of the three children survived and the deceased child was survived by one or more children, the two surviving children would each receive one-third of the property, and the grandchildren born from the pre-deceased child would share the final one-third. The problem arises when no children survive, but grandchildren survive. Some laws state that '*per stirpes*' requires that the grandchildren would share the property equally; other state laws state that the grandchildren in this example would receive only the share that their deceased parent would have received. Although this seems a highly technical point, the impact on the beneficiaries could be substantial and litigation could ensue if the trust agreement does not appropriately state the grantor's wishes.

The trust agreement should also define how to determine if someone is 'disabled' under the trust agreement. This need to determine disability may arise in several contexts. The grantor's disability in a revocable trust may trigger certain dispositive clauses; a trustee's disability may require the removal and replacement of that trustee; and a beneficiary's disability may require different distribution standards. In any event, if the term is not defined in the trust agreement, a court proceeding to declare a person disabled may be necessary to trigger these actions. This is an expense and delay – a painful proceeding – that can be avoided simply by defining what is meant. For example, disability can be determined by two physicians' certificates.

9. Conclusion

Courts frequently cite a time-honoured maxim that they will not "look outside the four corners of the trust instrument" in interpreting a trust. That is why it is imperative to review a trust to assure that it expresses a grantor's wishes, takes into account the assets funding it, takes advantage of tax strategies and provides the flexibility to stand the test of time. Therefore, it is critical that a trust review must begin with an understanding of what the trust is designed to accomplish as well as what assets are being placed in the trust.

The authors are deeply appreciative of the assistance of Joel C Krooks in the preparation of this chapter.

Annex 1: Document review checklist

For ________________				
Prepared by ____________				
Date _________________				
Initials				
		Circle appropriate letter		
1.	Review document for content.			
	This requires the reviewer to understand the intent of the Grantor.			
	Does it:			
	a. Express dispositive wishes correctly	Y	N	N/A
	b. Take advantage of tax techniques:			
	This assumes a knowledge of all applicable tax laws.			
	i. Formula for marital bequest	Y	N	N/A
	ii. Situs in proper jurisdiction	Y	N	N/A
	iii. QTIP trust	Y	N	N/A
	iv. Payment of estate taxes from proper source	Y	N	N/A
	v. Make charitable bequests to spouse w/necessary request	Y	N	N/A
	c. Take advantage of generation-skipping tax techniques:			
	i. Formula GST exemption shelter	Y	N	N/A
	ii. Appropriate general powers of appointment	Y	N	N/A
	iii. 90-day survival requirement	Y	N	N/A
	iv. Splitting trusts	Y	N	N/A
2.	Review trusts created under document. Do they:			
	a. Authorise invasion of principal to provide flexibility	Y	N	N/A
	b. Provide proper disposition of trust property upon termination	Y	N	N/A
	c. Avoid violating rule against perpetuities, if any	Y	N	N/A

3.	Consider whether document has exercised a power of appointment and, if not, whether it should.			
	This point requires the reviewer to examine other trusts created for the benefit of the Grantor.			
	If yes:			
	a. Are formalities of exercise observed	Y	N	N/A
	b. Are appointees permissible	Y	N	N/A
	c. Does exercise avoid violating rule against perpetuities	Y	N	N/A
4.	Review fiduciary appointment provisions. Does document provide:			
	a. Power to resign	Y	N	N/A
	b. Power to remove and replace corporate fiduciary	Y	N	N/A
	c. No termination fee upon resignation/removal	Y	N	N/A
	d. Appropriate trustee compensation	Y	N	N/A
	e. Appointment of appropriate office and jurisdiction	Y	N	N/A
	f. Adequate succession provisions	Y	N	N/A
	g. Adequate protection for fiduciary			
	i. Authority to rely	Y	N	N/A
	ii. Limitations on liability	Y	N	N/A
5.	Review fiduciary powers. Does fiduciary have power to:			
	a. Make any type of investment	Y	N	N/A
	b. Abandon worthless property	Y	N	N/A
	c. Terminate uneconomical trusts	Y	N	N/A
	d. Allocate receipts & disbursements in its discretion	Y	N	N/A
	e. Make loans/pledges	Y	N	N/A
	f. Employ and pay agents and advisers	Y	N	N/A
	g. Change situs and governing law	Y	N	N/A
	h. Merge similar trusts	Y	N	N/A
	i. Authorise investments in affiliated funds	Y	N	N/A

continued on next page

	j. Allow borrowing	Y	N	N/A
6.	Review definitions of:			
	a. Issue/descendants (adopteds)	Y	N	N/A
	b. Spouse	Y	N	N/A
	c. *Per stirpes*	Y	N	N/A
	d. Number/gender	Y	N	N/A
	e. Internal Revenue Code	Y	N	N/A
	f. Disability	Y	N	N/A
7.	Review trust agreements for:			
	a. Irrevocability/revocability language	Y	N	N/A
	b. Governing law provision	Y	N	N/A
	c. If charitable trust, conforming to IRS requirements	Y	N	N/A
	d. If directed trust, review direction language and trustee duties, etc and whether 'adviser' is a fiduciary			
8.	Check pagination			
9.	Check article and section sequence			
10.	Check internal cross-references for accuracy			
11.	Check names for accurate spelling			

Consider creating a private trust company

Todd D Mayo
UBS

Many wealthy families include trusts in their wealth structures. Using a trust inexorably involves selecting a trustee. Some families choose to form a private trust company to serve as the trustee of its trusts. A private trust company (sometimes called a family trust company or private family trust company) is a legal entity that is authorised to act as a trustee. It typically serves only one family; it does not serve the general public. Notably, it is controlled by the family that it serves. Some families find this quality appealing.

1. Understanding the options for trusteeship

For a family exploring the possibility of forming a private trust company, it is useful to begin with an understanding of the options for trusteeship and the strengths and weaknesses of each option. With that understanding, a family can better answer the question, 'Is a private trust company right for us?'

Broadly speaking, a family has three options for the trusteeship of its trusts. Those options are:

- individual trustees;
- commercial institutional trustees; and
- private trust companies.

Each of those three types of trustee can be further divided into subtypes. Each type (and subtype) of trustee has strengths and weaknesses. On many trusts, there are co-trustees and it is common to see two different types of trustees serving together as co-trustees of a particular trust.

1.1 Individual trustees

An individual trustee is a natural person who acts as trustee. There are two types of individual trustees:

- non-professional individual trustees; and
- professional individual trustees.

Non-professional individual trustees typically are family members, family friends and business colleagues. Professional individual trustees typically are lawyers, tax advisers and investment advisers who provide trust services in addition to other professional services.

In many cases, non-professional individual trustees bring a wealth of first-hand knowledge of a family, its financial situation and, perhaps most significantly, interpersonal dynamics. That knowledge can be invaluable in administering a trust in a manner that is faithful to the trust's purposes and the family's interests. Complementing that knowledge, non-professional individual trustees often are sincerely loyal to the family. On the flip side, they sometimes lack skill and experience in administering trusts, which can lead to missteps. For example, without sound professional advice, they may incur unnecessary costs or taxes. In addition, their loyalty sometimes crosses into bias and they wind up favouring some family members over others. They also can be more susceptible to allowing their personal beliefs and views to colour decisions, such as decisions concerning the purposes for which distributions are proper.

Professional individual trustees usually have some skill and experience with trust administration, although the degree of skill and experience varies from individual to individual. In some cases, they may have worked closely with the family through the years, gaining important knowledge of the family, their businesses and other aspects of their wealth. While working with a family can help to inform trust-related decisions, an individual's duties when providing professional advice can conflict with the duties when acting as a trustee. Also, some professional individual trustees don't know (or don't respect) their limits. They try to do too much. They provide services outside their area of core competency. For example, a private client lawyer may advise a family on wealth structuring, serve as a trustee of the family's trusts, and seek to manage the trust's investments. While the lawyer may be skilled at wealth structuring, he or she may have less skill at investing.

Individual trustees are susceptible to distraction. Non-professionals perhaps more so than professionals. Personal and business matters can intrude on the performance of their duties as trustee. Individual trustees also can lose their physical, emotional or mental capacity to fulfil their duties properly. Sometimes, the loss is gradual or sporadic. Individual trustees also die, sometimes unexpectedly. These issues can create challenges in effectively developing successors who have a solid baseline understanding of the family's trusts and circumstances.

1.2 Commercial institutional trustees

A commercial institutional trustee is a legal entity that is authorised to provide trust services to the general public. There are two types of commercial institutional trustees:

- banks; and
- independent trust companies.

Banks include banks with trust departments and bank-owned trust companies. They generally provide lending, investment management and other services. For many banks, trust services are ancillary services, offered for the purposes of encouraging clients to use its other services. Independent trust companies include trust service providers that also provide company administration services (and sometimes fund administration services) and multi-family offices that have an affiliated trust company. In some cases, they provide investment management services. For these companies, trust services usually are core services.

On the whole, commercial institutional trustees institutionalise trust administration. By design – and, to varying degrees, dictated by law – they generally aim to manage risks by minimising the opportunities for mistakes. This institutionalisation of trust administration includes establishing policies and procedures governing how decisions are made concerning trusts. This disciplined decision-making aims to ensure that a family's trusts are administered in accordance with their terms. It can also help lessen the impact of personal biases. Some decisions may require two people to agree; other decisions may require a committee's approval.

Smaller institutions often are more attentive, more personal and less bureaucratic than their larger counterparts, but that isn't universally true. On the other hand, small banks tend to lack the sophistication to handle more complex structures and issues that wealthy families commonly present. Larger institutions may offer more sophistication, broader experience and a wider array of services, which may be attractive to some families.

Commercial institutional trustees generally provide good continuity, serving as trustee over multiple generations. Unlike individual trustees, they don't die or become incapacitated. They, however, sometimes merge or discontinue services. Mergers involve change. Sometimes the change is for the better, enhancing service offerings and expanding capacity. Sometimes the change is for the worse, precipitating staff turn-over, scaled-back services or more bureaucratic decision making. The discontinuation of services likewise involves change. When an institution ceases to provide trust services whether universally or in particular geographic areas (as happened in the last decade with 'de-risking'), the change can be highly disruptive for a family.

1.3 Private trust companies

A private trust company is a legal entity that provides trust services typically to one family.[1] It does not provide services to the general public. It may be licensed or unlicensed. A licensed private trust company obtains a licence or charter from a banking regulator, which supervises the company's activities on an ongoing basis. An unlicensed private trust company is exempt from any licensing or chartering obligation, but generally qualifies for the exemption so long as it complies with certain requirements governing its organisation and operation. For some wealthy families, a private trust company marries the better qualities of individual trustees and commercial institutional trustees. It can provide bespoke, professional trust services that the family controls.

2. A private trust company's strengths

Why do wealthy families create private trust companies? Key reasons include:

- maximising family control;
- implementing a structure for holding complex assets;
- addressing trustee succession;
- complementing family governance; and
- insulating individuals from liability.

These reasons reflect some of the key strengths of private trust companies. Before discussing those strengths, it is worth addressing one thing that's largely a false narrative. Preserving a family's privacy sometimes is touted as one of the benefits that a private trust company offers. Proponents of this position assert that, by creating a private trust company, a family keeps information about its trusts – and potentially other aspects of its wealth – out of the hands of people in financial institutions. They claim that this limits the universe of people who see that information and consequently gives the family greater privacy. In practice, however, the universe

1 There are exceptions to the rule. In the United States, Florida and Wyoming allow a private trust company to provide services to two families.

of people with access to information about the family's wealth is unlikely to be materially different whether or not the family uses a private trust company. A family is likely to engage one or more financial institutions and other service providers to assist in running its private trust company. For example, a private trust company may engage a trust company to provide trust accounting and other trust administration services. Those third parties will have access to the family's trust-related information. Except in rare situations, a private trust company is thus unlikely to significantly reduce the universe of individuals who see that information. Regardless of whether a family establishes a private trust company, preserving a family's privacy requires proper contractual and technological safeguards to be in place.

2.1 Maximising family control

Control often is the primary reason that a wealthy family establishes a private trust company. The family controls the services that its private trust company offers and, sometimes as importantly, does not offer. The family decides when its private trust company adds or eliminates services. The family controls the hiring, cultivation and firing of the individuals who work for the family through the private trust company. Likewise, the family controls the selection of third-party service providers. With a commercial institutional trustee and, perhaps to a lesser degree, an individual trustee, the family may have limited influence over changes in the trustee's business strategy and service offerings, the assignment of individuals to handle the family's trusts, and the selection of service providers that the trustee engages.

Control can affect the day-to-day administration of trusts. For example, in connection with a proposed restructuring of a family's trusts and their holdings, a family may obtain tax and legal advice from a team of trusted advisers. An institutional trustee may insist on obtaining its own tax and legal advice. While a second opinion can be valuable – and, in some instances, even invaluable – it can also add unnecessary costs and delays. The institutional trustee may rationalise its position as fulfilling its fiduciary duties, but that's only part of it. An institutional trustee may seek its own tax and legal advice as a means of mitigating its potential liability for participating in the restructuring. With a private trust company, the family has more control over the hiring of advisers. It can choose to rely on its trusted advisers, forgoing a second opinion unless it feels that there is a compelling need for one.

2.2 Implementing a structure for holding complex assets

Wealthy families often own complex assets, such as interests in privately owned operating companies, real estate (sometimes in multiple countries), artwork, yachts and private aircraft. In structuring their wealth, many families hold complex assets through trusts. Some trustees, however, are hesitant to serve as trustee of a trust that (directly or indirectly) owns certain types of complex assets. This hesitancy manifests in different ways. Sometimes, it is a flat-out refusal to serve as trustee of a trust that holds certain assets, such as an interest in a privately owned operating company. Other times, it is an insistence on having what in the family's view is excessive amounts of insurance on certain trust-owned assets, such as artwork. By their nature, commercial institutional trustees tend to be risk averse, and their risk management practices aim to minimise potential liabilities (which can undermine profitability). In addition, their tolerance can change over time. A trustee that was once comfortable with a structure that held a particular type of complex asset may become unwilling to do so, or it may demand additional concessions to establish or maintain the structure.

Wealthy families tend to be more risk tolerant. Accepting risk is what often helped them become wealthy. (Of course, a family's risk tolerance may fade over the generations, especially if it no longer controls an operating company.) Although the family may want to hold complex assets within its trust structure, a trustee may be unwilling to do so, or a trustee may insist on indemnities, structural changes, additional insurance, or additional compensation that, in the family's eyes, is unreasonable or unwarranted. In short, a family's risk tolerance may clash with the trustee's risk tolerance. Such a clash may frustrate both the family and the trustee, and it ultimately leads to a deterioration in the relationship between the family and the trustee. That's not ideal. A family is best served when there is a close, strong and trusting relationship with the trustee of its trusts.

With a private trust company, a family has a trustee whose risk tolerance reflects the family's risk tolerance. Accordingly, a family can more confidently use trust structures to hold its complex assets. The family determines what level of risk it is comfortable accepting in its trust structures. Through its control of its private trust company, the family is assured that the trustee will also accept the risk and, importantly, won't unexpectedly become unwilling to accept the risk. Importantly, using a private trust company doesn't preclude the family from obtaining services from a commercial institutional trustee that would be unwilling to serve as trustee of the trusts that hold complex assets. The private trust company may engage a bank or independent trust company to provide trust administration or other services, which facilitate the private trust company's trusteeship of the family's trusts, including those holding complex assets.

For a family that has a private trust company, decisions concerning risk don't always occur in a vacuum. In the case of a licensed private trust company, the banking regulator is likely to raise concerns if the private trust company appears to be accepting imprudent risks. Although wealthy families tend to be more risk tolerant than commercial institutional trustees, most aren't foolish. Thus, this should be an uncommon issue.

2.3 Addressing trustee succession

Through the use of a private trust company, a family can address trustee succession. With an individual trustee, the individual eventually will become incapacitated or die. Consequently, there will be a need for a new trustee. Commercial institutional trustees generally provide better continuity of trusteeship, because they don't become incapacitated or die. They, however, don't completely avoid the issue. An institution may merge, or it may change how it provides trust services, or it may even cease to provide those services. In such circumstances, the family may find that it needs a new trustee. Unfortunately, the family cannot control when that need will arise.

A private trust company provides continuity of trusteeship. Unlike an individual trustee, it doesn't become incapacitated or die. Unlike a commercial institutional trustee, it won't merge or cease to provide trust services without the family's participation in the decision to do so. For a family that has had individual trustees of its trusts, it may seek to have some or all of those individuals continue to play a role with the family's trusts by serving as directors or officers of its private trust company. Of course, a private trust company has its own succession issues. It will have individuals serving as directors, and it may have individuals serving as officers and working as employees. Individuals eventually become unwilling or unable to serve in their particular roles. A private trust company's directors, officers and employees are no different. When designing a private trust company and on an ongoing basis afterwards, a family should consider how best to identify and cultivate talented, trusted individuals who can succeed the private trust company's directors, officers and employees.

2.4 Complementing family governance

A private trust company can complement a family's governance structure. It can play a role within the broader structure that the family has created for making decisions and managing the family's wealth. For example, many wealthy families establish family offices that manage the family's wealth and provide services to family members. A private trust company can complement a family office, providing trust and other fiduciary services to family members. Importantly, it provides a structure by which the family can make decisions concerning the administration of the family's trusts.

2.5 Insulating individuals from liability

A private trust company can insulate individuals from liability. A trustee is personally liable for any breach of trust. In the case of an individual trustee, the individual's personal wealth is thus exposed to any claims for a breach of trust. An individual whom a family would like to serve as trustee may be unwilling to do so because of the liability exposure. A private trust company can enable individuals to participate in the fiduciary decision-making process while generally insulating them from potential liability. As the trustee of a trust, the private trust company would be liable for any breach of trust that it commits. Moreover, family members may be less inclined to sue the family's private trust company, because it's like suing themselves.

A director or officer of the private trust company generally would not be liable for the private trust company's breach of trust, absent some personal malfeasance by the director or officer. Moreover, the private trust company generally can indemnify its directors and officers against any liability or cost in connection with a breach of trust or other claim. Those costs typically include attorneys' fees and litigation expenses. Thus, a private trust company can make it more attractive for trusted family members and advisers to participate in the administration of the family's trusts. It shields them from potential liability and provides a more efficient mechanism for covering the costs of defending against any claims.

3. A private trust company's weaknesses

As a part of a family's wealth structure, a private trust company can have some weaknesses. Those weaknesses include:

- echoing family disharmony;
- incurring costs;
- internalising responsibilities;

- inviting regulatory supervision; and
- playing to vanity.

3.1 Echoing family disharmony

A private trust company is ill-suited for a disharmonious family. Impressing a private trust company on a trust structure in which family members are already at odds risks exacerbating conflicts, creating at least the impression that some family members are trying to gain more control at the expense of other family members. A private trust company is best suited for a family in which the members work collaboratively. It potentially can be part of a solution for a family that has worked out its differences, creating an agreed-upon framework for collaboratively managing the family's trusts and associated wealth. It can help manage disputes that arise.

3.2 Incurring costs

Forming and running a private trust company requires a financial commitment. A private trust company will have start-up and ongoing costs. Start-up costs may include:

- capital;
- legal fees; and
- regulatory fees.

Ongoing costs may include:

- insurance premiums;
- audit fees;
- other service fees;
- director, officer and employee expenses;
- regulatory fees; and
- taxes.

A family typically runs its private trust company so that it breaks even financially. A private trust company usually charges trustee and other fees in an amount that it expects to cover its expenses.

Capital. In many jurisdictions, a private trust company must maintain a minimum amount of capital. The capital requirements tend to be higher in the United States than elsewhere.

Legal fees. Good legal advice is crucial in forming a private trust company. Through each stage of the formation process – considering whether to form a private trust company, designing the private trust company and (in the case of a licensed private trust company) obtaining the charter or licence from the banking regulator – a family needs good legal advice.

Regulatory fees. A licensed private trust company must obtain a licence from the regulator, and that process may require the payment of an application or other fee to the regulator.

Insurance premiums. A private trust company may maintain directors and officers (D&O) insurance, errors and omissions (E&O) insurance and fidelity insurance. D&O insurance generally insures the directors and officers against claims of wrongdoing in their management of the company, E&O insurance generally insures against negligence in administering a trust and other client accounts, and fidelity insurance (sometimes called a fidelity bond) insures against theft or embezzlement. It is good practice to have those policies as they can help finance the defence of claims. In addition, having adequate insurance can help to repel efforts to hold directors and officers personally liable for the private trust company's acts and omissions.

Audit fees. A private trust company may engage a firm to audit its financial statements or its compliance with its fiduciary policies and procedures. Even when a private trust company isn't under any obligation to conduct such an audit, it often is a good practice. The size and complexity of the private trust company and the trust structures in which it acts as trustee will affect the amount of the audit fees.

Other service fees. To the extent that it doesn't internalise functions like trust accounting, a private trust company will need to outsource those services. In some instances, it may outsource the services to a family office. In other instances, it may outsource the services to a third-party service provider, such as a commercial trust company.

Director, officer and employee expenses. A private trust company may have compensation and related expenses for its directors, officers and employees.

Regulatory fees. A licensed private trust company may be subject to an annual assessment, which effectively is a tax that is used to fund the regulator. The regulator may periodically examine a licensed private trust company, and the licensed private trust company must pay an examination fee. A licensed private trust company also may have to pay a fee when it seeks its regulator's approval to change its activities or its governing documents.

Taxes. In some jurisdictions, a private trust company may be subject to tax. In a jurisdiction that taxes an entity based on its net income, a private trust company typically will owe little or no tax, because it generally operates to break even, collecting trustee and other fees that roughly cover its operating expenses.

3.3 Internalising responsibilities

When a family uses a private trust company to act as trustee of its trusts, the family assumes the responsibility of obtaining the services necessary to administer the trusts. Many private trust companies engage third-party service providers – in some cases, banks or trust companies – to provide certain trust administration services. The private trust company will need to vet potential service providers, negotiate the terms of services and continuously evaluate the scope and quality of the services relative to its needs. In contrast, when a family appoints a third-party trustee (especially a commercial institutional trustee), it essentially is contracting for a bundle of services.

3.4 Inviting regulatory supervision

A licensed private trust company is subject to the ongoing supervision of a banking regulator. In fact, the regulatory scrutiny begins before the company's formation. As a part of the process of forming a licensed private trust company, a family generally must apply to the banking regulator for a licence or charter. After the private trust company's formation, the company must file annual or other periodic reports with the banking regulator, and the banking regulator generally conducts a periodic examination of the company. For some families, regulatory supervision is unwelcome governmental intrusion into the family's affairs. For other families, regulatory supervision is a welcome additional layer of oversight, which helps to ensure the proper administration of the family's trusts.

An unlicensed private trust company is not subject to the ongoing supervision of a banking regulator. In some jurisdictions, it may have an annual or other periodic filing obligation, such as a certification of its compliance with the requirements entitling it to exemption from licensing. In other jurisdictions, there isn't any filing obligation. The banking regulator may examine an unlicensed private trust company that may have engaged in improper conduct, such as offering or providing services to the general public. Similarly, other regulators may investigate an unlicensed private trust company that may have engaged in impermissible activities. For example, in the United States, the Securities and Exchange Commission (SEC) or a state securities regulator may investigate an unlicensed private trust company that may have offered investment services without qualifying for the family office exception or otherwise may have violated securities laws.

3.5 Playing to vanity

Private trust companies have become increasingly popular in recent years. Some families create private trust companies because they view a private trust company as a status symbol. They hear about private trust companies over cocktails at the club or a social event. They read stories about private trust companies in the *Financial Times* or *The Wall Street Journal*. They decide that, if the Joneses and the Smiths have private trust companies, they should have them, too. A family shouldn't form a private trust company simply because other families have. Like a family office, a private trust company isn't a good fit for every family. It is crucial that a family fully appreciates what's involved in forming and running a private trust company and is willing to make the commitments in time and money to run it properly. Vanity shouldn't cloud a thoughtful assessment of whether a private trust company will effectively serve the family and its needs.

4. Alternative structures

A private trust company isn't always the right answer. For some wealthy families, a well-designed trust structure can achieve their objectives with less cost and complexity. Nowadays, a family can structure a trust so that there are separate roles for managing and investing the trust property, making distributions and handling administrative matters. In some jurisdictions, a legal entity can act as a protector, enforcer or trust adviser and is exempt from any requirement to be licensed as a trust company. In addition to potentially shielding individuals from liability, that can also minimise the risk of having the trust subject to judicial proceedings in an unfavourable jurisdiction.

A family often can tailor a trust's governance structure so that the family has significant control over the trust.[2] The family can use directed trust or divided trust governance structures. Although the terminology is perhaps US-centric, these concepts encompass reserved-powers trusts and other settlor- (or beneficiary) controlled

---

2 For a more in-depth discussion of trust governance models, see Todd D Mayo, "Trust governance models", *The International Family Offices Journal*, June 2017, pp28–38.

trust structures. In a directed trust governance structure, the trustee is vested with all of the trustee powers, and other persons have the power to direct the trustee to exercise specific powers. For example, a person (perhaps called an investment director) has the power to direct the trustee concerning the management or investment of the trust property, and the trustee generally must follow those directions.

In a divided trust governance structure, the trustee is vested with some of the trustee powers, and other persons are vested with the other powers. For example, the trust instrument may vest the trustee with the powers concerning distributions, tax compliance and recordkeeping, and vest another person (perhaps called an investment adviser) with the power to manage and invest the trust property. Since the investment adviser is vested with the investment powers, the investment adviser can act directly, generally eliminating the trustee's direct involvement in investment matters. (As a practical matter, some third parties may nonetheless insist upon the trustee's participation – for example, by signing an account opening form or a subscription agreement – in certain situations.)

The trust structure also might include a holding company. By using a holding company, a family shifts significant day-to-day decisional and transactional activities out of the trust and down into the holding company. Instead of holding a portfolio of assets directly within the trust, those assets would be held in the holding company. The trust would hold the holding company, and it typically would also hold an operating cash account (which would be used to pay the trust's expenses and make distributions). This arrangement can simplify the administration of the trust. Many investment-related decisions would occur in the holding company. Similarly, investment-related inflows and outflows would occur in the holding company (or a subsidiary), rather than at the trust level.

Figure 1 illustrates an example of a directed trust governance structure that includes a holding company. In this example, the trustee is a commercial trust company, thereby providing the family with the benefits of professional trust administration. An investment committee has the power to direct the investment of the trust property. The settlor and other members of the family are members of the investment committee. The trust holds an equity interest in a holding company and an operating cash account. The investment committee has the power to direct the trustee concerning action involving the holding company, and its main directive is continuing to hold the equity of the holding company.

Figure 1. A directed trust with holding company

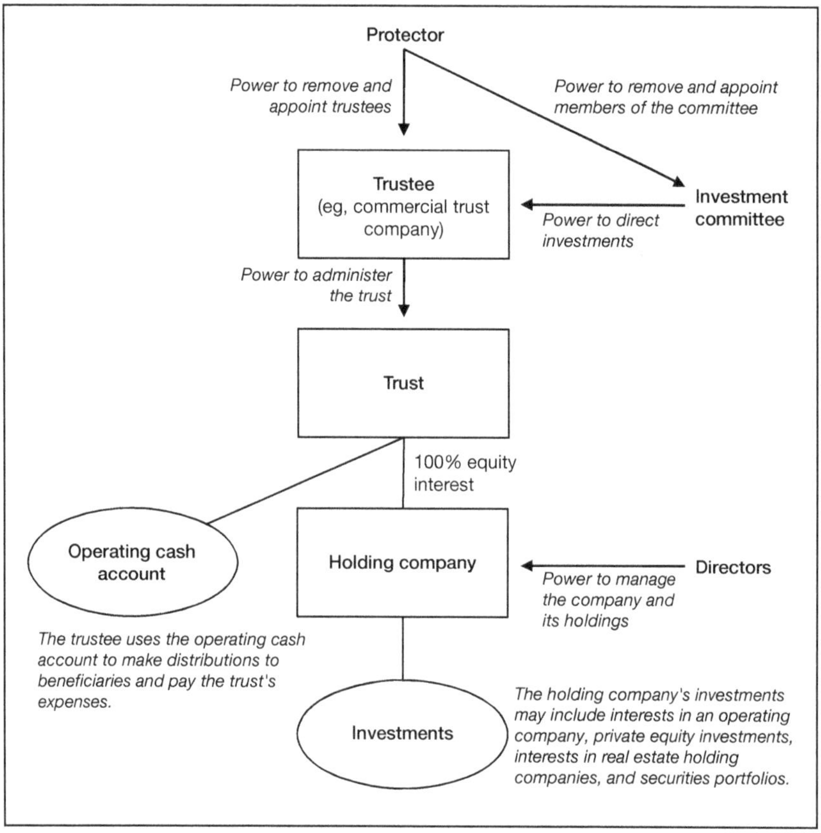

The company's directors manage the company and thus control investment decisions within the company.

As a check and balance within this structure, a protector oversees the trustee and the investment committee. The settlor potentially could be the protector (although that may have unfavourable tax or creditor protection implications), or the protector could be a committee of family members and close advisers. The protector has the power to remove a trustee and appoint a successor trustee. The protector also has the power to appoint any additional or successor member of the investment committee, and the power to remove any member of the investment committee. The removal powers provide a straightforward mechanism for resolving issues with the trustee's attentiveness, competency or unwillingness to remain true to the settlor's intent and wishes.

5. *Situs* selection

After a family decides to form a private trust company, it must decide where to form it. This important decision will affect the administration of the family's trusts and the options for designing new trusts. When considering where to form a private trust company, a family should look for:

- geographic convenience;
- favourable private trust company laws;
- favourable trust laws;
- favourable tax laws;
- good regulatory environment;
- good courts;
- good lawyers; and
- political and regulatory stability.

Each family is likely to weigh those factors differently. For most families, favourable trust laws and geographic convenience usually emerge as the most important factors.

5.1 Geographic convenience

For many families, geographic convenience is important. In some cases, families are looking for accessibility to their advisers and service providers. In other cases, families are seeking to minimise the risk of another jurisdiction asserting that the private trust company is engaging in activities outside of its home jurisdiction. In both cases, family members value the ease with which they can travel to the jurisdiction, so that they may conduct meetings there.

5.2 Favourable private trust company laws

As a threshold matter, a jurisdiction must allow private trust companies. Jurisdictions that allow private trust companies include Bermuda, the Caymans, Guernsey and Jersey. In the United States, states that allow private trust companies include New Hampshire, South Dakota, Tennessee and Wyoming. When evaluating the laws governing private trust companies, the factors that families consider often include:

- *Licensing.* Does the jurisdiction allow licensed private trust companies? Unlicensed private trust companies? Some families prefer one over the other. Other families may like the option of being able to switch from an unlicensed private trust company to a licensed trust company (or vice versa).

- *Permissible clients.* Whom may the private trust company serve? A private trust company typically can serve members of a particular family, as well as their trusts, companies and charitable entities. How does the jurisdiction delineate whom the private trust company may serve?
- *Capital requirements.* How much capital must a private trust company have?
- *Choice of entity and ownership structure.* What type of entity can a family use when forming a private trust company? Can a foundation be a private trust company? What type of structures are available for owning a private trust company? Does the jurisdiction allow the use of a perpetual purpose trust to own a private trust company? (For a discussion of foundations and other aspects of the ownership structure of private trust companies, see section 6 below.)
- *Directorships.* Are there any requirements or limitations on who may serve as a director of a private trust company? For example, does the jurisdiction require one or more resident directors?
- *Offices.* Are there any physical presence requirements? That is, does the jurisdiction require the private trust company to maintain an office within the jurisdiction?
- *Privacy.* How much information about the family – and possibly its trusts – can become public and under what conditions? This is an area of the law that has been evolving over the past several years.

For most families, a jurisdiction need only have workable private trust company laws, so long as the jurisdiction has good trust laws.

5.3 Favourable trust laws

Although it may seem counter-intuitive, the quality of a jurisdiction's trust laws probably is the most important factor that a family should consider when deciding where to form a private trust company. The quality of a jurisdiction's laws governing private trust companies usually are secondary to the quality of its laws governing trusts. On a day-to-day basis, trust laws are more relevant. Jurisdictions that have well-developed, progressive trust laws include Bermuda, the Caymans, Guernsey and Jersey. In the United States, states that have well-developed, progressive trust laws include New Hampshire, South Dakota, Tennessee and Wyoming.

5.4 Favourable tax laws

When evaluating a potential *situs* for a private trust company, a family should consider two possible incidents of tax. First, the family should determine whether the potential *situs* would impose tax on any of its trusts administered there. Jurisdictions with favourable trust laws typically don't impose taxes on trusts. Secondly, the family should determine whether the potential *situs* would impose any tax on the private trust company. To the extent that a jurisdiction might impose a company-level tax, it typically is based on the activities within the jurisdiction. The potential impact of a company-level tax generally is limited, because a private trust company generally operates so that it doesn't have any profits.

5.5 Good regulatory environment

A hospitable and reputable regulatory environment is vital. That is true for all private trust companies, even though it is more significant for licensed private trust companies. Good laws aren't worth much if the regulator is unwelcoming or acts in an arbitrary manner. Getting a read on a regulator can be challenging. Local advisers often are the best source of information, although some seem to be cheerleaders for their jurisdiction regardless of how a regulator is behaving. Good laws also aren't worth much if the jurisdiction has a reputation for tolerating questionable or illicit activities. A jurisdiction that attracts bad actors – or even appears to attract bad actors – can create risks for a family.

5.6 Good courts

A family ideally will never find itself embroiled in litigation involving its trusts or its private trust company. When evaluating where to form a private trust company, however, a family should consider the quality of a jurisdiction's judicial system. Do the judges have experience handling complex litigation? How much experience do they have with trusts? Do they have a reputation for being thoughtful and impartial? Is there a court that specialises in trust disputes? Do the judges have the time to give proper attention to the matters that come before them?

Hope for the best. Plan for the worst.

5.7 Good lawyers

The availability of quality legal advice is important. When forming and operating a private trust company and when establishing or administering a trust, a local lawyer's insights can be invaluable.

A local lawyer can often provide a perspective that cannot be discerned from reading a statute or a court's opinion. A local lawyer thus can play a vital role in a family's team of legal advisers. In some jurisdictions, there are many good lawyers. In others, there are only a few. A dearth of good lawyers can create challenges for families.

A jurisdiction that has a number of good lawyers generally is preferable to one that does not. First, families sometimes want a second opinion. Even though a family may have a high degree of confidence in its local lawyer, the cost of getting something wrong may be too high. Thus, the family may want the added assurance of a second opinion. Secondly, should a dispute arise, the family's go-to lawyer may have a conflict that precludes him or her from representing the private trust company. Or the family's go-to lawyer doesn't handle trust disputes. A lawyer who is skilled in wealth structuring isn't necessarily adept at handling a controversy. In a jurisdiction with few good lawyers, a family may be unable to find someone who can effectively advise or represent it. Thirdly, where there are a number of good lawyers, they tend to create an ecosystem in which good laws develop. They talk, and they share stories about their experiences. This can create a generative process for cultivating ideas for improving the laws. This can be good for families with their trusts and private trust companies in that jurisdiction.

5.8 Political and regulatory stability

For many families, political and regulatory stability is an essential quality of a *situs* in which to form and operate a private trust company. Forming a private trust company involves a meaningful commitment of time and expense, and moving the private trust company – and the trusts of which it serves as trustee – to another jurisdiction isn't an insignificant undertaking. Thus, families and their legal advisers (who, as a lot, tend to be conservative in the advice that they give) generally value certainty, avoiding jurisdictions in which there is (whether actual or perceived) a heightened risk of a change in the laws or their application.

Some families will mitigate this risk by forming private trust companies in two (or more) jurisdictions or forming a private trust company in one jurisdiction and opening one or more trust offices in other jurisdictions. Sometimes getting a good read on the political and regulatory stability of a jurisdiction can be difficult, because the people who often have the best vantage points also have a personal stake in families forming their private trust companies in the jurisdiction.

6. Ownership structure

Who should own the private trust company? Since ownership carries an element of control, the answer determines who can control the private trust company. A good ownership structure will aim to safeguard control, preventing control from slipping to people who, whether purposely or through inattention, allow the private trust company to operate in a manner that isn't consistent with settlor intent or the family's interests.

There are four common ownership structures. They are:

- single-trust structure;
- dual-trust structure;
- purpose trust; and
- foundation.

For a private trust company organised as a company, corporation or limited liability company, a family would typically use a single-trust, dual-trust or purpose trust structure for the purposes of owning the private trust company. Since the private trust company is likely to have an indefinite life-span, any trust owning a private trust company's equity should be perpetual. A foundation does not have any owners, so it avoids the necessity of a more complex structure.

6.1 Single-trust structure

In a single-trust structure, a single, perpetual trust holds the private trust company's equity interests. The trustee typically is a commercial institutional trustee. The beneficiaries typically are the family members. Figure 2 overleaf illustrates this structure.

The key advantage of this structure is its simplicity. There's one trust, and it holds the private trust company. The key disadvantage is that the trust has beneficiaries. The trustee owes various fiduciary duties to the beneficiaries, and a beneficiary who is unhappy about how the private trust company is operating could exert pressure on the trustee – for example, by asserting that the trustee had breached its fiduciary duties by failing to monitor the private trust company properly – in an aim to influence how the private trust company operates. For this reason, the purpose trust usually is a better structure.

6.2 Dual-trust structure

In a dual-trust structure, two perpetual trusts hold the private trust company's equity interests. For example, one trust might hold voting interests in the private trust company, while the other trust holds

Figure 2. Single-trust structure

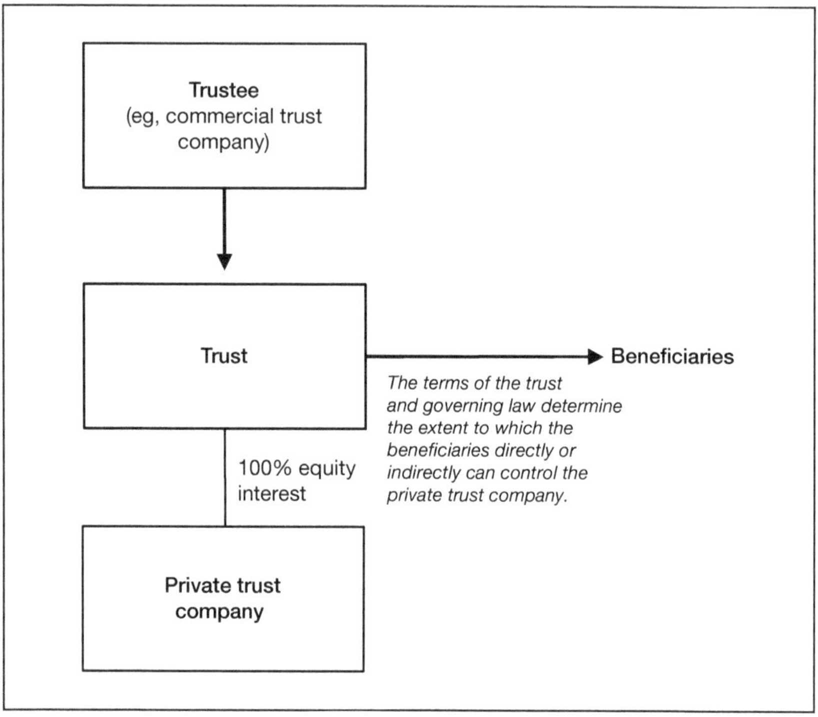

non-voting interests. The trustee often is a commercial institutional trustee. The beneficiaries typically are the family members. Figure 3 illustrates this structure.

The dual-trust structure is perhaps more common in the United States, where families seek to design private trust companies in a manner to avoid potentially adverse tax consequences. One approach involves having a private trust company issue voting and non-voting interests and using separate trusts to hold those interests. In 2008, the Internal Revenue Service (IRS) issued proposed guidance, which outlined a simpler approach.

6.3 Purpose trust

In a purpose trust structure, a perpetual purpose trust holds the equity interests in the private trust company. A purpose trust is a trust that is formed for one or more non-charitable purposes. It typically does not have any ascertainable beneficiaries. Figure 4 illustrates this structure.

Since it does not have any beneficiaries, a purpose trust may be better suited to owning a private trust company. It eliminates an alternate path to challenging the administration of the family's trusts.

Figure 3. Dual-trust structure

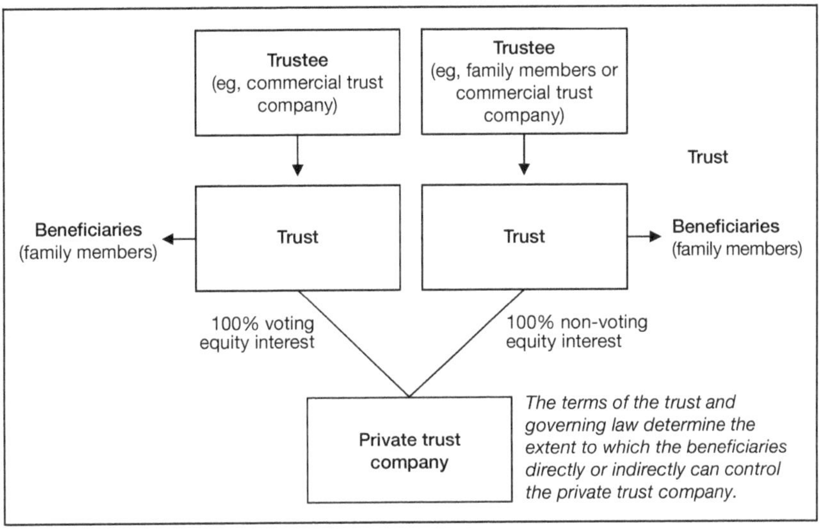

Figure 4. Purpose trust structure

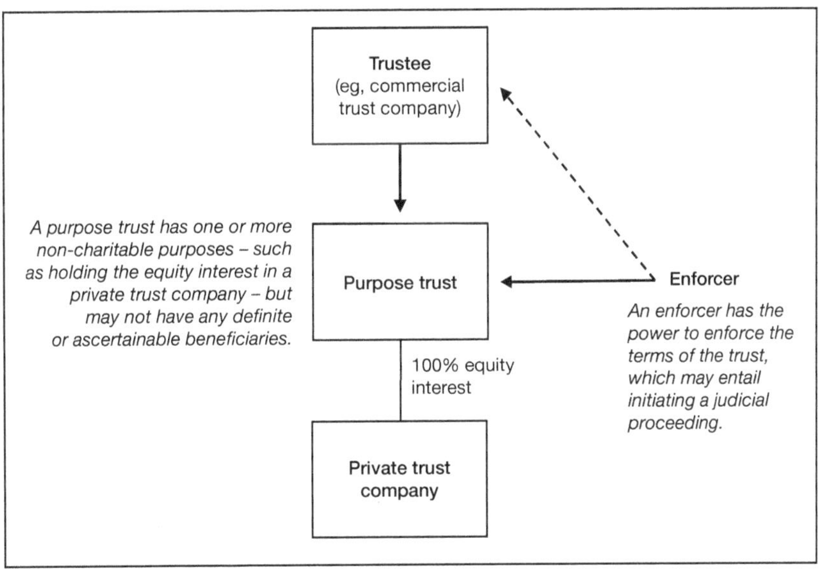

6.4 Foundation

In a foundation structure, a family organises the private trust company as a foundation. A foundation is a legal entity that operates for one or more non-charitable purposes. Notably, a foundation does not have any owners. Thus, using a foundation as a private trust

Figure 5. Private trust company organised as a foundation

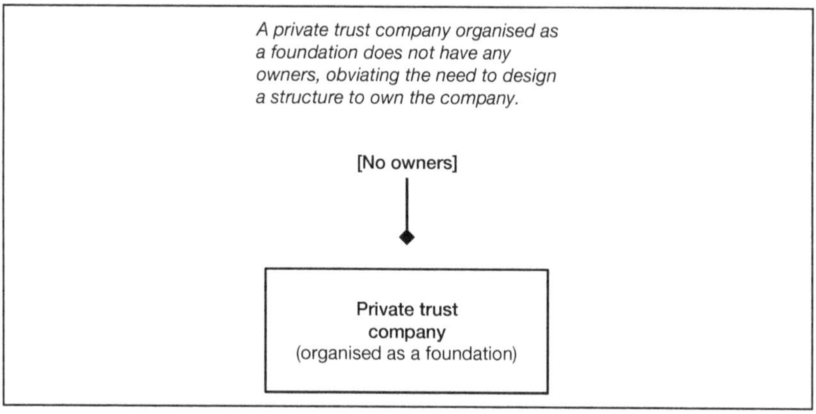

company can simplify the structure, obviating the need to design and maintain a structure that can own the private trust company through the generations. Figure 5 illustrates this simple structure.

Bermuda, the Cayman Islands, Guernsey and Jersey allow a private trust company to be organised as a foundation. In the United States, New Hampshire allows a private trust company to be organised as a foundation. (Wyoming allows foundations but currently does not allow them to operate as private trust companies.)

7. Governance and administration

A private trust company typically has a board of directors, which oversees the company and its management. Depending on governing law and the private trust company's organisational documents, the directors may have day-to-day management powers, or the company may have officers who have those powers. Likewise, the directors may form one or more committees to which they delegate specific powers and duties. The private trust company may hire staff to perform various functions, or it may outsource those functions to a family office or one or more third-party service providers. With respect to the governance and administration structure, the level of complexity varies from family to family. Figure 6 illustrates an example of a private trust company's structure.

In the example in Figure 6, the private trust company has a board of directors. (If the private trust company is organised as a limited liability company, its 'directors' would be managers to whom the governing documents grant the powers and duties substantially similar to those of a director of a corporation.) The board has three committees. A trust committee typically has the

Figure 6. Governance and administration

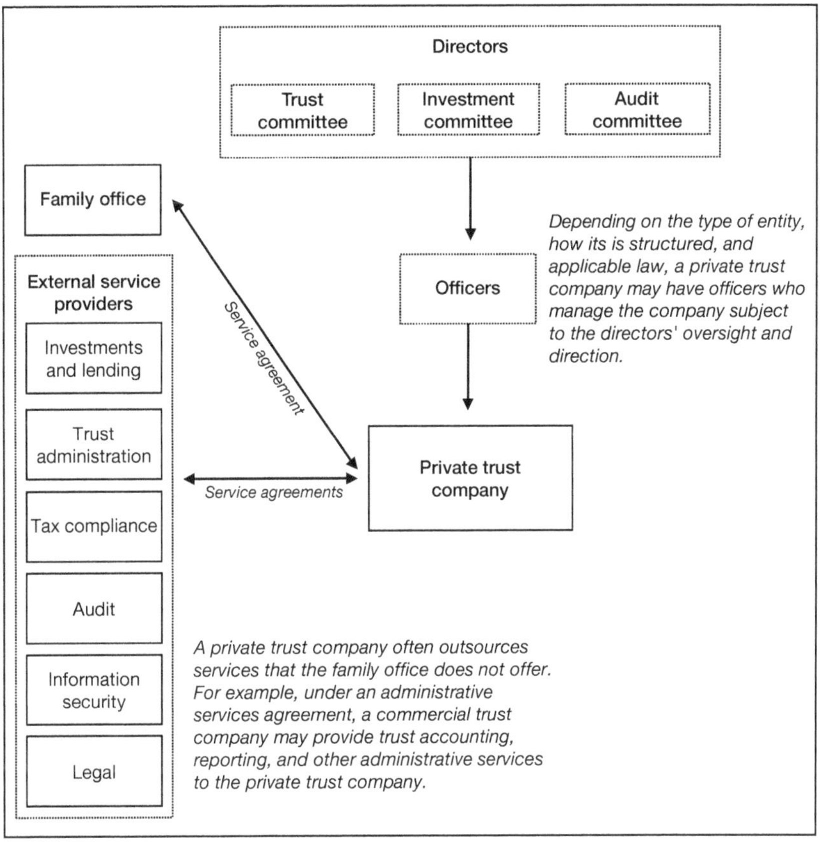

duty to oversee the exercise of the private trust company's fiduciary powers. The trust committee would approve the acceptance of new trusteeships and other arrangements, would decide whether to exercise the private trust company's discretionary powers as a trustee, would annually review each trusteeship and would review the termination of any trusteeships. An investment committee typically has the duty to oversee the exercise of any investment powers that the private trust company has over the trusts of which it serves as trustee. This usually entails periodically reviewing the trust's investments and any delegation of investment powers to a third party. An audit committee generally has the duty to oversee the private trust company's finances, engage an auditor to audit the company's financial statements, and engage an auditor or similar service provider to audit the company's compliance with applicable laws and its policies and procedures. Some families eschew the use of auditors, while others embrace audits as an additional layer of protection for the family's trusts.

The directors should meet regularly, and they should take minutes of their meetings. This is simply good governance. Having regular, formal meetings helps to ensure that the directors take their duties seriously, and it helps to ensure that there is good oversight of the private trust company's activities. For a wealthy family, inattentiveness in the administration of its trusts or the oversight of the administration can lead to unwelcome consequences. For these same reasons, the committees likewise should meet regularly and they too should take minutes of their meetings.

The directors should adopt policies. Again, this is simply good governance. For example, the directors should consider adopting policies concerning trustee and other fiduciary activities, compliance with anti-money laundering and anti-terrorist financing laws, information security and third-party risk management. The scope and specificity of a policy should reflect the scope and complexity of the private trust company and the trusts of which it is trustee. A private trust company that has a significant staff and is trustee of complex trust structures generally should have more detailed policies than a private trust company with little (or no) staff and simpler trust structures. When adopting policies, the directors should avoid setting unrealistic standards. A private trust company's failure to comply with its policies may be evidence of its culpability in administering a trust or performing other duties.

In the preceding illustration, the private trust company has officers. In some cases, that's necessary. Some jurisdictions require a private trust company to have certain officers, such as a president, secretary and treasurer. Others do not. In either case, a family may decide that it is useful for the private trust company to have officers, who have specific sets of duties. This choice often reflects how complex the family's business interests and other holdings are. It also reflects the degree to which the family wishes to internalise various functions rather than outsource them.

In addition to a president, secretary and treasurer, a private trust company's officers may include:

- *AML/ATF officer.* The AML/ATF officer is responsible for overseeing the private trust company's compliance with anti-money laundering and anti-terrorist financing laws. This responsibility typically includes overseeing the implementation of relevant policies and procedures. The officer's specific title and responsibilities can vary from jurisdiction to jurisdiction. In the United States, the company's bank secrecy act officer (also called the BSA officer) would typically have those responsibilities.

- *Chief compliance officer.* The chief compliance officer oversees compliance with the company's policies. The chief compliance officer seeks to verify whether people within the private trust company are performing their duties in accordance with the company's policies.
- *Chief information security officer.* The chief information security officer oversees compliance with the company's information security policy. With the increasing importance of information security, this is becoming a more important role.
- *Trust officers.* A trust officer typically handles the day-to-day administration of the trusts of which the private trust company is trustee.
- *Investment officers.* An investment officer typically handles the day-to-day investment of assets in the trusts over which the private trust company has investment powers.

A private trust company may outsource some of its functions to a family office. The private trust company may have a service agreement with the family office, under which the family office provides facilities, information technology, human resources and other services to the private trust company. In addition, the private trust company may delegate certain investment powers to the family office, thereby enabling the family office to manage the trusts' portfolios. A private trust company also may outsource some of its functions to third-party service providers. For example, it may engage an independent trust company to provide trust accounting services. Likewise, it may engage tax advisers to provide tax advice and tax compliance services, lawyers to provide legal services, and information security specialists to help safeguard the family's trust-related records.

7.1 US tax considerations

For families who include US persons, tax laws can influence a private trust company's governance structure. For US tax purposes, a family's control over a private trust company – and, by extension, the trusts of which the private trust company is a trustee – may have tax implications, especially for the settlors of those trusts. The IRS has not issued any definitive guidance on how to structure a private trust company without creating adverse tax consequences. In 2008, however, it published a proposed ruling.[3] The IRS has not finalised the ruling. The proposed ruling thus is not official guidance upon which families may rely. It is nonetheless useful, because it does provide some insight into the IRS's thinking and concerns.

In the proposed ruling, the IRS generally approved a structure in which the private trust company establishes and maintains two committees:

- discretionary distribution committee; and
- amendment committee.

In addition, the private trust company's governing documents must delegate to the company's officers all personnel decisions, including decisions regarding the hiring, discharge, promotion and compensation of employees. The governing documents also must prohibit reciprocal agreements between family members concerning discretionary distributions from trusts of which the private trust company is trustee.

The discretionary distribution committee must have the exclusive power to make decisions regarding discretionary distributions from each trust for which the private trust company serves as trustee. (The proposed ruling did not discuss whether this requirement applies to a directed trust or divided trust in which a person other than the private trust company is vested with discretionary distribution powers. It presumably does not.) Although any family member may serve as a member of the discretionary distribution committee, a member must be barred from participating in any decisions concerning a trust in which the member or his or her spouse is a settlor or beneficiary.

The amendment committee must have the exclusive power to amend the following aspects of the private trust company's governing documents:

- The creation, function and membership of the discretionary distribution committee;
- The creation, function and membership of the amendment committee;
- The delegation of personnel decisions to the private trust company's officers; and

3 IRS Notice 2008–63.

- The prohibition of reciprocal agreements between family members.

A majority of the amendment committee's members must be persons other than family members and persons who are related or subordinate to any of the private trust company's owners. (The proposed ruling assumes that one or more family members would (directly or indirectly) own the private trust company.)

Under the proposed ruling, a private trust company with this structure can serve as a trustee of a trust of which a family member is a settlor or beneficiary without causing the trust property to be includible in the family member's estate for US estate tax purposes or causing other adverse US tax consequences. The proposed ruling, however, was the subject of some criticism.[4] In some respects, its requirements probably are overly restrictive. Even as a rough roadmap, it is useful in structuring a private trust company so that it is unlikely to cause any adverse US tax consequences.

8. Conclusion

Although forming and running a private trust company requires a commitment of the family's time and money, it affords the family greater control and more flexibility, and it can complement the family's governance. For some wealthy families, those are compelling reasons to use a private trust company as the trustee of their trusts.

Disclosure

This chapter is provided for informational and educational purposes only. Providing you with this information is not to be considered a solicitation on our part with respect to the purchase or sale of any securities, investments, strategies or products that may be mentioned. In addition, the information is current as of the date indicated and is subject to change without notice. Neither UBS Global Wealth Management nor its employees (including its financial advisers) provide tax or legal advice. You should consult with your legal counsel and/or your accountant or tax professional regarding the legal or tax implications of a particular suggestion, strategy or investment, including any estate planning strategies, before you invest or implement.

---

4 See, eg, American College of Trust and Estate Counsel, *Comments on Notice 2008–63*, 4 November 2008, and New York State Bar Association, *Comments on Notice 2008–63*, 4 November 2008.

Consider a family office

Barbara R Hauser
Independent family adviser

1. What is a family office?

The first question is to define what a family office is. As they are quite tailored to each particular family there is a humorous saying in the industry that "if you've seen one family office ... you've seen one family office". But of course they do have common features. All family offices are created to serve the needs of a particular family. The family might be small in number or might include 50 or more family members in multiple generations. At some point they decide that they would benefit from hiring outside staff to take care of some of their needs. Those needs are often tied to portfolio investments but are not limited to that area.[1]

Although 'family office' is a fairly recent term, which developed primarily in the United States where it became heavily marketed in the 1990s, the services provided by a family office have been provided without using that name for centuries all over the world.

When a family is wealthy enough to pay others for services that are dedicated to that one family, they are receiving the benefits of a family office. From the historic literal 'gatekeepers' in Asia to the home servant staff in English manors, dedicated service is the hallmark of the family office.

The older models usually developed gradually: one butler would later supervise a full staff for upstairs and downstairs. This increase could take place over several generations. The main measure of a family's wealth was often in the land, the castle, the farm or the ranch. Hence portfolio management of liquid investments was a much smaller concern, and was often handled by outside advisers.

In the United States it often happened in the 20th century that the family's operating business would share some of its staff to help with the family's personal matters. This could range from help with

1 For a detailed 80-page manual, see Keith Drewery and Barbara Hauser, *Setting Up a Family Office*, Special Report, Globe Law and Business, 2020.

travel plans to shopping to party planning. As the personal liquid investments would grow, often from dividends, the financial officers in the business might also help out with basic investment decisions. Without conscious direction, some part of the company staff would begin to take on functions that would today be classified as family office functions. The range of services was as broad as the needs of the entire family: obtaining financing for an adult child to purchase a home; hiring and firing household staff; planning private business/social events; keeping bank accounts in order; paying household and personal bills; getting tax returns filed; and so on.

As the needs increased, it became increasingly awkward to fulfil all of the family services through the operating company staff. At a minimum, to preserve the tax deductibility of business salaries and overhead expenses for the company it was necessary to maintain internal allocations of time. The personal time should have been paid for in some other way. In most cases, though, this was probably not done.[2]

From a family perspective, it also became increasingly awkward to have their personal finances scrutinised and organised by operating company staff. If one or more family members were actively involved in managing the company, other family members faced the additional problem of concealing confidential matters from those members who were managing the company.

The relationship between the family and the operating company was often very opaque. Unsure of their rights as family owners of the company, younger family members in particular were hesitant about asking for personal assistance. The operating management team was often unclear about what, if any, involvement the family members should have in the direction of the business. Using internal company staff to handle family office functions often looked like a bridge between these two groups.

Ultimately, though, the confusion of roles, overhead allocation, tax rules and concerns of confidentiality would often prompt a split. A physically separate family office would be created.

Another catalyst for separating the personal family services from the operating business would be if the family business came to a stage where it wanted to be attractive to outside investors (to be listed or to go public); then the family would start to separate its

---

2 A notable exception is a publicly traded US company that houses the family office in the corporate headquarters, disclosing the personal costs by footnote.

services from the business. Sometimes this was done by allocating an internal charge for the family owners to pay personally for their partial use of the business executives and/or of the business's physical space. What functioned as a family office could be viewed as an 'embedded' family office, ie, an office that was embedded within the operating company.

If the family services became substantial enough, the family and business would often decide at some time to separate the family services from the business physically. This would be the birth of a family office.

It is common for the family to give a special name to its new separate family office. It might be based on a favourite vacation site or some other private family meaning.[3] Even when they have formed a separate family office, families generally prefer to stay very private. This includes a preference not to have the family's name mentioned anywhere. In some countries families are also concerned with their physical safety – another privacy function that can be provided by the family office.

The other principal catalyst for the creation of a separate family office has been when the operating business is sold or goes public.[4] This transaction has two major effects on the family owners. First, they suddenly have much more liquid wealth than ever before. Secondly, they no longer have access to company staff to take care of their personal and family needs.

Many owners become paralysed at this point. The activity they knew so well – operating the business – is gone. The liquid wealth is not something they have had much experience with, and they do not know whom to trust. A surprising number of the suddenly liquid owners in the United States simply put the money into ordinary Treasury bills while wondering what they need to learn about the sophisticated investment world. Their day-to-day conveniences are also gone: no more secretary, no more office to go to every day, no more staff and so on. This sudden transition can be very difficult.

Consultants are often hired at this stage to give advice on how to set up a family office to take care of the new financial needs. Facing the family office market for the first time can be bewildering for a family. Other family offices wishing to expand will offer to add the new family to their original family group base. Large institutions

---

3 For example, the Cargill family office is called 'Waycrosse', which is a combination of two place names special to the family.

4 This is referred to in the industry as 'a liquidity event'.

will compete for the financial management services and promise that they can be the family office substitute themselves.

This is a very confusing time for a family. Those who are able to speak directly to other families who have been through similar experiences are extremely grateful. Families have found particularly helpful the opportunities to participate in off-the-record small group discussions of many of the issues that need to be addressed when creating a family office.

Those who have been through this process caution that a family should start small, and grow as needed. The family might add any number of services over the years and grow to having a staff of 50 or more.

There is an assumption that a family must have a certain amount of wealth to justify creating and funding its own family office. Current estimates are that a family should have an investment pool of at least US$100 million. In practice it is more accurate to quantify the cost of the chosen services that are desired, and to arrive at a budget by way of that process. The first step is to decide which services should be provided, keeping in mind that additional services can always be added.

2. What services will the family office provide?

There is an incredible variety of services that can be provided by a family office. As so many family offices, especially in Europe, are focused on investments, those offices tend to look down on the full-service offices. A shorthand description of a family office that is primarily focused on investment services is that they 'do not walk the dog'. In many ways those offices would be more accurately named 'private investment offices'.

Deciding what services should be provided is a very personal evaluation. It should not matter what most other family offices provide. What matters is the unique needs of a particular family. For example, one investment professional hired by a new family office complained that this was not a 'real' family office – because on the organisational chart most of the positions related to looking after six international homes and their staff, including local nannies. In that case there was still a successful operating business, with a relatively small amount of liquid investments. Nonetheless this was a good example of a real family office. The services were built to serve the current needs of the family.

The following are some of the services that are provided, to some degree, by family offices:

- income tax planning to minimise taxes;
- coordination of all individual financial matters;
- cash-flow management;
- preparation of financial reports;
- oversight of brokerage transactions;
- family philanthropic strategies;
- investment services;
- asset allocation;
- management of debt/leveraging;
- retirement planning;
- estate tax planning;
- bill paying;
- payroll tax administration for household help;
- cyber security training for the family;
- health and well-being coverage for the family;[5]
- coordination with bankers, attorneys and insurance brokers;
- oversight of real estate investments;
- wealth transfer strategies;
- mediation of intergenerational conflicts;
- assistance with succession transitions;
- serving as trustee;
- family education;
- facilitation of family meetings;
- family governance;
- family council structures;
- preparing a total wealth audit, to understand the family's holdings on a comprehensive basis;
- monitoring all risk coverage, from property and casualty to substantial life insurance programmes;
- developing a detailed kidnap policy;
- offering offshore solutions as appropriate;
- overseeing and monitoring outside trustees;
- creating educational programmes for the next generation, giving them the skills needed for independent evaluations in connection with the family wealth, and also preparing them to serve as valuable board members for other organisations;
- facilitating family meetings, at the foundation or the family council; and
- managing art collections, and other collectibles.

5 See, for example, Qineticare (www.qineticare.com), describing itself as the first global family health office.

Many families have a strong interest in philanthropy, and this is another area in which the family office can provide a number of services. The family office, for example, can evaluate all of the requests for charitable grants, and make recommendations to the family. If there is a family charitable foundation or trust, the family office can organise the meetings and make sure that all the records are properly kept, and that any income tax filings are properly prepared. Families that previously had operating businesses often prefer to have a more active role in their charitable giving. Often referred to as 'venture philanthropy' the family in effect starts another venture, this one based on philanthropy. For example, a family might decide to build a school, hospital or mosque. The family office can handle the oversight and administration of such projects. This ability of the family office to help with charitable activities extends to the recent interest in 'impact investing'.

When the family has shared assets (a yacht, plane, compound, foreign vacation home, etc), the family office can oversee their staffing, insurance, maintenance and agreements for their shared use. These assets often cause a fair amount of friction within families, so having the family office involved can be very helpful.

In terms of liquid investments, the appeal of combining their investment funds is generally that as a larger fund they will be able to negotiate discounted fees, can qualify to enter funds with larger minimums, and can have access to top national and international managers. From time to time one or more family members might decide that they would rather handle their investments on their own, and may leave the family office entirely.

All wealthy families are aware of the importance of the next generation in planning for the future. Some family offices will establish educational programmes to ensure that everyone has a background in the areas they think they should know, which can certainly vary by family.

As part of the family services most family offices will oversee estate planning, which is usually carried out by outside lawyers. This includes family trusts, wills, prenuptial agreements, postnuptial agreements and marriage dissolutions.

Another role played by some family offices is simply to be the 'glue' that keeps the family connected with each other. This can be especially important when a family business has been sold. At that time many family members are anxious about losing that connection with each other.

The family office may organise regular gatherings of the entire family. In some cases the family office will hire outside advisers to help the family create its own family council, mission statement or family constitution, all of which are designed to keep the family closely connected.

3. What are some alternatives?

After a family has spent time deciding which services it would like to have provided to them, they would be wise to consider the alternatives in the marketplace. It may be that an existing firm would provide all or most of the services without involving significant investment. For any service, the family will want to decide whether they should 'buy or build' that particular service.

Looking at alternatives to a single family office, the first type of service provider that may be the most visible in the marketplace is any number of financial institutions. From the largest global firm to the smallest local firm, nearly all of them now market that they provide 'family office' services in addition to their investment management. These offerings should be examined very carefully, especially with respect to their fees. If their fees are based, for example, on the investment assets they are given to manage, their incentives are likely to focus on the investments, and not any of the other family services that have been described. A number of firms offered family office services and then learned that the cost of providing the 'walk the dog' services was simply too costly. This is a very fluid marketplace, so a current search and comparison is always advised. There are several consultants who can help a family evaluate the various firms.

The next alternative to consider is an existing 'multi-family office'. As the name denotes, these are family offices that service more than one family. In the case of a newly wealthy family (eg, after a liquidity event) looking at alternatives to manage the family wealth, they are likely to consider joining an existing multi-family office.

The most appealing type of multi-family office to many families would be one that itself began as a single family office, and then grew to create a structure and staff large enough to support additional families. These are offices with the experience of handling multi-generational issues in families.

The advantages of a multi-family office are a perceived reduction in operating costs, the use of qualified, experienced family office staff, increased investment capabilities and the ability to share in some areas with the other client families. A more recent phenomenon is when a single family office decides to outsource various functions to a qualified multi-family office but to otherwise maintain itself as a single family office. For example the multi-family office might handle the various tax and administrative requirements, leaving the single family office more available to interact with the family.

The principal perceived disadvantage of a multi-family office is that the family office staff is shared with other families. This means giving up that single dedication that is the hallmark of a traditional single family office, as well as giving up total control by a patriarch or matriarch. If the multi-family office began as a single family office, there is often a concern about whether the new clients will have an equal priority. Sometimes there are also concerns about privacy, although most multi-family offices adhere to strict privacy principles.

4. Where should it be located?

Assuming that due diligence has occurred, and the alternatives have been examined, the next question is where the family office should be located. An excellent summary has been prepared by Jan Van Beuren and Thomas Ming, from FOSS Family Office Advisory in Zurich.[6] They begin with a look at the family members who will need services and ask where the family members are and where their assets are:

A good starting point for drafting a longlist of potential jurisdictions for the establishment of a single-family office is analysing those jurisdictions in which the family will need to receive support. This support relates to the jurisdictions in which family members live and in which assets are held.[7]

They give as an illustration the different factors that might apply in two different families.[8]

We assume that family number one lives in Germany and consists of a couple with three adult children, of which two are married. All the family members live in Germany, and they all hold a German passport (only). Their assets consist of the family business and real estate investments, both located in Germany. They also hold bank accounts in several jurisdictions. As this family is centred in Germany, Germany

6 Jan van Bueren and Thomas Ming, "Family Office Jurisdictions: Choosing the Right One", *The International Family Offices Journal*, Globe Law and Business, March 2018, pp39–44.

7 *Ibid.*

8 *Ibid.*

clearly should be on the longlist. Moreover, as the family office staff should be well acquainted with German legal and tax issues (which are relatively complex) and preferably fluent in German, jurisdictions such as Austria, Liechtenstein, Luxembourg and Switzerland should also qualify for the longlist.

Depending on the proximity with respect to where the family is physically located, one of those jurisdictions might be ranked higher on the list than others.

The second family in their example is a family with a Russian background:

The family consists of a couple with two children, one already of legal age and one a minor. The father owns a large company in Russia and is primarily based there. The minor attends a boarding school in the United Kingdom, where the mother also resides. The young adult is a student at a university in the United States. He intends to stay in the US when he finishes university. They all hold a Russian passport. The mother and minor have a residency permit in the UK. The young adult holds a visa to study in the US.

In that case and solely based on where the family is residing, Russia, the UK and the US should be put on the longlist of potential family office jurisdictions.

In some cases the family might choose to split the family office functions into two separate offices. One office would be physically very convenient to the main family members and the other office would be closer to a major financial centre, such as London or Singapore. In some cases a family office may have several offices based near their preferred financial centres. Some families want to avoid regulation; some families welcome the safety that comes with oversight.

An innovative model in terms of location is the promotion of a 'virtual' family office, without any physical location.[9] It is challenging to operate such a personal set of services without a fair amount of personal interaction.

5. Hiring the right people for the family office

Being employed by a family office is quite different from working in a traditional financial services firm. There are a few search firms

9 See Thomas Handler, "Global virtual family offices" in *Family Offices: The STEP Handbook for Advisers*, 2nd edition, Globe Law and Business, 2019, p47.

that specialise in family office hiring.[10] Unlike a traditional financial services firm, the staff of a family office, no matter how impressive their educational credentials are, will often be asked to take care of any number of personal errands. One family office head was called out of an acquisition closing to help the Christmas card committee. There must be an unusually strong service attitude. Another difference is that there might not be an upward career path, which is something the potential employee should clarify and understand. Finally, the compensation can be tricky, both in terms of finding comparisons in the marketplace and not being able to include stock options. The emphasis on family confidentiality can also make it difficult for family office staff to access current educational information. An important function, which is where this chapter began, is to act as a strict 'gatekeeper' for the family.

6. Managing the office

Managing the office well should include participation by the family and the accountability of the family office personnel. For example, there should be professional governance in place: a board of directors, with appropriate committees tailored to the needs of the family. Ideally the board should include some independent outside directors, though as a practical matter most families are reluctant to have a true outsider privy to the family's financial information. A good practice is for the family office staff to report to the family on at least a quarterly basis.

7. Life cycle of a family office

In the United States many of the visible single family offices were created in the late 19th century by several extremely successful entrepreneurs during the 'Robber Baron' era. John D. Rockefeller founded his office in 1882.

As single family offices age they tend to have three alternatives going forward.[11] The first is to add additional families, and so become a multi-family office, as discussed above. The second alternative has been to wind down the office and close it. This often occurs

10 See MJ Rankin's "Tips for long-term hires" in *Setting Up a Family Office,* Globe Law and Business, 2020, p52.

11 See Leslie Voth, "The lifecycle of the family office" in *Family Offices: The STEP Handbook for Advisers*, 2nd edition, Globe Law and Business, 2019, p233.

when the next generation begins to question the amount of costs involved. The third alternative, which seems to be occurring more in the United States in recent times, is to align the single family office with a larger multi-family office that can take care of all of the 'back office' needs of tax, accounting and general administration. This leaves the smaller staff with more capability to spend time on the non-investment issues. See, for example, the website of multi-family office Pitcairn, where we find a direct appeal to single family offices:

> *When a single family office is powered by Pitcairn, it can take advantage of all the resources offered on our world-class platform, achieving significant economies of scale and serving family members more effectively and efficiently. A single family office powered by Pitcairn harnesses the value of a true partnership that can be tailored to fit any family office at any stage of its evolution.*[12]

8. Conclusion

The future of family offices looks secure. After the global financial crisis in 2007–2008 many families wanted to find a safe place for their family wealth. The number of trustworthy investment firms had decreased and the number of ultra-wealthy families had increased. Later scandals in the investment world added to the seriousness of the search for capable trustworthy management. The number of single family offices has shown a constant increase. One estimate is that there are 12,000–15,000 family offices globally.[13] The predictions are for that increase to continue.[14]

For wealthy families who want one, and are willing to pay for it, creating their own private family office can be a rewarding solution to the many needs of the family. The secret to success seems to be to have a focus on the actual needs of a particular family and then find the right staff to provide those services.

In closing we can return to the timeless needs of wealthy families. To have a truly dedicated staff, who can be trusted completely, has been and continues to be a valuable luxury. A single family office can be at the top of the list for a wealthy client.

---

12 At www.pitcairn.com.

13 See *A Guide to Establishing a Family Office*, at www.privatebank.citibank.com/ivc/docs/A-guide-to-establishing-a-family-office-Citi-Private-Bank.pdf.

14 Kirby Rosplock and Barbara R Hauser, "The Family Office Landscape: Today's Trends and Five Predictions for the Family Office of Tomorrow", *Journal of Wealth Management*, Winter 2014.

Managing declining capacity

Keith Drewery
Drewery Consulting

Since originally writing the majority of this chapter in 2017 for *The International Family Offices Journal*,[1] there have been several further studies and pieces of research that are supportive of the general proposition of this chapter. Very simply, my sense is that the family's decision-making framework should be accommodated to provide for 'supported decision making'. Families and their family offices are comfortable with the idea of collective decision making and, with thought, can adjust those frameworks to accommodate family members who may be suffering from cognitive decline. The idea of supported decision making is compared to the use of 'substitutes', such as attorneys and guardians, whose role should follow on from a 'supported decision-making' process.

The focus on the individual and their needs and concerns is vital for any advisory relationship but it yields great results in dealing with people who are struggling with their own sense of identity and decision-making capacity.

1. Introduction

Each year, Alzheimer's Disease International (ADI), a London-based not-for-profit organisation focused on Alzheimer's disease management, publishes its *World Alzheimer Report*. In 2019, the report explored attitudes to dementia[2] and found that while small changes had occurred in the way that Alzheimer's was perceived, it continued to be viewed as a condition arising as a consequence

1 Keith Drewery, "Managing Declining Capacity: the Role of the Family Office", *The International Family Offices Journal*, December 2017, p44.

2 Alzheimer's Disease International, *World Alzheimer's Report 2019: Attitudes to Dementia*. Developed in conjunction with London School of Economics, the survey received responses from over 70,000 participants, making it the largest survey of its type ever undertaken.

of ageing and not as a disease requiring significant governmental resources and attention.

What the report also showed very clearly was how much public perceptions of the disease leave sufferers themselves feeling empty and disregarded and frequently ignored by health professionals when in the company of caregivers. The point being that it is very easy for wealth advisers to view their advice framework as being simply to protect the individual without having understood the extent of the individual's decline. The skill of the wealth adviser is to recognise the individual and assess their capacity to remain engaged in discussions concerning their future and the future of their family and its ownership of wealth, while at the same time recognising the need to ensure that the individual concerned remains safe and protected.

Within the executive summary of that report, the following was noted:

> *In 2019 ADI estimates that there are over 50 million people living with dementia globally, a figure set to increase to 152 million by 2050. Someone develops dementia every three seconds and the current annual cost of dementia is estimated at US$1trillion, a figure set to double by 2030.*

Dementia Australia estimates that by 2028 the number of people living with dementia in Australia will be 590,000.[3] The number of people diagnosed with dementia increases by around 250 every day and the burden on their families, social frameworks and the economy continues to increase. In most cases, the onset of the disease is gradual and the individual struggles to even contemplate or appreciate the nature of their condition. Often it is left to the caregiver, the spouse, close friend or relative to gradually assume responsibility and seek help and assistance from professionals on his behalf. The impact of the disease is felt across all spectrums of society, rich and poor. However, the fact is that as a client's wealth increases, the complexity of his or her affairs, the nature of his or her governance structures and frameworks for decision making become far more complex. In general, the capacity of professional service providers to engage with their clients as they face up to the effects of diminishing memory remains a challenge to their conventional practice and highlights a need for them to develop deeper collaborative relationships with a whole range of different service and care professionals. Using examples drawn from their

---

3 www.dementia.org.au/statistics.

experience in advising clients with diminishing capacity and working with their families and other care professionals, this article examines the issues facing professional service providers in their responsibilities to their client, the practicalities of developing professional legal relationships and how the service provider may need to rethink their model for service delivery to move from an agent to a position of 'fiduciary'.

A Shakespearean tragedy serves as a metaphor for the impact of declining capacity on family capital:

Does any here know me? This is not Lear:
Does Lear walk thus, speak thus? Where are his eyes?
Either his notion weakens, his discernings
Are lethargied – Ha! waking? 'tis not so.
Who is it that can tell me who I am?

(William Shakespeare, *King Lear*, Act 1: Scene 4)

The descent into madness of Shakespeare's ageing King Lear offers many insights into the consequences of declining capacity on the transmission of wealth and power wielded by a wealthy family.

An ageing king, concerned about the conflict that may arise between his three daughters, and their husbands and consorts, on his death, makes a misguided decision to determine a strategy around the succession of his kingdom among his three daughters (Goneril, Regan and Cordelia).

As in many unfortunate cases, the transition to retirement and the clumsy management of the division of the kingdom turn out to have terrible ramifications, far removed from the original intent. Lear's actions end up destroying his family, tearing apart the kingdom, and creating extraordinary conflict, with the death of many of the play's characters, including all of Lear's daughters, either by murder or their own hand.

As a play, *King Lear* may be seen as an examination of the consequences of creeping senility and declining capacity on decision making at a political level but even more so for the impact it has on family relationships.[4]

---

4 For a discussion on this point, Lou-Ellen Barkan, "What Alzheimer's Caregivers Can Learn from King Lear", *The Huffington Post* (9 November 2014), available at https://guce.huffpost.com/copyConsent?sessionId=3_cc-session_871a235b-cd32-49e5-b5fc-88687b388bf7&inline=false&lang=en-us provides a provocative analysis of the nature of the condition and the response to be made by care givers.

2. The extent of the problem

The incidence of dementia in 2015 was estimated to be 46.8 million sufferers worldwide.[5] In that year alone it was calculated that 9.9 million, or one person every three seconds, were diagnosed with the disease. Using similar incidence rates, the global population of sufferers of the disease will double roughly every 20 years with an estimate that, worldwide, there will be 131.5 million people living with the condition by 2050.

According to a report[6] commissioned by Alzheimer's Australia:

- There are over 250,000 Australians with dementia, and over 1,300 new cases are confirmed every week;
- By 2030 there will be over 560,000 people with dementia and by 2050 almost one million;
- Dementia is the third largest cause of death after heart disease and stroke; and
- Dementia is already the single largest cause of disability in Australians aged 65 and over, and is responsible for one in every six years of disability burden for this group.

The reaction of the insurance industry in the United Kingdom to the effect of dementia and Alzheimer's on UK business illustrates the financial impact of the disease on business and society in general and thus the potential cost to insurers.[7] Touched by the experience of relatives, several members of the Insurance United Against Dementia board have been actively promoting and funding research into the cause and prevention of Alzheimer's disease.

Based on the Office of National Statistics report "Deaths Registered in Engalnd and Wales (series DR) 2017" dementia and Alzheimer's disease accounted for over 12.7% of all deaths registered in the UK and is the leading cause of death in the United Kingdom, having overtaken heart disease in 2015.[8]

---

5 www.alz.co.uk/research/statistics.

6 Deloitte Access Economics, *Dementia Across Australia 2011–2050*, 9 September 2011, available at www.dementia.org.au/publications/access-economics-reports.

7 According to a 2019 report, "Projections of older people with dementia and costs of dementia care in the United Kingdom 2019–2040" produced by the London School of Economics and Political Science, p6, "The total costs of dementia in the UK in 2019 amount to £34.7 billion at 2015 prices".

8 Office for National Statistics, Deaths Registered in England and Wales (series DR) 2017, released 23 October 2018, Main Points.

3. The impact on financial decision making and the rise of elder abuse

With the decline in capacity and cognitive function, the risk of financial abuse increases. According to the NSW Law Society,[9] some of the more common ways in which older people are at risk include:

- Forced changes to a will or other legal document including the making of a new will in favour of a new friend or another family member;
- Power of attorney may be obtained improperly from a person without decision-making capacity;
- Forging of signatures – on bank accounts or legal documents; and
- Misusing enduring power of attorney.

Not unsurprisingly, it is the wealthy who are often at most risk of financial abuse simply by virtue of the benefits that can accrue to the manipulative or unscrupulous.

Among several high-profile cases, the family of the former Lord Mayor of Adelaide and wealthy property developer, John Roche, were involved in a bitter battle over his estate amid allegations that he was not of sound mind when he signed his will. One of his three daughters argued that he "lacked testamentary capacity and was not of sound mind" when he executed a 2006 will that cut her out of his legacy. John Roche died in April 2010, leaving his fortune to his two other daughters, for them to effectively run the family's property development business. The company is thought to be worth around AU$250 million. Lawyers acting on behalf of the estate said "Mr Roche changed his will after Shauna had threatened legal action to secure her 25% entitlement from a AU$30 million family trust". They said Mr Roche "had a complete grasp of his assets and the claims on them, and a reasonable and rational response to those claims when he drafted the will at his lawyer's office".[10]

Throughout all jurisdictions, the incidences of claims against estates and their dramatic fall-out are increasing, spurred on perhaps by ever more aggressive marketing campaigns targeting disaffected claimants launched by legal practitioners promising to charge on a success fee basis.

---

9 The Law Society of New South Wales, *When a Client's Mental Capacity is in Doubt: A Practical Guide for Solicitors*, 2016.

10 Reported in the *Adelaide Advertiser* on 17 November 2015.

4. Planning and managing the impact of declining capacity

Rather than examining the nuances of the legal frameworks in New South Wales, and Australia more generally, that deal with 'mental capacity', the rest of this chapter discusses the manner and means by which family offices may consider managing the impact of declining capacity for family members.[11] In particular, it covers the following areas:

- Advisory relationship management in cases of declining capacity;
- The role of the family office;
- Identification, recognition and monitoring of health and well-being; and
- Developing decision making – substitute versus supported decision making.

It then offers some concluding comments.

5. Advisory relationship management in cases of declining capacity

The presentation of symptoms indicating a decline in decision-making capacity creates significant issues for the providers of professional services. Such issues include:

- The validity of the creation of a binding legal agreement securing the delivery of the professional services;
- The need for review and continuation of pre-existing agreements;
- A re-examination of the nature of the professional service arrangements;
- The identification of relevant support professionals; and
- The review and management of pre-existing substitute arrangements.

Within the environment of the single family office (SFO) there are typically very few contractual arrangements existing between the family and the family office at the initial stages of the SFO's development from the first to second generation. There would not

11 For a summary of the issues affecting Commonwealth laws, see Australian Law Reform Commission, *Equality, Capacity and Disability in Commonwealth Laws*, ALRC Report 124, November 2014.

typically be, for example, a contract created between the group of advisers employed inside the SFO and the founders themselves.[12] At the very least, regardless of the circumstances facing the individual, it would be important to make sure that there is a clear understanding of what role the family office serves, the scope of services (within the skills of the family office resources to deliver) and some sense of the expected costs for delivery of those services.

In developing service standards, it is clearly important to identify 'who is doing what to whom' and in this regard the nature of and relative complexity of the family office structure would need to be fully appreciated.

In particular, where the family office provides services to individuals, directors of private companies, trustees of discretionary trusts and pension funds, and the shareholders and beneficiaries of these legal entities, the SFO (as a service supplier) should ensure that it is intimately aware of what service is being provided and for whom. In so doing, the risk and risk mitigation around decision making can be formalised.

More challenging perhaps for a service professional is meeting the demands and complexity of a services relationship that declining capacity may impose and being aware of the limitations of their own skills and capabilities. In this regard, it is possible that the trusted adviser who has typically served the family over several years may be as well placed as any to the extent that they are not necessarily seen as solely delivering 'subject matter expertise'.

In his paper, "The Shifting Sands of Professional Accountability",[13] Michael Perkins highlighted the change in client service expectations that may confront advisers and the definition of their role. In the introduction, Perkins explains:

> *With the retirement of the Baby Boomer generation, the longevity of their parents and increasing fiscal transparency in the global economy, private client focused professionals [executives of family offices] are being challenged to engage with the consulting and general counsel expectations of their clients.*

---

12 As the SFO increases in size to serve an increasing number of family members across generations, the need to develop formal service relationships increases. Here there will be a need for service level agreements to be established and a more formal professional service relationship created. This is covered by Family Office Exchange, *50 Best Practices for an Enduring Family Enterprise*, 2008.

13 Michael Perkins (Perkins Fahey Rosenblum), "The Shifting Sands of Professional Accountability", paper presented to the 2nd International Conference on Private Capital and Intergenerational Wealth (Hong Kong), 2016.

The paper further explains that:

As families become the client segment of focus for private client focused professional practices [family offices] there is an increasing need to define cross disciplinary and multidisciplinary approaches to professional practice where efficient delivery of professional services to a family does not require parallel delivery of specialist services directly to the client. A more balanced approach that mediates the general client care with specialized service delivery as needed has to be developed.

With an awareness of the issues affecting the delivery of professional services to an ageing client base, the family office will need to understand the way in which it will respond to the management of this risk and either incorporate broader service capability inside the family office or build partnerships with relevantly experienced professionals. For example, the family office may wish to engage with health and well-being professionals as part of its response, perhaps partnering with a provider such as the Hong Kong-based Qineticare (see www.qineticare.com).

6. The role of the family office

If we accept that a consequence of the ageing process is the increased prevalence and presentation of mental deterioration, it would seem important that the family office understand the potential exposure of the family's capital in the event of an impulsive or ill-considered decision, potentially by someone who would lay claim to his or her right to make such decisions. Wealth has not been shown to act as a shield to the potential impact of the disease but the existence of wealth does potentially make the impact of declining capacity far more profound.

The Australian family office experience has been that many SFOs exist because of the success and single-minded determination of the wealth creator and typically the founder of the family office.

At any particular point in time, the life-span of a family office is largely unknown and the formalisation of policies dealing with the retirement of senior personnel are often *ad hoc*, at best, particularly at the level of the first generation wealth creator.

For the founder, the capacity to appreciate the potential for the problem to exist and actively manage the situation requires an enhanced level of 'emotional intelligence'. However, it is not surprising that the number of self-referred incidences of dementia are relatively rare. The chances of a founder being at once both sufficiently self-aware and of a sufficiently high level of emotional intelligence to call into question his or her own decision-making capability would be similarly slim.

For this reason alone, planning for the risk of the incidence, either to the founder or beneficiary member or delegated decision maker, should form part of the family office's standard risk management process.[14]

Perhaps a solution is to articulate carefully the potential downside to capital and/or business risk that may arise and, through an examination of the 'system' by which the family office operates, to develop proactive planning and reporting protocols to reduce these risks.

As an example, if the family governance system is particularly autocratic and the 'autocrat' becomes incapacitated, the very real risk is that either a poor decision is made, as that person's judgement declines, or no decision is ever made, as the individual withdraws. It could even result in a contractual relationship being created which is rendered unenforceable.

In cases I am aware of, quite often the founder of a business stays too long in his or her role and in doing so, directly or indirectly, overcommits the enterprise and its capacity to fulfil its obligations. On my rethinking the circumstances that prevailed in these matters, I recognise that it was often a failure to act or fully discharge their responsibilities rather than a specific poorly made decision that created the problem. Either way, insufficient oversight existed as many 'compromised' decision makers simply did as they were told, albeit by well-meaning and considered advisers.

By developing a policy to mitigate a scientifically proven and calculated risk, the risk becomes objectified and this may serve several distinct purposes:

- The risk is identified as being 'one arising in the ordinary incidence of the management of family capital';
- As an identified risk, appropriate mitigating strategies can be developed and implemented; and
- Perhaps most importantly, the founder and other decision makers can turn their minds to the impact of declining capacity on their family's capital and future while circumstances allow.

---

14 In its 2006 paper, "Recasting the Central Role of the Family Office as Risk Manager", the Family Office Exchange expressed the development of a six-step process for managing family risk:

1. Define long-term family goals and objectives;
2. Identify risks associated with family objectives;
3. Prioritise risks by likelihood of occurrence and potential impact;
4. Create mitigation strategies for top-priority risks;
5. Commit resources for implementing mitigation strategies;
6. Continuously monitor the risk landscape and results of mitigation efforts.

However, that document did not identify ageing and the impact on decision making as a specific risk.

To help develop the risk protocols necessary to mitigate the impact of declining capacity, an examination of the roles played and the skills and responsibilities of personnel inside the family office should be completed.

Clearly, the level of complexity and sensitivity required increases where the roles of the office are being filled by family members.

By undertaking this review, appropriate safeguards, checks and balances can be considered and developed. These may include:

- Access to health and well-being resources and the introduction of statutory medicals;
- Review of decision-making authority to ensure no single point of decision making;
- Review of delegated authorities including appointment of relevant 'powers of attorney' and a move towards support-based decision making (see below);
- Development of policies to ensure all material financial decisions are approved by two or more directors/responsible officers; and
- Introduction of step-down or step-back clauses for participants of a certain age, if not triggered earlier.

It is not too inconceivable that a family office could also develop a complete inventory of the family's capital to incorporate the 'value' of human and social capital, to be delivered as part of its regular reporting protocols. Several family offices already undertake education as part of their service syllabus which looks to invest in the future management and control of the family's capital.

Including, as part of that inventory, a report on the continued capability of senior personnel may be a systematic way to identify potential depreciation in the 'value' of the family's human capital.

7. Identification, recognition and monitoring of health and well-being

While risk protocols can be developed and integrated into the family office's risk framework, it is still vitally important for the family office to help the family in the identification of symptoms associated with a decline in mental capacity.

In her chapter for the *Wealth of Wisdom*[15] anthology, Patricia Annino made the observation, "Frequently there is no clear

15 T McCullogh and K Whittaker, *Wealth of Wisdom: The Top 50 Questions Wealthy Families Ask*, John Wiley and Sons, 2018.

demarcation between competence and incompetence until the day when the demarcation line is very clear, and incompetence is definite. The challenge is to handle the issue with the planning process when there is no need to".[16]

It is perhaps at the family office that several of the traits can be more easily recognised, as those in close proximity to the individual can often sense several of the key indicators and hopefully, having done so, feel they have the right to suggest they are present.

People vary in their ability to understand and make decisions, and these abilities can change over time. A person has a right to make decisions about their own life if they are considered able to understand the relevant information and express a choice in some way. The law[17] refers to a person's 'decision-making capacity', and applies specific tests to determine this, asking:

- Can the person understand the nature and consequences of the decision?
- Can they weigh the relevant information in order to express a preference?
- Can they retain the relevant information long enough to make a decision?
- Can they communicate their decision in some way?

The concept of decision-making capacity, while necessary in legal activities (eg, contracts and wills), has been criticised because it can exclude people with cognitive impairments from everyday decisions about their lives.

The United Nations Convention emphasises that all individuals have the right to make their own decisions in the context of relationships, and that a person's decision-making ability can be increased through support and education.

The following principles about decision-making ability are well established in common law in Australia and apply nationally:

- A person is presumed to be capable of making decisions about their life, unless there is evidence to the contrary;
- A person's decision-making ability can fluctuate and change over time;

---

16 Patricia Annino, "How Families Can Prepare for Longevity and Mental Incapacity Among Family Members" in McCullogh and Whittaker, *Wealth of Wisdom*, p75.

17 United Nations, Convention on the Rights of Persons with Disabilities, 2006. www.un.org/development/desa/disabilities/convention-onthe-rights-of-persons-with-disabilities.html.

- An assessment of a person's decision-making ability is specific to a particular time and a particular decision; and
- Assessments of a person's decision-making ability should occur in the context of the actual task or decision that is being undertaken.[18]

At a practical level, according to the Alzheimer Society of Canada:[19]

The disease will affect mental abilities, emotions and moods, behaviour and physical abilities.

Mental abilities

Alzheimer's disease or another dementia can affect a person's communication, decision making and thought-processing abilities. This may include:

- *Trouble remembering or understanding others*
- *Confusion*
- *Difficulty performing simple tasks*
- *Poor judgment*

Emotions and moods

Dementia can affect the way a person experiences and expresses emotions. This may include:

- *Appearing uninterested and apathetic*
- *Losing interest in things you once enjoyed*
- *Becoming more withdrawn*

Behaviour

A person with dementia may start reacting different to his environment. This may include:

---

18 Attorney General's Department, *Capacity Toolkit*, NSW Government, 2008, www.justice.nsw.gov.au/diversityservices/Documents/capacity_toolkit0609.pdf.

19 See https://alzheimer.ca/en/hpe/We-can-help/Information-and-referral/Information-for-the-person-with-dementia.

- *Repeating the same action or words*
- *Hiding possessions*
- *Physical outbursts*
- *Restlessness*

Physical abilities

The disease can affect a person's physical coordination and mobility, leading to a gradual physical decline.
This may include trouble with:

- *Eating*
- *Bathing*
- *Getting dressed*

It is obviously extremely difficult to broach the subject of declining capacity with an individual who may be exhibiting some of the symptoms described above. For those close to the individual over a number of years, they may observe a dulling of the insight brought to bear by that person and are arguably well-placed to ask discrete questions bringing to light this seeming change in the character of the individual and their engagement with the problem.

Here the adviser must be careful; too firm a hand may result in the victim becoming defensive and asking "why are you seeking to take away my decision-making capability?" Too light a touch and the impacts of the impairment of decision making become more profound and potentially irreversible.

Instead, family office executives and decision-making processes may need to be reconsidered with the development of a 'choice' framework that allows the individual the dignity of continuing to be involved in making decisions with the safety of the decision and the choices available being reviewed.

Building awareness and training inside the family office around identification of symptoms will become increasingly relevant. While such training may seem overly prescriptive, bear in mind that very few business-like environments are quite as all-embracing as the SFO or the headquarters of the private family-owned business.

Founders, owners and family members, particularly at the first and formative stages of an SFO, are extremely hands-on and engaged in the day-to-day operation of the office and the staff are also highly loyal and in many cases close to the founder and the family, as trusted advisers.

Understanding of the complexity of the problem, and potential difficulties in diagnosis, are key first steps in understanding how to engage with the individual and his or her family and help to garner support for a review and consideration of the family decision-making process in light of the identification of a potential problem.

Such training is no substitution for medical diagnosis, of course. To this end, the training provided to the legal profession is often useful as a basis for developing some practical guidance for family office staff.

In Australia, the legislation regarding a person's capacity to make his own decisions differs in each State/Territory. The Queensland legislation sets out the definition very clearly. It states that capacity for a person for a matter (ie, any matter you may need to make a decision about), means that the person is capable of:

- understanding the nature and effect of decisions about the matter;
- freely and voluntarily making decisions about the matter; and
- communicating the decisions in some way.[20]

In a very useful booklet *Dementia and Your Legal Rights*,[21] the authors clearly spell out some of the key legal matters:

- First, it is internationally accepted that an individual should be regarded as having a 'presumption of capacity'; and
- Secondly, that capacity is decision specific and even if someone has been diagnosed with dementia it does not mean that all decisions they make are affected. It relies on an understanding of the place and circumstances and is then only reversible if challenged.

Continuing this theme, the Law Society of New South Wales in its publication *When a Client's Mental Capacity is in Doubt*[22] offers guidance to solicitors under "Key Principles".

---

20 Schedule 4 to the Guardianship and Administration Act 2000 (Queensland).

21 Sue Field and Colleen Cartwright, *Dementia and Your Legal Rights*, Alzheimer's Australia, www.dementia.org.au/files/NATIONAL/documents/Dementia-and-your-legal-rights.pdf.

22 The Law Society of New South Wales, *When a Client's Mental Capacity is in Doubt*.

8. Developing decision making – substitute versus supported decision making

Engaging in a conversation about diminishing decision-making authority can be problematic and difficult, particularly where the former decision maker was, or remains, autocratic in his or her decision-making style and less open to allowing others the authority to make decisions.[23]

For all practical purposes and depending upon the extent of the condition, a key outcome for a family office should be to understand how an individual can remain engaged in the decision-making process, to ensure his or her experience and rights are respected, while acknowledging that the views of others may be important through this key transition of governance.

It is helpful to understand in general terms the nature of the pre-eminent decision-making models and understand their application in cases where declining capacity is observed.

The Australian Law Reform Commission review of 2014[24] contained several recommendations that are directly relevant to the development of new decision-making models.

> ***National Decision-Making Principles***
> *1.4 The ALRC recommends that the reform of relevant Commonwealth, state and territory laws should be consistent with the following National Decision-Making Principles:*
>
> ***Principle 1: The equal right to make decisions***
> *All adults have an equal right to make decisions that affect their lives and to have those decisions respected.*
>
> ***Principle 2: Support***
> *Persons who require support in decision making must be provided with access to the support necessary for them to make, communicate and participate in decisions that affect their lives.*
>
> ***Principle 3: Will, preferences and rights***
> *The will, preferences and rights of persons who may require decision-making support must direct decisions that affect their lives.*

---

23 For several good articles on the question of dealing with individuals undergoing significant change events associated with ageing, see the blog of Danielle Robertson of DRC Care Solutions, available at www.daniellerobertson.com.au/single-post/2017/01/16/Understanding-the-loss-of-independence-in-ageing.

24 Australian Law Reform Commission, *Equality, Capacity and Disability in Commonwealth Laws*.

Principle 4: Safeguards
Laws and legal frameworks must contain appropriate and effective safeguards in relation to interventions for persons who may require decision-making support, including to prevent abuse and undue influence.

A key push in the Australia Law Reform Commission's report was the development of supported decision making as a priority over the more common appointment of a substitute. Indeed, in the Key Principles articulated by the Law Society,[25] resorting to the substitute decision making was considered to be a step of last resort.

While directed towards a similar intention, to provide a mechanism by which those suffering a disability can be represented, supported decision making and substitute decision making are quite different in approach.

Substitute decision making gives the decision maker complete legal authority to act in relation to particular types of decisions on behalf of the individual, typically through the form of a power of attorney. The substitute decision maker should act in consultation with the individual to the extent that it is possible to do so. However, once capacity is lost, the substitute must follow written or verbal instructions, if they have been provided and communicated to the substitute.

However, in some circumstances, the substitute may need to make the decision on his or her own, for example if the wishes of the individual in a particular situation were unclear, vague or unknown. In some rare cases it may be that the substitute believes that he or she should make a decision in opposition to the individual's views as expressed. In such a case, the substitute decision maker will need the authority of the board or tribunal before he or she can do so. Sometimes, there is conflict between the substitute and someone else, perhaps another family member or friend, and often the only way to resolve the issue is to make an application to the guardianship board – or tribunal in NSW – which will decide the matter.

The appointment of a substitute has traditionally been the most common approach to managing decisions on behalf of someone lacking capacity but may be an inferior alternative to supported decision making where there are already well-defined terms of reference such as a family constitution or charter. Both are becoming

25 The Law Society of New South Wales, *When a Client's Mental Capacity is in Doubt.*

increasingly common in their application by family businesses and family enterprises of wealth.

Such documents may well need to include comment on or make reference to what the family should consider in cases where the decision-making capability of an individual may be compromised.

Supported decision making is a framework that has arisen from concerns about the increasing number of cases of disconnect between substitute decision making and the affected individual and the compromised position that can often eventuate. There are several recently reported cases in Australia where the actions of the substitute have been critically examined. Indeed, on a worldwide scale the problem continues to increase as the number of reported incidents attests. Supported decision making may be based on a formal agreement between the individual with questionable capacity and his or her supporters, or an informal network of people, who support that person in making his or her own decisions based on his or her own views and wishes.[26]

A handbook published by the Sydney-based Cognitive Decline Partnership Centre[27] provides the following explanation:

> *Supported decision making has been defined as: "the process whereby a person with a disability is enabled to make or communicate decisions with respect to personal or legal matters". The term 'supported decision making' also refers to the legal systems that protect the rights of people with impaired decision-making ability.*

The adoption of a supported decision-making framework inside family offices would seem to be a fairly natural fit for many SFOs. However, in adopting this framework, SFOs need to consider what staff training should be undertaken. Are current attorneys/ guardians properly trained in the responsibilities that such roles require?

What broader levels of skills and resources will we need to manage a support-based decision-making framework and how will the family office and the client engage with those services (ie, insource or outsource)?

---

26 This form of decision making is more in keeping with obligations under the United Nations' Convention on the Rights of Persons with Disabilities. Australia is a signatory to this convention.

27 C Sinclair, S Field, K Williams, M Blake, R Bucks, K Auret, J Clayton and S Kurrle, *Supporting Decision-Making: A Guide for People Living with Dementia, Family Members and Carers*, Cognitive Decline Partnership Centre, 2018, p8.

What the adoption of a support-based framework will require is the development of a broad-based holistic service capability that works in sympathy with the family as a client as a whole.

9. Concluding comments

Members of families of wealth and their family offices are not immune from the impact and consequences of impairment of capacity of family members.

It is accepted that the incidence of a deterioration of mental capacity will increase and while there may be steps that can be taken to decrease the rate of deterioration, the effects of that impairment and the rate of future deterioration are largely unknown.[28]

Faced with an increase in the likelihood of the risk, and being unable to quantify the impact of the risk, family offices should develop responses to mitigate that risk by considering the following:

- Raise the issue for formal evaluation as part of the family office's risk management framework;
- Review pre-existing service relationships with an examination of 'Who is doing What to Whom';
- Develop in-house protocols dealing with decision making inside the family office;
- Consider incorporating mental health and well-being as a risk managed inside the family office;
- Review pre-existing family governance arrangements, including a review of family constitutions and charters to determine appropriate responses;
- Consider how pre-existing decision making and governance supports the adoption of 'supported decision making'; and
- Identify appropriate health professional and relevantly experienced service professionals to support the family office.

The author acknowledges the support and work of Michael Perkins, of Perkins Fahey and Rosenblum, and specifically his time and comments in developing the themes presented. In addition, the author would like to thank Danielle Robertson, CEO and Founder of DRC Care Solutions, for her insights into the management of individuals suffering from cognitive impairment and her work in supporting families to help manage the needs of elderly relatives.

---

28 For an examination of the nature of the condition from someone diagnosed with early onset dementia and living with the condition, see www.christinebryden.com/books/book-before-i-forget/.

The philanthropy framework

Melissa Berman
Rockefeller Philanthropy Advisors, Inc

1. Introduction

Complex families with significant resources think more holistically now about their businesses and their assets, their activities, their commitments, their legacy and their successors. As expectations grow for the wealthy to be engaged, knowledgeable and committed to making a difference in issues such as inequality and climate change, family office leaders must be prepared to help their principals form strategies and action plans. Their role in philanthropy goes well beyond facilitating donations.

Across the world, philanthropy is undergoing a rapid transformation that offers both exciting opportunities and complex challenges. As a more unified global culture around giving and social investment emerges, new players, vehicles, strategies and approaches are creating commitment, enthusiasm and optimism. Yet shifting attitudes towards philanthropy, intense debates about power and effectiveness and difficult operating environments require philanthropists and social investors to demonstrate their value to a wide range of stakeholders. And, as many philanthropists broaden their activities from grant-making to impact investing, knowledge-building, advocacy and coalition-building, they face the need to change how their organisations assess and allocate non-financial resources.

With so much in flux, emerging donors and established funders are seeking new models not only for funding strategies and impact measures, but also for organisational design and management systems that will serve them well into the 21st century. Family office advisers have a critical role to play in helping families leverage the opportunities and manage the risks.

In response to these interests and needs, Rockefeller Philanthropy Advisors developed the 'philanthropy framework', a tool to give an emerging or established philanthropy (whether in the form of a foundation, trust, funder collaborative, LLC, donor-advised fund or direct giving) a structure to align resources for maximum impact.

Figure 1. The philanthropy framework

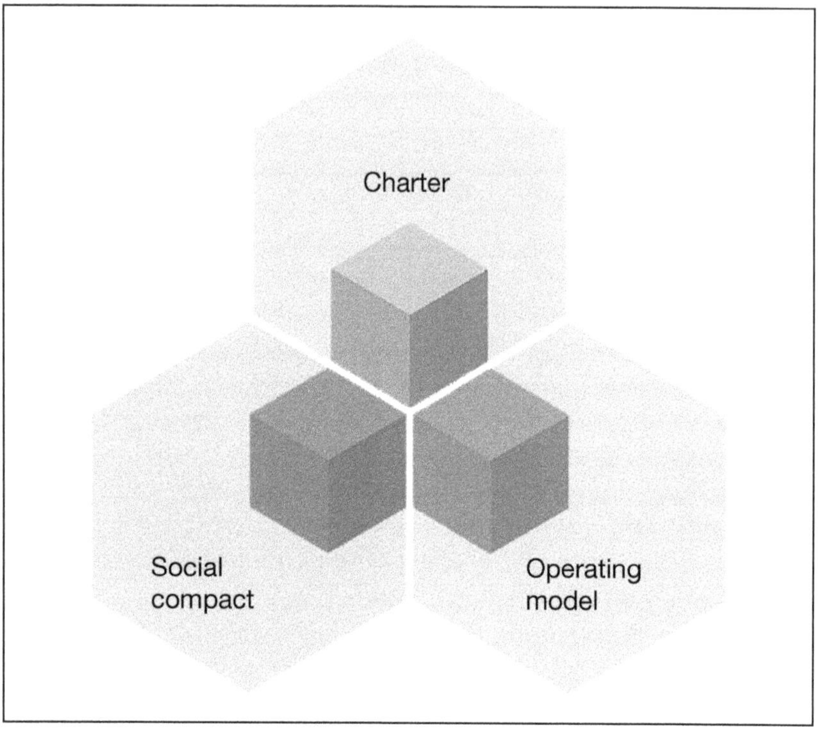

The framework comprises three core elements:

- Charter – the organisation's scope, form of governance and decision-making protocol;
- Social compact – its implicit or explicit agreement with society about the value it will create; and
- Operating model – the approach to the resources, structures and systems needed to implement strategy.

2. Genesis of the philanthropy framework

Philanthropy is in a remarkable era of expansion in many senses:

- As a culture of giving spreads globally, more wealthholders are engaging in philanthropy earlier in their lives, and more deeply.
- The concept of what philanthropy entails is expanding to include impact investing, and there is a renewed interest in advocacy, capital aggregation and partnerships.

- How philanthropy connects with communities increasingly incorporates community-based decision making and participatory engagement.
- 'Giving while living' and spend-down philanthropy are on the rise, expanding concepts of how impact occurs.
- Corporate interest in 'social business' models is changing the scope of corporate giving and Corporate Social Responsibility to focus on societal impact.
- Foundations and other giving vehicles are expanding their ideas about how to source and develop talent, how to develop and share knowledge and learnings, and how to use their voice and reputational capital.
- Newer vehicles for philanthropy, including donor-advised funds and LLC umbrellas in the US, allow for more donor flexibility.
- Many traditional grant-making foundations are taking a bigger role in shaping and operating programmes rather than just underwriting them.
- Expectations of philanthropy and donors themselves are expanding, both from public sector officials who sometimes seek to shrink philanthropy's sphere of action, as well as from critics of private philanthropy's role and privilege.

New models are essential to helping philanthropic leaders manage the opportunities and risks of this expanding space.

In light of these trends, Rockefeller Philanthropy Advisors launched a multi-year programme of collaborative research called the Theory of the Foundation, co-developed and supported by more than 50 funders to date. The initiative was inspired by iconic management expert Peter Drucker's seminal article "The Theory of the Business",[1] which called on business leaders to assess their fundamental assumptions in response to changing conditions. Drucker's challenge is highly pertinent to philanthropy and is particularly urgent in this era of innovation and re-evaluation. After interviewing more than 75 foundations and hosting dozens of working sessions with funders, experts and research partners in the US, Europe, Asia and Latin America, Rockefeller Philanthropy Advisors developed the philanthropy framework. This establishes,

1 Peter F Drucker, "The Theory of the Business", *Harvard Business Review*, 17 October 2016, hbr.org/1994/09/the-theory-of-the-business.

as Ford Foundation President Darren Walker calls it, "an exciting idea and an important framework for bringing more rigor and a depth of analysis to understanding philanthropy's role".[2]

Since launching this project, Rockefeller Philanthropy Advisors has published articles in SSIR.org[3] and the Foundation Review[4] and co-published reports with partners at the Marshall Institute of the London School of Economics[5] and Foundation Center's GrantCraft series.[6] This chapter synthesises our findings, along with lessons learned from participating foundations that have used the philanthropy framework. We are deeply grateful to all the foundations that have contributed, and to our many advisers, co-authors and partners.

3. Elements of the philanthropy framework

The philanthropy framework provides new tools for analysing how a philanthropic organisation makes decisions, interacts with others and the broader society, and utilises its capabilities and resources. Together, these elements define the organisation's culture, inform its structure, and shape how it carries out its strategy. By examining the questions and topics raised in the framework, foundations and other philanthropic entities can better:

- assess, validate or crystallise identity, structure and approaches;
- align trustees, board and staff around core concepts and values;
- manage organisational inflection points, such as leadership transition, restructuring, change in time horizon, shifts of focus, new strategic direction or a new operational approach;
- allocate financial and non-financial resources to maximise impact; and
- realise aspirational goals, including launching a new philanthropic endeavour, by helping identify and articulate the current state and future vision of an organisation.

2 Melissa Berman *et al*, "Frameworks for Private Foundations", *GrantCraft*, 27 June 2017, https://grantcraft.org/content/guides/frameworks-for-private-foundations/.

3 Melissa Berman, "The Theory of the Foundation", *Stanford Social Innovation Review*, 21 March 2016, ssir.org/articles/entry/the_theory_of_the_foundation.

4 Melissa Berman, "Enhancing Foundation Capacity: The Role of the Senior Leadership Team", *The Foundation Review*, 8(2) 2016, Article 9, https://doi.org/10.9707/1944-5660.1299.

5 Marshall Institute and Rockefeller Philanthropy Advisors, *The Theory of the Foundation: European Initiative 2016*, www.rockpa.org/wp-content/uploads/2017/02/ToF-European-Initiative-report.pdf.

6 Berman, "Frameworks for Private Foundations".

4. Charter

An organisation's charter tells its origin story and defines its intended scope, form of governance and procedural guidelines. The charter includes both written and unwritten elements, such as history, governance, decision-making processes, culture and values. Risk tolerance – the type and level of risk considered acceptable – is also embedded in every charter. Many organisations in the philanthropic space describe themselves as 'risk-taking', but the term's meaning isn't always adequately unpacked across programmes, governance and staff.

A philanthropic organisation's charter may also define key geographic and issue areas (such as the arts, the City of Cleveland or the well-being of children), or a set of beliefs (such as social justice, the enterprise system, a faith or a particular type of leadership). It may include broadly understood norms (such as an aversion to advocacy, or commitment to a particular field) that may or may not echo the entity's formal documents. A few of these components are explored below.

4.1 Founding legacy as origin story

Origin stories, including the role of the founding legacy, are central to a philanthropic organisation's charter. They serve as a reference point and source of inspiration, typically informing both culture and programmatic areas.

This is illustrated by the Wellcome Trust. According to one team member, the legacy of founder Sir Henry Wellcome, an American-born pharmaceutical entrepreneur, "has been and still is quite a strong source of philosophy and inspiration in terms of the breadth

Figure 2. Charter components

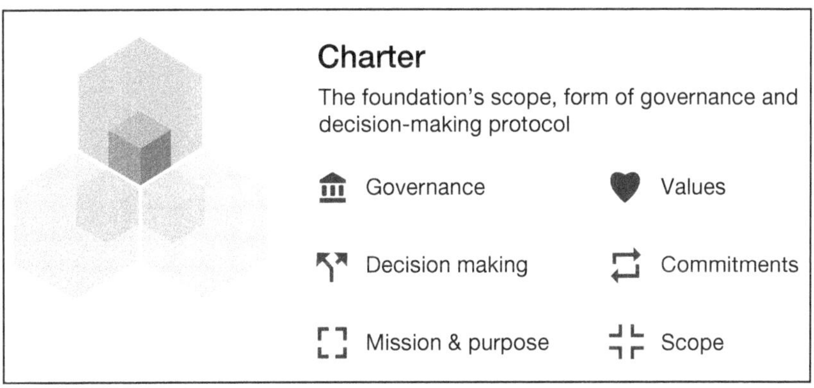

of what the organization does. [His legacy] also shapes how the organization interprets concepts such as health and medicine, beyond just the medical, because of the way that Henry Wellcome thought about the world".[7]

While some organisations view their original charter as a mandate to honour forever, others expect change based on shifting conditions, new observations or emerging leadership interests. Massimo Lapucci, secretary general of the Fondazione CRT, provides a clear example of the interplay between his organisation's original charter and ongoing flexibility. "We have a very clear charter: we are a foundation of banking origin, established by law. The foundation has a statute and by laws that legally define our mission, endowment and geographic focus. That said, we do adapt our approaches over time – and we use our charter as a guide, to ensure that we are achieving meaningful results."[8]

4.2 Charter continuum

Philanthropic organisations typically trace their roots and founding stories to an individual or group of donors, a philanthropic family, a corporation or company, public or private institutions or the government. The way in which an organisation connects to its founding donor(s) can be described as a point on a continuum. While this may change over time for any given entity, philanthropic organisations can fall into one of the following categories.

(a) Founder-led

In founder-led organisations, the living founding donor(s) sets the mission, priorities, allocation of resources and forms of engagement. While these elements may evolve, they directly represent the desires and goals of that donor or donor group, which, of course, may change. For corporate and public foundations, decisions typically follow the values and goals of the organisation's founding source or a legislative/regulatory agreement.

(b) Stewarded

Stewarded organisations are founder-determined, and often still led by those who knew the founder(s) well or feel a profound sense of responsibility to carry out the wishes of the founder(s). While

7 Rockefeller Philanthropy Advisors, *Profile: Wellcome Trust*, 2018, www.rockpa.org/profile-wellcome-trust.

8 Berman, "Frameworks for Private Foundations", p12.

the original founder(s) may no longer be alive, their decisions continue to shape the organisational mission, programme areas and approach, whether legally or by custom.

(c) ***Founder-connected***

Founder-connected organisations include successors – sometimes family members, sometimes not – of the founder or group of founders, who honour the original vision and approach without feeling tightly constrained by them. The successors see themselves as interpreters of tradition: not bound to specific policies, but walking the path of the organisation's original directives.

(d) ***Open***

In open charter organisations, board members and organisational leaders – whether descendants of the founder(s) or not – feel empowered to make decisions based on their collective assessment of external forces and internal capacity.

4.3 Charter parameters

Another way to look at an organisation's charter is to define:

- How clearly the charter is set out;
- How narrow or broad the charter is;
- Whether the organisation's rules are written or unwritten; and
- The strength of the charter's ties to history.

Figure 3. Charter parameters

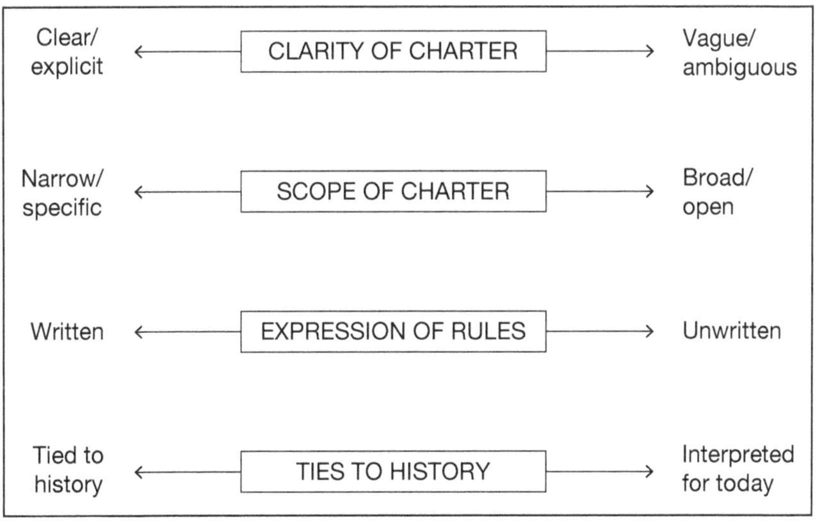

Unwritten norms or rules of the charter may play a critical role in both inspiring and challenging philanthropic organisations. For instance, the Hewlett Foundation has such a long-standing commitment to the environment that its leadership cannot imagine abandoning this issue – although how the foundation engages with the issue may change. Another major foundation interviewed as part of the Theory of the Foundation project reports that, for many years, its board reviewed individual grant summaries – but not the foundation's strategy. Eventually, a new leader recognised that this unwritten rule of not reviewing strategy no longer served the board, staff or partners of the foundation. This fresh perspective opened the organisation up to regularly evaluating its strategic direction.[9]

Another important charter consideration is time horizon. The charter of an in-perpetuity or a long-horizon organisation will look markedly different than one of a spend-down philanthropic venture. The chosen time horizon plays a significant role in shaping an organisation's governance, decision making, intrinsic risk tolerance, culture, written and unwritten rules and areas of work. A change in the spending timeframe of an entire organisation or a programme should ideally trigger a reassessment and adjustment of the charter.

Moreover, as impact investing is gaining traction as an extension of philanthropic approaches, more and more organisations are re-evaluating and fine-tuning core elements of their charter to allow for the use of this new instrument.

5. Social compact

An organisation's social compact is its agreement with key stakeholders about the specific value it will create in society. A social compact is formulated along six dimensions: accountability, legitimacy, transparency, direction of influence on society, independence and approach to risk.

The time horizon of a philanthropic organisation has profound implications for its social compact, in that it can shape the targets and expression of accountability, has the potential to enhance or hinder legitimacy and can influence an organisation's approach to collaboration or risk. Also shaping an organisation's social compact beyond the six dimensions explored below are the political and economic systems in which it operates, including prevailing views about private wealth and public responsibility.

---

9 Rockefeller Philanthropy Advisors, *Theory of the Foundation Bellagio Briefing Book*, 2017.

Figure 4. Social compact components

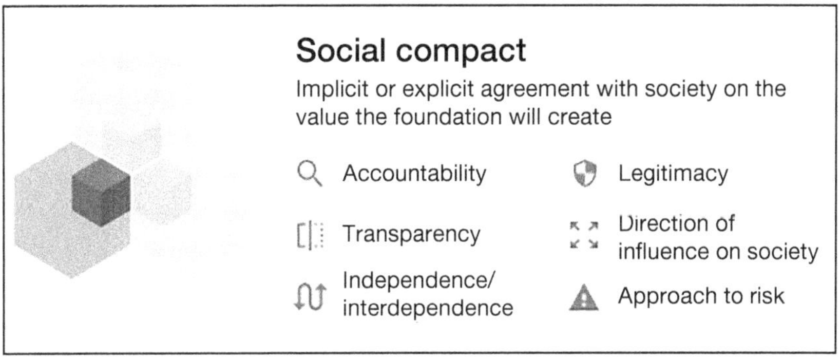

5.1 Accountability

Some philanthropic organisations find power and freedom in the absence of mechanisms holding them accountable to broader society. Others see the same absence – and the lack of input from outside voices – as potentially problematic.

Organisations can be accountable to the legacy of the original founder, populations and communities they support, a geographic region, a chosen cause or a set of values. Most foundations are formally accountable to their boards and to regulatory authorities. Many feel informally accountable to various stakeholders, including grantees, the general public or future generations. And how each organisation chooses to honour that accountability varies widely.

Other organisations are intentionally accountable to very few. For example, Kresge Foundation's President and CEO Rip Rapson observes, "By definition, we're really not accountable to anybody. And so, it is only the intentionality of our ability to be transparent, listen to criticism and adjust course that ultimately serves as a check on our innate authorities".[10] However, despite this described lack of formal accountability, the Kresge Foundation operates with a balance of internal and external measures in mind. Internally, it has articulated values of stewardship, respect, creativity, partnership and opportunity as its organisational guideposts. Externally, the foundation's effectiveness in achieving its goals serves as the final arbiter of its success.

---

10 Rockefeller Philanthropy Advisors, *Profile: Kresge Foundation*, 2018, www.rockpa.org/profile-kresge-foundation.

5.2 Legitimacy

As conceptions about what constitutes public good shift, philanthropic organisations are under increasing pressure from various sources to demonstrate value and consider what makes them credible. There are attempts by a number of governments to undermine philanthropy and restrict its scope and impact. Moreover, the power of private philanthropy and the right of private wealth to exert influence on society is the subject of intense debate, with organisations finding themselves under pressure to justify their existence, the value they add and the use of private wealth for public good. Philanthropists also face criticism for profiting from and representing the engines of inequality. This includes possible divergence between their charitable activities and investment choices, which may further impact legitimacy.

Accordingly, philanthropic organisations often wrestle with whether to engage in public discourse about and with the communities and programmes they support – and, when they do, how to do so effectively. Some organisations are seeking new ways of enhancing their credibility within their communities through new networks, technologies, convenings, advisory groups and boards.

As part of the concern around legitimacy, a growing number of organisations are becoming intentional about their external expression of diversity, equity and inclusion. The dimensions of these considerations may vary from region to region but generally include race, ethnicity, gender and belonging to vulnerable, marginalised populations. This not only reflects the increasing diversity of today's world and the communities supported, but also recognises that a focus on diversity, equity and inclusion are crucial to fulfilling and building legitimacy and trust, particularly where philanthropic activities most impact vulnerable or marginalised communities. Thus, more and more organisations are proactively seeking representation of populations supported in their work and in decision making.

The oft-heard phrase "nothing about us without us", initially made popular by the disability rights movement, captures the essence of this growing trend. Connected to this, interest in involving communities served in participatory grant-making is growing. Listening to communities can improve effectiveness, more clearly identify needs and enhance trust and credibility. To achieve this, a robust feedback loop is essential. Fund for Shared Insight's Listen for Good initiative[11] is one example of this practice. It uses the Net Promoter System to receive feedback from people and communities served. Similarly, the

---

11 Fund for Shared Insight, Listen4Good Initiative, www.fundforsharedinsight.org/listen-for-good.

Center for Effective Philanthropy's Grantee Perception Report[12] uses an online grantee survey to provide funders with honest feedback from their constituencies.

5.3 Transparency

An issue related to legitimacy in our current era of heightened public scrutiny is transparency. In some jurisdictions, individuals or foundations receive tax incentives for their philanthropy, creating an explicit or implicit obligation to prove that they are indeed providing public benefit. Even without tax incentives, many societies expect some level of information to be available to the public to ensure that such privileged resources are being appropriately used. For some organisations, fulfilling expectations of transparency might mean sharing insights to improve the overall philanthropic sector. For others, the desire for privacy might override any external calls for public disclosure, leading them to communicate very little with the outside world.

5.4 Direction of influence on society

Foundations hold a wide range of attitudes towards other parts of society, namely government and the private sector. Some seek little interaction with either, explicitly funding only activities that lie outside the scope of those sectors. Others see themselves as 'canaries in the coal mine', raising the profile of key issues so that they are recognised by state actors as important to the greater good. Still others strive to fund innovation that is potentially scalable through corporate or public sector funding. In recent years, general interest in collaboration has risen as various entities target large-scale problems that could have a substantial influence on societal structures.[13]

5.5 Independence/interdependence

To what degree does the organisation rely on societal support, and to what degree does it act independently? Most philanthropic organisations consider themselves independent actors: they're free to chart their own strategic course, identify their programmatic

---

12 The Center for Effective Philanthropy, *Grantee Perception Report*, https://cep.org/assessments/grantee-perception-report/.

13 Rockefeller Philanthropy Advisors's Scaling Solutions initiative explores this topic in depth: *Scaling Solutions Toward Shifting Systems: Approaches for Impact, Approaches for Learning*, 2018, www.rockpa.org/wp-content/uploads/2018/10/10-20-RockPA-Scaling-Solutions-02-WEB-1.pdf.

focus and goals and determine how and where they operate. However, there is a growing recognition that meaningful impact requires an ecosystem of external partners and stakeholders, which can include: grantees, populations and communities served, other funders in the sector, policy makers, thought and opinion leaders, government actors and corporate entities. Partnership activities range from consulting and learning to co-creating, co-investing and co-funding, with shared rather than independent decision making. Indeed, many organisations and leaders have come to view convening and facilitating connections among funders, grantees and stakeholders as their primary purpose.

5.6 Approach to risk

Some philanthropic organisations believe that an obligation to maintain public trust can constrain their ability to take action on matters that might be deemed risky or controversial to key stakeholders. Other foundations believe that as independent actors in society, they are obligated to take risks, engender controversy and experiment with ideas that no one else can – or will. For many, risk is innate to philanthropy, deeply tied to the sense that a philanthropist should also be an innovator, and that philanthropy is risk capital. As one interviewee put it, "A foundation ought to be using its resources to look to new horizons, to experiment, to try out new things and to offer working models that others can take on".[14]

Foundations often welcome the idea of risk because the term is used as shorthand for risk and opportunity. Being a 'risk-taking foundation' has implications for its social compact because it may open doors for other funders who don't self-identify as risk-takers. For many philanthropic organisations, adopting a more nuanced view of risk has been useful, separating out operational, strategic, reputational and other risk types. This can give the philanthropic organisation a unique role in a particular field, or in society at large.

6. Operating model

The third component of the philanthropy framework is the operating model: the combination of resources, structures and

14 Marshall Institute and Rockefeller Philanthropy Advisors, *The Theory of the Foundation: European Initiative 2016*, pp45–46.

systems that enable a philanthropic organisation to deliver on its mission, strategy and goals. Some philanthropic organisations use one operating model for all of their work, while others use different operating models for specific programmatic areas, for instance, choosing different approaches for their environmental and cultural goals.

An operating model defines where and how key tasks happen, when critical resources should be brought in from outside, how parts of the organisation connect, how resources are deployed and how work is distributed. The operating model encompasses financial and non-financial assets, talent and knowledge development, internal and external collaboration and organisational structure. In essence, an operating model defines how an organisation deploys its capabilities to implement strategy and achieve results. An operating model can be looked at through two lenses: operating approaches and operating capabilities.

6.1 Operating approaches

Operating approaches include how an organisation functions with respect to its operations. Philanthropic organisations, leaders told us, need to establish and calibrate a specific set of operating approaches around resourcing, decision making, initiative, flexibility, programming and relationships. Decisions about these approaches can be thought of as points along a spectrum. While there is no 'right' place to be on any of these spectrums, each choice has important implications for an organisation's operations.

Figure 5. Operating model components

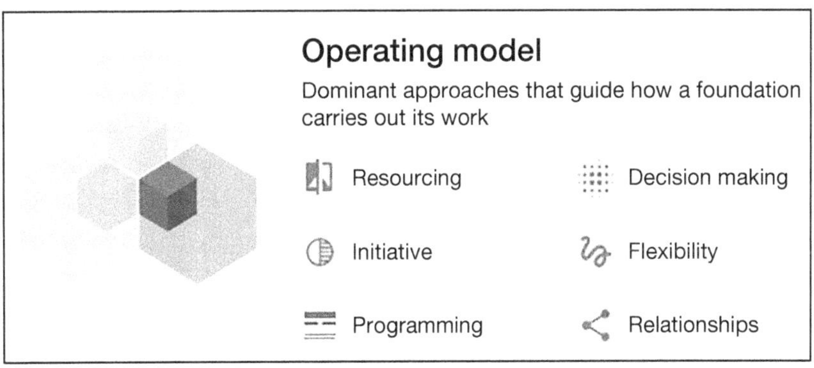

Figure 6. Operating model parameters

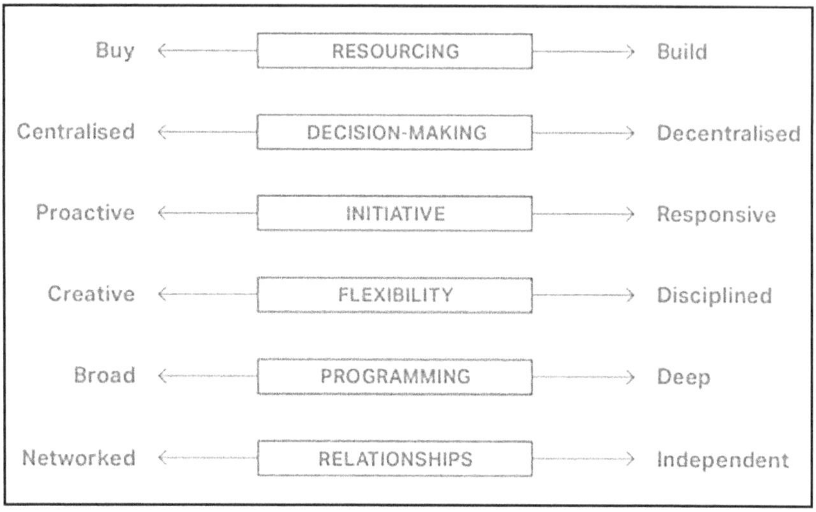

(a) ***Resourcing: buy vs build***

For functions such as programmatic expertise, advocacy, communications and operations, an organisation must choose whether to develop in-house expertise or to outsource through consultants. It may choose to act entirely as a grant maker and/or investor (buying external expertise or action taken on its behalf), or to act, in effect, as an operating foundation by building internal capability in service of its mission. The decision to buy or build may be different for internal operations and external programmes, or even among programme areas. Many organisations view their people, skills, approach and tools as more important than their financial assets, so the cultivation and deployment of these non-financial resources is a critical decision.

For example, The Heron Foundation took a hard look at its operating capabilities, and then took steps to shift them towards the 'build' end of the spectrum. As its former president Clara Miller noted, "We decided that we needed to do more than just conduct financial transactions; we also needed to leverage these transactions by being out in the investment community, by building and helping others to make deals. So we've moved beyond thinking of transactional relationships with grantees as the prime influence – we now put other voices to our work, not as a broadcast, but as a community. We hired a VP of Knowledge and Influence who is essentially community organising around this work".[15]

(b) *Decision making: centralised vs decentralised*

How a philanthropic organisation makes decisions can deeply affect its approach to social change. When and where are decisions made? Do various programmes operate independently, or are key programme strategy and design decisions made centrally, with each programme taking on an implementation role? How much latitude do individual programme officers have? How much effort goes into integration across programme areas or functions? Many foundations grapple with internal silos between functional and programmatic teams, and are increasingly looking at ways to intentionally create cross-foundation work in order to bridge those divides.

Adopting a centralised decision-making approach allows an organisation to marshal all of its resources towards major long-term initiatives and creates internal focus, synergy and alignment around vision and a shared agenda. This approach is most conducive to large-scale, systems change.

However, challenges of such an approach may include forced alignment and synergy, or a potential disconnect between designed solutions and the realities on the ground. In a decentralised approach, programmatic decisions and solutions are more closely linked to the affected communities and realities on the ground. However, decentralisation may risk creating silos and/or a lack of shared organisational vision, priorities and values.

(c) *Initiative: proactive vs responsive*

Some organisations take a responsive approach to their work, supporting goals and initiatives defined by leaders in their field or community. Others see themselves as creators of solutions, designing their own goals and initiatives in service of their theory of change. Some fall in the middle of this spectrum, with a generally responsive grant-making strategy complemented by select proactive initiatives.

Organisations operating in conflict zones, for example, where urgent issues change rapidly and dramatically, are likely to need to be responsive. Issues requiring longer-term arcs of change, including

---

15 Rockefeller Philanthropy Advisors, *Theory of the Foundation Bellagio Briefing Book*, 2017.

human rights, generational poverty or other areas where solutions may take decades, tend to lean towards the proactive approach.

An organisation that favours a proactive approach typically has a long-term trajectory that makes it less susceptible to the winds of change, or trend surfing. However, it should be mindful of the dangers of becoming insular. Thus, consideration should be given to a concerted effort to clearly communicate the vision and justification for choosing this approach. On the other end of the spectrum, a responsive organisation is more open to input from communities it serves and to partnering with a broader ecosystem of stakeholders. However, it can fall victim to the latest trends and fixate on short-term objectives rather than long-term goals.

(d) ***Flexibility: creative vs disciplined***

For many years, funders have been drawn to the discipline of the logic model, or a theory of change. They therefore want to stick to their implementation blueprint, especially because long-term commitments are critical to making sustainable systems change. Other funders prefer to assess and adjust very frequently. Some want to give staff the ability to make tactical decisions within a broad framework. And some keep some funding capacity in reserve to respond to emerging opportunities, including collaboration. Clearly, being neither completely rigid nor totally ad hoc is optimal, but there are many thoughtful, valid approaches between those two extremes. Each approach, though, requires alignment of staffing, budgeting and reporting systems.

Organisations on the creative end of the spectrum are most successful when they have tolerance for experimentation and failure, as well as systems and processes light on bureaucracy, in order to encourage creativity. They should be aware that while the sought-after creativity can sometimes yield unexpected solutions, innovations and new approaches, it can be difficult to assess progress, especially in the short term. Disciplined philanthropic organisations that require clear timelines and deliverables can, on the other hand, easily track progress, but they risk a disproportionate focus on short-term objectives and becoming isolated from the realities on the ground and change.

(e) ***Programming: broad vs deep***

Some organisations favour having well-defined programmes with clear boundaries, while others define their role in terms of a broad social change agenda with a variety of modes of implementation among the groups they support. Some foundations seek to create impact in highly specific areas, intending to create ripple effects that reach the systems level; others pursue 'big bet' or field-building grant-making with the intention of seeding an approach, movement or strategy for change.

Those that favour broad programming tend to focus on long-term change and the broad forces that shape the world. However, they should be careful to guard against superficiality, ambiguous focus, diluted resources and a mismatch between resources and problems. To address this from a staffing perspective, they should seek out individuals with strong strategic and analytical capacity, who are comfortable being generalists and working across many subject areas and functions. For organisations that lean towards the deep approach, the deep and narrow focus does not automatically preclude collaboration or a deep understanding of the whole system. They can in fact create change that others can learn from, adopt and adapt for broader applications as long as they are intentionally aware of how their work fits into the larger system and avoid working in isolation.

(f) Relationships: networked vs independent

How a foundation sees its role and interactions within a community of peer funders, applicants, grantees and other stakeholders is a crucial question. Collaborations are of significant interest to many foundations in principle; however, foundation leaders often have concerns about the time, investment and political dexterity needed to deliver them. Some foundations prefer to take solitary or unilateral action, which they may define as exhibiting leadership, risk-taking and/or ownership of an issue.

Others tend to take a networked approach with a focus on collaboration and even co-creation, seeking buy-in, leverage and a larger sphere of influence and impact.

Networked organisations gain invaluable exposure to ideas and approaches generated by others and benefit from the multiplier effect of collaboration. This approach makes it easier to address highly controversial issues, mitigate risks and create movements and coalitions. However, organisations adopting this approach must make an effort not to dilute their activities, resources and organisational identity by joining too many coalitions.

Organisations that fall towards the independent end of the spectrum are more likely to experiment and risk failure, as they can more easily align internal resources, set their own agenda, demonstrate leadership and maintain a unique voice. Such independent organisations, however, may risk becoming isolated and irrelevant.

6.2 Operating capabilities

In addition to reviewing operating approaches, it is important for an organisation to take stock of its entire range of operating capabilities. This can help validate its trajectory or help identify potential tension points, misalignments and gaps. Operating capabilities include the organisation's arsenal of activities, assets and resources – internal and external, as well as tangible and intangible. Among these resources are:

- talent;
- financial tools (impact investing, PRIs, grants, etc);
- knowledge and strategic insights;
- reputation and influence;
- networks and relationships; and
- project management.

The topic of talent has gained increased attention in the philanthropic sector. There is a growing recognition of the need to build teams that reflect the populations served, understand and espouse the values and needs of the organisation, and possess the specialised skills and knowledge needed for their roles. Organisations are also becoming more cognizant of the need to shift internal culture to promote, empower and enable talent, break down silos and create a team-based culture.

Globally, philanthropic organisations are placing a sharper strategic focus on overcoming limited diversity within the sector and embedding diversity, equity and inclusion on an organisational level. In addition to recruiting talent representative of groups that have been traditionally excluded and marginalised, the concepts of diversity and equity increasingly come to include diversity of thought and political perspectives, as well as equity of power and equity of pay. There is recognition that greater prioritisation of diversity, equity and inclusion involves increasing diversity at the leadership and decision-making level, as well as educating staff, senior leadership and board members on issues related to diversity and inclusion. To achieve equitable and competitive salaries, a growing number of organisations are becoming committed to conducting regular compensation studies and encouraging conversations about pay transparency.

7. Conclusion

Today, millions of foundations and non-profits are working across a highly developed, multi-sector constellation of institutions, fields and networks. Collaboration at scale has become both possible, given this rich supply of external capacity, and increasingly feasible, as our collective imagination and adaptive capacity have begun to catch up to game-changing advances in technology. At the same time, knowledge and resources are fragmented and a loss of trust in major societal institutions is on the rise globally. It is vital for family office advisers to enable their clients to articulate their role in society, their operational strategies and their relationships to others to more effectively implement change. The philanthropy framework is intended to help family offices and philanthropic organisations navigate these challenges and opportunities.

The essential infrastructure for wealth preservation

Natasha Pearl
Aston Pearl

This chapter describes the Wealth Preservation Infrastructure™ required by wealthy clients. It will enable the reader to diagnose existing infrastructure, to understand the profound negative consequences of deficient infrastructure and to recognise the value of strong infrastructure. The chapter outlines the systematic process to build and strengthen infrastructure, and the benefits of doing so: improved quality of life, lower risks, fewer surprises and significantly higher probability of wealth preservation.

1. Introduction

Wealth preservation. Many wealthy clients, and all too often their advisers, believe it is all about investing. But that is only one component. Having observed more than 95 wealthy clients since 2003, I have identified a serious barrier to wealth preservation, one that is rarely discussed or acknowledged. Infrastructure.

A surprising number of wealthy clients lack infrastructure. Not bridges, roads and harbours, but Wealth Preservation Infrastructure™. These are the processes, systems and resources required to provide consistent service levels, improve quality of life, reduce risk and avoid surprises. Examples include consolidated investment reporting, up-to-date cybersecurity measures and residential preventive maintenance checklists.

This Wealth Preservation Infrastructure™ enables clients to make efficient decisions and to participate in opportunities, investment-related and otherwise.

What, exactly, is infrastructure? The *Oxford Dictionary* defines it as "[t]he basic physical and organisational structures and facilities needed for the operation of a society or enterprise".[1]

1 "infrastructure", www.lexico.com/definition/infrastructure.

Given this definition, how could it be possible for a wealthy client to operate without sufficient infrastructure? Well, in many cases the client is focused on wealth creation, rather than on wealth preservation. And what is needed to support wealth creation is very different from what is needed to support wealth preservation – wealth preservation requires a conscious effort to build infrastructure.

Some clients point to their executive assistant, or chief of staff, or their attorney, and insist that 'all is under control' due to that person's excellent work. But infrastructure is not dependent on any one specific person; rather, it consists of processes and systems that operate in the absence of any specific person.

If infrastructure is not built by the wealth creator, it is even more difficult for the next generations to build it, dramatically increasing the likelihood that the wealth will not be sustainable.

Infrastructure can enable opportunities, including participation in sophisticated investment and estate planning strategies. Infrastructure can prevent disasters: careless spenders depleting their inheritance, residential maintenance breakdowns causing leaks or fire, cybersecurity breaches, and compliance issues leading to lawsuits, to name a few.

Without infrastructure, wealth preservation is actually a game of chance. Why does this matter to advisers? It matters because clients lacking infrastructure will not be able to implement sophisticated or even simple strategies that advisers recommend. And these clients are unable to take advantage of opportunities that would support long-term wealth preservation.

While advisers are of course not mandated, legally or otherwise, to take action with regard to their clients' infrastructure deficiencies, advisers surely have an interest in their clients' successful wealth preservation. Therefore, advisers should assist clients in understanding the status of their infrastructure and by recommending that clients address significant infrastructure issues.

2. Diagnosis

How do clients and their advisers know if infrastructure is a problem? Look for symptoms, then determine the possible causes before seeking a solution. A frequent error clients make is jumping ahead to a quick fix, before completing thorough problem definition and diagnosis. If the root cause is ignored, the solution may actually turn out to be "a shinier, more expensive, differently organized version of the same problem that you had before", in the words of Dan Markovitz, an organisation performance consultant.

Humans, he says, have a natural tendency to be "jumpers", but in order to solve problems effectively, we need to be "analysts".[2]

Here are problems we have heard about while working with more than 95 clients since 2003:

We set up our single family office (SFO) to manage our investments, but that's the least of it. We aren't getting the support we need with the rest of life, from medical care to cybersecurity to jewellery and art, to renovations, to managing our private staff.

Every capital call comes as a surprise, and requires a 'liquidity scramble'.

We arrive at our third (or fourth, fifth or ninth) home, and the milk is sour, the flowers are dead and the wifi is down.

We don't have a process for making decisions that affect the family, and two of the next gen are frustrated and stirring up the others.

I was excited to drive my favourite car, but the registration had expired and tyres were almost flat.

Our attorneys have set up multiple entities holding our assets, but we are not sure that all the paperwork is in order, that the complex set of taxes are paid on time, etc.

We're worried about the artwork that we have in storage. How do we know it is all still there and in good condition?

There are several snacks that I really enjoy. But our homes, vehicles and aircraft never have these to hand; instead they offer foods that have been 'off my list' for years.

We can't seem to retain our housekeepers ... drivers ... estate manager ... personal assistant ... chef ... as soon as they learn how we do things, they quit and the replacement staff have to be taught all over again.

We want to have a 'green' home. Yet every time we look in the utility closet, we see cleaning products containing harmful chemicals.

Our elderly parents can remain in their home forever, but we have no way of knowing if the 24/7 caregivers are giving them the proper care.

What all of these problems have in common is deficient infrastructure. Are you hearing about or observing similar issues with your clients? Are your clients frustrated or even kept awake at

---

2 Dan Markowitz, *The Conclusion Trap*, D & L Publications, 2020.

night with problems like these? If the answer is yes, then your client has an infrastructure challenge.

Advisers may feel that some of these problems are trivial. But one client's 'trivial' is another client's 'monumental'. And even the trivial can cause distraction and frustration, diverting the client's attention from strategic thinking, creativity and uncovering investment and other opportunities. Instead clients are immersed in petty, low-impact activities.

Clients may have infrastructure that is strong in certain areas but weak in others. This may be more difficult to diagnose, as the stronger areas may be on display while the weaker are hidden from view. Sometimes this takes the form of strong investment management coupled with weak residential maintenance. Or, expense management is strong, but family decision making is not.

The first step of the diagnosis is to identify the type of infrastructure deficiency. And then determine why these deficiencies exist.

Table 1. Types of infrastructure deficiencies

Type	Examples
Crumbling (old, outdated, overused, not maintained)	"We have maintenance checklists that were created 10 years ago, but have never been updated despite renovations and new fixtures. So there is no programme of preventative maintenance for our homes." "We do track our expenses, but the categories were created years ago and are no longer relevant."
Insufficient (lacking resources, or 'bandwidth' to handle the volume)	"The IT Help Desk at our SFO is so busy with the office that they have no time to assist with our personal devices, or the wifi in our homes." "We don't have enough staff at our residences to cook and do laundry for our large, active family."
Non-existent ('no bridge – you can't get there from here')	"We don't have a consolidated list of our private investments, and cannot respond quickly enough to capital calls." "We are constantly running out of pantry essentials, and literally can't cook breakfast sometimes."

Table 2. Reasons for infrastructure deficiencies

Reason	Example
Accumulation	"We started with two residences, three cars and a boat; now we have five residences and have lost count of all the rest."
Short-termism	"We have so much to do today and can't take the time to plan long-term infrastructure." "I will be working at this office for only a few more years, and it will take all of that time or more to develop the needed infrastructure. Let my successor worry about it."
Focus on cost reduction	"In our SFO, we minimise expenses in every way possible; there is no way that 'infrastructure investments' will be approved in our budget."
Lack of expertise	"There isn't anyone in this SFO who is capable of developing and implementing the infrastructure that we require."
Fear of change and its consequences	"This is the way we have always done things, and if we changed it, we would have to terminate some long-serving staff."
An underlying feeling that it is somehow wrong to allocate resources for personal comfort and quality of life	"It doesn't feel right to spend money for this. Surely there must be higher priorities than my personal comfort."
Wealth creator or entrepreneurial mindset	"My investing is entirely focused on my operating company, and I have no plans to diversify, as I believe that wealth is created through concentration."
'One time thing-ism'	"Whether it is bill pay, tax administration or residential maintenance, 'it's a one time thing [that] just happens a lot'.[3] I don't need a 'process' for bill pay, tax administration or home maintenance because of a few isolated incidents."

3 Suzanne Vega, "Cracking", *Suzanne Vega*, 1985.

Advisers can use the list of reasons in Table 2 to help identify the reason for the infrastructure issue, and apply appropriate persuasive arguments. It is possible that the client is not aware of the reason, and may welcome this assistance. If, however, the client is resistant and unwilling to take action, advisers should assess whether they are likely to have a positive impact given the deficient infrastructure.

3. Infrastructure example: consolidated investment reporting

Consolidated reporting of investments is a fundamental component of Wealth Preservation Infrastructure™. Yet some wealthy clients lack this, and some actively resist it. Why?

- *I have enough funds to cover expenses and make desired investments, so precision is unnecessary.*
- *I am sure a competent professional is handling this on my behalf.*
- *I am sure my spouse is handling this on my behalf.*
- *I am disorganised and can't identify all of my investments and expenses ... my desk drawer is stuffed full of statements, and my email inbox is overflowing with investment notifications.*
- *It's boring – my interests lie in areas other than keeping track of my assets and expenses.*
- *I don't have an investment policy statement (IPS), which is a bit embarrassing given my net worth, and this will be immediately apparent when the consolidated report is prepared.*
- *I place a high value on privacy, and worry that if my information is consolidated my privacy could be more easily compromised.*
- *I worry that my operating companies will not want to share their key performance indicators (KPIs) with the SFO finance team, and that I will have to intervene to resolve a conflict.*
- *The valuations aren't accurate anyway, so why bother?*
- *My assets may be less than I think, or maybe I am spending too much, and I fear the truth.*
- *My exposure to risk is too high, and I am overly concentrated – and I might be forced to do something about that.*
- *It will be too costly to create a useful report.*

Wealth preservation requires actions that are virtually impossible without the infrastructure that consolidated investment reporting provides. Such actions include:

- optimising entity structure;
- measuring investment returns in order to take action if needed;
- managing risk exposure across multiple assets and asset classes;
- running comprehensive 'what if' scenarios;

- maintaining desired asset allocation;
- forecasting the liquidity needed for upcoming expenses, philanthropy, gifting and capital calls;
- optimising taxes; and
- detecting warning signs of fraud and theft.

Clients who lack this reporting infrastructure typically have either too much liquidity, as they overcompensate due to their lack of knowledge, or not enough. Clients without enough liquidity may be chronically late for capital calls, miss short-term investment opportunities and be pressured to create liquidity in a suboptimal way through unplanned asset sales. While this could potentially be overcome with creative use of credit, it is unlikely that such a client would have a credit line readily available, since that would require proactive planning and action. On the other hand, clients with excessive liquidity 'just in case' may be missing opportunities to deploy those funds more productively.

An ever-present threat to wealth preservation is an unexpected severe shock, such as a prolonged recession or a 'black swan' geopolitical or other disaster. If the client requires liquidity at the same time as everyone else in the market, unless they understand their own holdings and have forecast the steps to be taken they are unlikely to emerge intact.

4. Consequences of deficient infrastructure

The troubling thing about infrastructure is that it is unlike a … factory machine with squeaks, where you go, 'Ooh, this machine is squeaking, I need to put some oil on it'. Bridges and roads and sewer systems don't squeak. They just exist and wear away and then in time collapse.[4]

Deficient infrastructure has five negative consequences for wealth preservation:

- Inconsistency and workarounds. Inconsistency is a frequent consequence of insufficient infrastructure. Service levels may be excellent one day and terrible the next. Typically this inconsistency occurs because of workarounds. The *Merriam-Webster Dictionary* defines a 'workaround' as "a plan or method to circumvent a problem without eliminating it". *Ad hoc* and reactive attempts to patch infrastructure with

4 Robert Inman, "Bigger Than Potholes: Why Fixing America's Infrastructure Should be a Priority", *Knowledge@Wharton*, 22 June 2018.

workarounds are time-consuming, are often costly and detract from the important focus on wealth preservation.

- The most common workaround is to hire more people. All advisers have seen SFOs with a large staff and many vendors – yet the client complains that they are not receiving what they need. Staff are working hard and 'scrambling', but are ineffective.
- Workarounds often lead to surprises, including financial exposure, legal penalties, lawsuits and bad publicity. Some surprises have health, safety and security implications, such as leaks, mould and fire, along with reputational damage, to name just a few.

- Distraction. Infrastructure issues described above are unpleasant surprises, or have the potential to cause distress. Surprise and distress are distractions. Distractions impair quality of life, but also obstruct the client's focus on their most important priorities, including wealth preservation, strategic thinking and creativity.
- 'Communications blizzard'. The issues that arise when the infrastructure is inadequate prompt a flurry of urgent emails, texts and calls in order to resolve the issue. These communications are unstructured, uncategorised and not measured or analysed.
- Non-compliance. Lack of infrastructure can lead to missing deadlines, errors on tax returns and other filings, misclassified staff and other labour law violations, lapsed registration or insurance on vehicles. Penalties, sanctions and lawsuits may follow.
- Collapse. There is a real risk that the existing infrastructure, however long it has been in place, may collapse entirely, and this is where wealth preservation may be most at risk. Excessive spending, deferred maintenance, insufficient controls and lack of business continuity or disaster planning can have profound negative consequences.

"How did [everything fail]?" Bill asked.
"Two ways", Mike said.
"Gradually and then suddenly."[5]

5. Is an SFO necessary for Wealth Preservation Infrastructure™?

No, an SFO is not necessary. In fact, it is theoretically possible for wealthy clients to build and manage their own infrastructure without

5 Ernest Hemingway, *The Sun Also Rises*, Charles Scribner's Sons, New York, 1926.

any external support at all. But clients rarely have the expertise, time or interest level required to accomplish this as a solo endeavour.

Rather than employing staff directly, wealthy clients may rely on staff within an operating business. Alternatively the client may outsource to a multi-family office, or deploy a virtual model using outsourced providers. This approach to infrastructure can be effective, but requires controls and oversight, including a rigorous process to qualify and oversee the selected providers. Under this scenario, clients should identify a qualified and objective manager who is proactively overseeing the providers, reviewing periodic reports and performance metrics to ensure the services are delivered per the contractual arrangements, and confirming that the providers continue to meet the needs of the client.

6. Is an SFO sufficient for Wealth Preservation Infrastructure™?

No, an SFO is not sufficient. An SFO has the potential to provide essential infrastructure for wealthy clients. But this depends on its objective and activities. SFOs are sometimes built by wealth creators for a 'single purpose': to oversee the client's investments, to pay the client's bills or to assist with financial and tax administration. And even those limited single purposes may have woefully inadequate infrastructure.

If the SFO is not consciously designed with the objective of wealth preservation, it may be an expensive mistake that only adds to the client's clutter and distractions, rather than providing support through repeatable, documented systems and processes.

7. Benefits of strong infrastructure

Table 3 (see p205) provides examples of the benefits.

8. What is the minimum infrastructure required for wealth preservation?

It is surprisingly controversial to suggest that there are specific systems and processes – in other words, infrastructure – that every wealthy client should have. Some view this as inconsistent with every client being unique. To be sure, each wealthy client is different and of course has different requirements. However, this stubborn insistence on uniqueness is sometimes used as an excuse for the absence of key elements of infrastructure.

The author's experience with numerous wealthy clients has enabled the identification of the minimum infrastructure that all wealthy clients require, found in the list overleaf. There is ample opportunity for customisation; this is a foundation.

1. Entity structure optimisation.
2. Decision making (governance), meeting facilitation and conflict resolution capabilities.
3. Client education/preparation – proactive management of human capital including education, training in conflict resolution and budgeting.
4. Compliance support and expertise (tax, human resources, vehicles).
5. Financial controls/fraud prevention.
6. Consolidated investment reporting.
7. Expense management – analysis of spending by entity and category; comparison to contract terms and to prior periods.
8. Liquidity management for living expenses, philanthropic commitments, capital calls, etc.
9. Risk management.
10. Residential service and maintenance processes.
11. Human resources procedures for private and SFO staff.
12. Security – physical and cyber (including social media and deep web monitoring).
13. Health and wellness oversight and monitoring.
14. Reputation management.
15. Emergency planning.
16. Wellness management.
17. 'Infrastructure to improve the infrastructure':
    - Ongoing monitoring, measurement and improvement of the infrastructure components. Since an important goal of Wealth Preservation Infrastructure™ is to prevent distractions, any high impact issues that arise must be tracked and analysed in order to determine root cause, and to be prevented in the future. Just as clients have an investment committee, clients who want world-class Wealth Preservation Infrastructure™ should have an ongoing Infrastructure Committee.

9. How can advisers motivate clients to create or improve their infrastructure?

Advisers should use their knowledge of their client to encourage the client to take action. Some will respond to 'carrots' such as a positive desire for sustainability, while others will need a 'stick' in the form of the negative fear of theft or collapse.

- Benchmarking – identify other clients who would be willing to meet with your client in order to demonstrate their processes and systems;

Table 3. Examples of a strong infrastructure and benefits

Example of strong infrastructure	Description	Benefit
Residential operations management	Manage residences more like a multi-site business, while ensuring ease and comfort. Document roles and responsibilities, update position descriptions, formalise human resources activities, implement inventory systems for food and household supplies, recruit professional management.	Improves service, increases consistency, increases safety, improves staff retention.
Fleet management	A systematic process to ensure that registrations, insurance and inspections are current for all vehicles, boats and aircraft, and that all maintenance is proactive and timely.	Improves safety, compliance and service.
Collections management	Consistently updated inventory, along with preservation, appropriate documentation and location tracking for art, jewellery and other valuable items.	Reduces risk of deterioration and unexplained 'missing' items. Preserves asset value.
Information technology support, including cybersecurity measures	Ensure that technology, such as wifi and devices, is in 'ready state' at all times, with detailed checklists for this purpose. All software updates executed timeously. Proactive testing of cybersecurity defences.	Reduced risk of downtime for critical technology, and of cybersecurity breaches.
Eldercare	Professional care management to ensure that both ongoing and emergency needs will be met, and seniors can 'age in place' if they choose.	Higher quality of life for seniors, and peace of mind for relatives.

continued on next page

Example of strong infrastructure	Description	Benefit
Inventory management	Systems to ensure sufficient supplies of everything from paper towels to cleaning supplies to medications; ensures that changes in preferences are updated.	Ensures that critical items are always in stock, and that personal preferences are honoured. Also provides early warning of theft by staff.
Medical management	A trusted medical adviser and a proactive wellness programme for all family members including a focus on nutrition, exercise and stress management.	Improves quality of life, and likely to prolong strong cognition and longevity.
Project management	Wealthy clients have many simultaneous projects underway, ranging from residential renovations to planning family meetings. When projects are documented, tracked and managed, with updated status reporting, clients can be confident that projects are proceeding on time and on budget. This can be accomplished with project management software, or with simpler systems such as the Aston Pearl proprietary 'Tracker'.[6]	Minimises worries about vital projects 'falling through the cracks'. Reduces reactive, one-off 'communications blizzard' emails and texts.

6 The Aston Pearl 'Tracker' consolidates all of the client's current projects and initiatives into a single report format that can be updated on a regular basis, and be sorted by priority, due date and person responsible.

Example of strong infrastructure	**Description**	**Benefit**
Consolidated investment reporting	A statement containing all of the client's investments, as well as KPIs for operating businesses, with current valuations.	Enables accurate asset allocation, risk management and tax and entity optimisation.
Expense management/ bill pay/GL	Analysis of the client's spending, using actionable categories, with comparisons to prior time periods. Enables calculation of run rate and assessment of long-term viability.	Enables visibility and corrective action if run rate is too high to be supported. Early warning of theft by staff and vendors.
Human capital management	An educational development plan for the client, family members if applicable, SFO staff and residential staff. Plan should include objectives, milestones and specific skills and knowledge to be attained. Communication skills, conflict resolution and process thinking are critical, along with an understanding of the client's values and legacy.	Helps clients and staff achieve their full potential; enhances performance; reduces the likelihood of unresolvable conflict.
Regular meetings	Scheduled meetings, with objectives and agenda, at regular intervals to review project status, investment returns, run rate or other performance measures; opportunity to discuss issues and concerns, between clients and SFO, clients and staff, and/or client family members if applicable.	Enables structured communication of information and issues, along with analysis and resolution. Progress can be tracked. Reduces volume of reactive texts and emails.

- Missed opportunities – point out investment and estate planning strategies that are impossible due to insufficient infrastructure;
- Sustainability – help the client think through what could happen when the wealth creator or current client is no longer present, if the infrastructure has not yet been implemented;
- Business continuity – alert the client to the potential consequences if systems and processes are undocumented and unable to be replicated;
- Audit trail and controls – some clients, particularly those who are 'hands-off', may be responsive to the need for controls in order to reduce risk of fraud and theft;
- Frustration – enable the client to see that repeated 'errors' can be prevented, eg, bill pay errors such as lapsed subscriptions and power cut-off, late response to capital calls; and
- Fear – warn the client of potential negative consequences, particularly the risk of collapse.

10. How to build infrastructure: the seven-step plan

10.1 Step 1: identify the areas that require infrastructure improvement

The highest priority areas will be different for every client. If the client consists of a family or multiple households, there will be differences among the individuals. Here are some suggested starting points. An approach that has been successful for some clients is to convene a group session where participants write down their issues and concerns with the areas listed below, then review them together and create a combined list of potential improvement areas.

Be sure to identify which areas are working well for the client, and to analyse why. This will provide insights that are helpful in improving the problem areas. In addition, it will help ensure that any changes made to address problems do not inadvertently damage the areas that are high-functioning. Note that this list includes the 17 listed above that are the minimal requirements.

1. Entity structure optimisation.
2. Decision making (governance), client meetings and conflict resolution capabilities.
3. Client education/preparation – proactive management of human capital including education, training in conflict resolution and budgeting.
4. Compliance support and expertise (tax, human resources, vehicles).

5. Financial controls/fraud prevention.
6. Consolidated investment reporting.
7. Expense management and bill pay – analysis of spending by entity and category; comparison to contract terms and to prior periods.
8. Liquidity management for living expenses, philanthropic commitments, capital calls, etc.
9. Risk management.
10. Residential service and maintenance processes.
11. Human resources procedures for private and SFO staff.
12. Security – physical and cyber (including social media and deep web monitoring).
13. Health and wellness oversight and monitoring.
14. Reputation management.
15. Emergency planning.
16. Wellness management:
    - medical (a gentle voice reminding family members to obtain checkups and preventive medical services; management and oversight of significant medical issues);
    - nutrition;
    - exercise;
    - stress management.
17. 'Infrastructure to improve the infrastructure':
    - Ongoing monitoring, measurement and improvement of the infrastructure components. Since an important goal of Wealth Preservation Infrastructure™ is to prevent distractions, any high impact issues that arise must be tracked and analysed in order to determine root cause, and to be prevented in the future.
18. Fleet (aircraft, yachts, vehicles).
19. Scheduling and calendar.
20. Collections management for art and other items.
21. Care management for family members requiring assistance (elderly and the disabled).
22. Travel coordination.
23. Event planning (including book clubs or play-reading groups, or a travel club to visit special places).
24. Information technology:
    - devices;
    - software;
    - privacy.
25. Philanthropy.

10.2 Step 2: prioritise on a five-point scale

First, rank each area by its current status (1 = excellent; 5 = terrible). For each area requiring improvement, rank it by impact (1 = least impact; 5 = highest impact). Clients and SFO executives may have differences of opinion, which may require facilitation to resolve.

10.3 Step 3: quantify current resource allocation and document current processes

Who is doing what? Are resources available, but not allocated towards the priorities? Are resources insufficient? Or are skills missing?

What activities are taking place? Which activities are the most staff-intensive or error-prone, and which are of highest impact to the client? Focus on these processes.

10.4 Step 4: identify the infrastructure gap and score by ease of implementation

Compare the current status and the desired outcome. Rank the ease of implementing each desired improvement on a 1–5 scale (1 = easiest to implement; 5 = very difficult to implement) and reprioritise them, based on level of impact but incorporating ease of implementation.

Focus initially on the quick wins – those improvements that were rated highest impact in Step 2 and easiest to implement in Step 4.

10.5 Step 5: create a plan and obtain agreement from stakeholders

Develop a strategic and tactical plan to implement the prioritised infrastructure improvements. Ensure that stakeholders are in agreement to move forward.

The use of project planning software, such as Microsoft Project (there are many others), is recommended in order to document progress and to provide early warning of unexpected barriers and delays.

10.6 Step 6: implementation (hint: this is the hardest step!)

- When there is no existing SFO, implementation takes the form of finding an experienced SFO recruiter to identify candidates for leadership roles, and/or identify appropriate vendors and service providers to provide what is missing.
- Where there is an existing SFO, identify change management resources with SFO experience. Organisational change is challenging and there are many forces that will try, consciously or otherwise, to stop it. Trained expertise is essential.
- Identify an implementation 'owner' who will lead the process and ensure accountability.

- Convene an Implementation Steering Committee (ISC), consisting of SFO executives and clients, to oversee and manage the implementation process.
- The organisation may appear to need additional human resources, but first assess and analyse existing resources to determine if they can be trained or retrained. Some existing resources may need to be terminated, and an attorney who is experienced with employment issues must be consulted.
- Whether the SFO is already in existence or not, competent 'engineers' are needed for implementation, and it is vital to identify internal or consulting resources who have 'built that type of bridge before'. The alternative is to spend a lot of time and money building a bridge, only to see it fail when cars drive over it for the first time.

10.7 Step 7: ongoing monitoring, measurement and accountability

Ongoing monitoring is needed to ensure accountability. The ISC composition should change to ensure the right type of expertise is present so that it can provide oversight.

Specific actionable metrics, with appropriate standards, should be created and tracked, with the continued oversight of the ISC. For example, track 'preventable maintenance issues', such as appliance repairs, that could have been proactively prevented.

As part of the measurement of the impact of infrastructure, incorporate positive financial impacts, for example:

- Tax reductions as a result of entity optimisation or other means;
- Reduced insurance premiums due to preventive maintenance and installation of best-in-class early warning systems (eg, heat detection); and
- Reduction in staff expense as some processes are automated;
- Increased ability to participate in sophisticated investment and estate planning strategies.

Do not underestimate the potential measurable value of infrastructure. One SFO reported that annual savings from their infrastructure implementation more than paid for the annual cost of the SFO.

11. Example: SFO infrastructure improvement

What can we learn from a client with multiple entities, including operating companies, and a high volume of transactions, including personal bills, capital calls, distributions and philanthropic gifts?

Before starting the infrastructure improvement process, the client's SFO CEO targeted and prioritised the work.

- Be clear about what services the client needs, and what it costs to provide these services:
  - Confirm the client requirements – the desired services, processes and activities;
  - Determine whether customisation, or additional customisation, is needed (for example, if there are multiple clients or family members with varying requests/requirements);
  - Determine whether additional scale is needed, now or perhaps in the future if additional clients will be served by the SFO.
- Document the current services, functions and activities.
- Identify the 'gap' between the client's desired services and what is actually taking place.

In this case, there was a wide gap between the desired services and the current activities. It was also clear that more customisation was needed, as some client family members wanted to review bills prior to payment but only if the invoice exceeded US$1,000 and others set a rule of prior review only if the invoice exceeded US$5,000, while others preferred to review a quarterly report with no prior review.

In order to close the gap, the SFO implemented a major infrastructure improvement, a comprehensive general ledger system. This enabled setting customised 'rules' for the different family members, eliminating time-consuming manual review and the challenges of keeping track of 'this one wants this, and that one wants that'. The system is scalable, so that additional generations and new family members can be added at no additional cost.

The SFO CEO highlighted the importance of 'quick wins'. An early infrastructure success was the establishment of a document-naming protocol. This had high impact, and was relatively easy to implement. Too much time was being wasted by SFO staff searching for documents that had not been named in a consistent and searchable way. Productivity increased significantly once the document-naming protocol was implemented.

The SFO CEO pointed to multiple benefits of the infrastructure implementation:

- Reduced time the SFO CEO and principal spend on routine tasks;

- Increased time available for strategic planning and creativity;
- Enabled investing in more sophisticated alternative assets with potentially higher returns;
- Enabled scaling – can easily add more family clients (eg, next gen) and more entities;
- Enabled customisation within a complex environment – treating different family clients and entities differently, without scrambling, higher staff costs and 'reactive repair';
- Reduced staff costs;
- Eliminated careless errors; and
- Reduced the 'one-off parade of emails and texts' as the client is receiving timely reports and needed services without having to make special requests.

12. Case study

- John and Susan are first generation wealth creators in their mid-60s. There is an operating business that continues to generate substantial income.
- They had a significant liquidity event, US$480 million, 10 years prior. John continues to be involved in the family's operating business while also serving as CIO for the family's wealth.
- Susan has visited multiple doctors regarding her troubling health issues and has not received a definitive diagnosis.
- Richard and Ellen, adult children, are aged 32 and 30; they are frustrated as they do not know how much of the wealth they will receive and when. They are bombarded with business plans and investment opportunities from acquaintances and find this awkward and uncomfortable.
- The principals own three homes in Los Angeles, Aspen and Hawaii; each has a part-time caretaker/handyman and various contract workers who clean and perform other services as needed. The family recently terminated one of the contract workers, who is now threatening a lawsuit alleging that he was misclassified as a contract worker when he should have been an employee.
- John and Susan view themselves as strategic philanthropists, but have not developed the strategy. In the meantime they are relentlessly targeted by charities offering to honour them at awards galas, appoint them to the board of trustees, and so on.

- There is a small SFO, which is co-located and shares staff with the operating business. Marge, John's assistant, has been with him for over 20 years. None of her activities are documented.

Analysis: This family is facing multiple risks to wealth preservation. The most immediate is the possibility that John might be 'hit by a bus', with no back-up for his role as family CIO, at a time when Susan's health is uncertain, and the children's roles have not been defined. There are compliance concerns that could lead to penalties and payouts to staff, given the lack of human resources and legal oversight. Lacking an estate manager who would oversee preventive maintenance and service levels for the three residences, there is the possibility of deterioration, insufficient security, fire and other issues. Marge might retire or be 'hit by a bus', leaving John's needs unmet.

The existing minimal SFO is embedded within the operating business and does not put the family's personal priorities at the forefront. If John were to pass away suddenly, where would the family members turn for the support and assistance they would require?

Action plan: This family has reached a tipping point and needs a separate and distinct SFO with an experienced leader and sufficient resources that are fully dedicated to their personal requirements. This SFO will act as a gatekeeper, handling philanthropic requests, investment opportunities and any other external inquiries appropriately. Its processes and procedures will be documented so that there is no longer a critical dependence on a single person (Marge). Each of the issues listed above leads to an item on the list in Step 1, and then prioritised in Step 2 of the seven-step plan to build infrastructure.

13. Conclusion

In conclusion, infrastructure may not seem to have a major impact on wealth preservation. Indeed, some may ask how infrastructure could be mentioned in the same breath as asset allocation, manager selection or investment performance. Yet the risks described in this chapter clearly illustrate why infrastructure is essential to wealth preservation. None of the great wealth creators and philanthropists would have been able to achieve what they did without an underlying infrastructure and the peace of mind that comes from reducing risk and improving quality of life.

The future of finance

Craig Pearson
Private Wealth Systems

1. Introduction

My father passed away in January with a total estate valued at under US$3,500. This is a man who inherited multi-generational wealth that survived through a great depression and a world war. The root cause of the destruction of my father's wealth was friction of information caused by multiple advisers implementing multiple strategies across multiple financial products. My father never had a platform that allowed him or his advisers to understand his total exposure to any given investment, theme, manager, sector or asset class. When isolated and viewed independently, investment strategies he approved appeared aligned with his goals. However, if he had had a total consolidated view across his entire wealth the concentrated risk would have been identified and corrected. Sadly, without such a platform my father's wealth was destroyed, and with it the breakup of a once-close family. As a teenager I lived through the implications that come with the loss of wealth. This is why today, many decades later, I remain committed in purpose and pursuit to solve the structural challenges that allow for the destruction of family wealth.

Private Wealth Systems was founded with the commitment of empowering ultra-high net worth wealth owners and their trusted advisers with the information they need to gain actionable oversight and control over the management of their wealth regardless of size, complexity or global jurisdiction. This is why we have taken the time and made the capital investment to build a system that is structurally different than any other accounting or reporting system. One private banking executive said we have created the first meaningful innovation in the private wealth industry in the past 40 years – we are creating a new paradigm in global finance by shifting the power of information and action from the heavily concentrated pool of financial services companies back into the hands of the millions of wealth owners, eliminating the destructive nature of friction caused by silo-based information and ill-informed action.

2. Introducing Private Wealth Systems

Many ask if we are disintermediating the financial intermediaries. My premise is that global finance is at an inflection point and that traditional banking and investment management organisations of the future will comprise ultra-high net worth individuals and consortiums of wealth owners, and not the banking and investment houses we think of today. We already have ultra-high net worth individuals and family office clients who act as both consumer and producer of financial services, a trend that no doubt will grow stronger during these unprecedented times. Wealth owners need to have control as to who they lend money to, borrow from, invest in, with the freedom to create new forms of financial products that will transform how financial services are created, delivered and managed.

I can imagine a time in the not-so-distant future when my son, on his way to a business presentation in Chennai, receives a mobile alert notifying him of a US$1.2 million distribution from his investment in a Hong Kong real estate fund he made with a family office in China that created their wealth in real estate. Using our application's cognition, he will be presented with several points of action to reinvest or spend those funds. He will be alerted that he is below his target allocation for high yield loans in Brazil to help fund emerging companies across South America, below his target for socially responsible investing in healthcare clinics in India – not as a means for charity, but for-profit businesses that are improving the safety and health across the most impoverished regions of the country – and underexposed to leveraged buy-outs in the United Kingdom to drive consolidation and efficiencies across the United Kingdom's middle market business segment. Based on his preferences, which allows other family offices and financial sponsors to provide investment information based on his specific criteria, he can view the list of products that meet his needs. He might then decide to invest BRL855,387 in bank loans with a family office in Brazil, invest INR16,741,237 in a special purpose investment vehicle created by a family office in India, and invest £175,370 in a buy-out fund through a new family office he was introduced to by his advisers at Goldman Sachs and JP Morgan. He also might invest US$200,000 across four fintech start-ups he viewed in his Private Wealth Systems' venture capital marketplace that he evaluated because of his expertise in early-stage financial technology. He uses the remaining balance to purchase a new boat that he has been researching just in time for a summer vacation.

What would have taken weeks to research and transact is now completed in a matter of seconds on a single platform – Private Wealth

Systems. Our system is designed to improve upon the accuracy and comprehensiveness of a multi-asset, multi-bank, multi-currency accounting system, the interactivity of a portfolio management system, and the flexibility, engagement and personalisation of a reporting system – capturing, correcting, calculating and presenting every component of every transaction across every financial and non-financial instrument in any currency regardless of ownership structure, and delivering true intelligence to those who are best able to control their financial destiny.

3. Family fortune

For context, my father was part of a multi-generational ultra-high net worth family that made substantial wealth over a century ago. He grew up very comfortably in Greenwich, Connecticut – an idyllic and affluent American town just over the border from New York. My father was the descendant of a prominent Swiss family that made its mark during the turn of the century in wheat harvesting, grain elevators, real estate and other business interests. My father had a very comfortable life, attending the right schools, living in the right town and being afforded all the privileges of wealth. Sadly, the one thing he did not have was a method of centralised oversight over the management of his wealth. My father and his advisers had no way of understanding or managing the collective risks he was assuming in the investment choices that his multiple investment managers were taking on his behalf. That lack of oversight ultimately led to the destruction of our family's wealth, and with it the legacy and unity of our family. The loss of wealth has an inherent and profoundly destructive nature and I do not want anyone to experience what my family went through.

I still remember at age 16 working as a landscaper during the day and clearing tables as a bus boy at night. I worked every minute I could and earned a few thousand dollars which at the time I thought was all the money in the world. I was so happy watching the balance in my bank account grow. But those savings were needed for more important purposes, and I could tell it broke my father's heart when he asked me, his youngest son, for the money I earned in order to pay rent. The one thing I learned is that those who inherit wealth often lack the ability or nature to rebuild wealth. My father was smart, strong and proud, but he lacked the ability or – more importantly – the burning drive that his ancestors had to create wealth. Handing my father my entire savings from that summer was the first time I cried in many years. In some ways it broke me and in some ways it made me the person I am today – focused with relentless determination, but equally empathetic. You do not know the true story behind a family unless you ask and listen. Listen to what you hear but also listen for the nuances in how the story is told, the inflection in the voices of the family members who tell the story, the comfort and discomfort as you learn about the events that led a family to demand oversight over their wealth.

As the third-generation beneficiary of a family fortune, my father did not take an active role overseeing the assets that had been amassed or the managers that were being paid to manage the assets. In the 1980s my father's advisers were all doing what most investment managers still do today, managing to the same asset allocation models, chasing the same risk strategy in hopes of excess returns with zero accountability or participation in financial loss. In the course of one year, as markets shifted, my father's wealth was gone. There was no recourse – each adviser was individually doing the right thing, though unfortunately they were all doing the same thing, which my father was blind to. He lacked a consolidated view of his holdings. We fell into dire financial straits and no one should experience what I did as a teenager. My family's story is not unique. It has been reported that roughly 90% of wealth gained in one generation will be lost by the third. We lost more than money. Our financial challenges led to my parents' divorce and no doubt played a role in what became my brother's struggle with addiction that ultimately took his life last summer.

4. Family offices, expertise matters

Amazingly, in 2019 a 25-year-old with US$10,000 in savings has a multitude of tools and platforms at his or her disposal to track every penny spent and every dollar invested. Yet for those who have multi-generational wealth, for those who influence the world's economies, there have never been such tools – until now. According to Wealth-X, there are over 262,000 individuals who have US$30 million or more in personal wealth controlling over US$31.7 trillion in global investment power. This is the most concentrated and most powerful consumer segment on the planet, yet this segment remains unserved and reactive waiting for their quarterly reports from their multiple managers to tell them what happened to their wealth in the prior quarter. The reason this market segment has not participated or benefited from the fintech revolution is because the inherent complexity of extreme wealth creates organic barriers to entry that prevents financial applications from adequately supporting this market. You need decades of experience working with hundreds of family offices across multiple continents to truly understand the root issue causing friction of information and action. There are numerous examples of fintech companies that had great intentions of serving ultra-high net worth families, but after burning through tens of millions and even hundreds of millions of dollars in capital they understood that in the ultra-high net worth segment it is experience and knowledge, not just capital, that determines longevity and success. I have been told on many occasions that our company has an unfair advantage because we have worked with more family offices in more countries longer than anyone else, and it is this collective experience that informs our approach to solving the structural issues that foster information friction and place great wealth at risk.

5. A new system

After spending two decades working for some of the largest and most respected financial software companies in portfolio management, asset allocation, trading and family office reporting, while working with hundreds of family offices around the world, I learned that in order to drive a meaningful transformation in global finance a new system had to be created from scratch, built on lessons learned with a complete understanding of the capabilities required to empower wealth owners with the information they need to engage and control the destiny of their wealth. Albert Einstein put it best, saying we cannot solve our problems with the same thinking that created them. In order to truly transform global finance we had to focus on solving the industry's structural challenges around data, globalisation, scale and security. To solve the challenge of data we knew we had to capture more data than other systems, so we have taken the time and made the investment to build proprietary data connections to major banks throughout the world, which has allowed us to capture more data than other systems. Our platform has over three times more transaction codes than other systems so we can process every component of every transaction in every asset class across every currency. From equities, fixed income, private equity, currencies and hedge funds to complex bank loans, derivatives, art and real estate, Private Wealth Systems captures, corrects, calculates and presents meaningful intelligence so wealth owners know who and what is driving risk, return, income and expense. Because private wealth is global, our system had to be global. Most systems built outside the United States do not support tax lot level information and the majority of systems built inside the United States do not support multi-currency transactions. Our system solves the industry's structural challenge of globalisation by supporting the trade currency, settlement currency and base currency on every transaction at the time of the transaction, and allows users to select a reporting currency. In addition, our system can separate principal currency from income currency, and our currency calculation supports all 16 decimal points to eliminate rounding errors, providing more comprehensive and more accurate data for better control and decision making. It is important to note that data capture is just part of the solution. Data that is not accurate is harmful – which is why our system provides daily transaction-level reconciliation and we reconcile on more data elements to ensure the highest level of accuracy and trust. Custodial data feeds have error rates up to 18% daily. For example, one global custodian data feed showed an adjustment to the cost on a client holding by US$22 million – in error. Another custodian misapplied the exchange rate on a dollar/yen trade, misrepresenting client exposure to the currency and country. A large custodian truncates accrual calculations, resulting in a lower market value and understating true performance. Another custodian misapplied cash on a trade which would have overstated a client's liquidity. There are many more examples, but this sample shows there is a 'must-have need' to capture and correct custodial data before it gets to the decision makers in order to prevent bad decisions being made because of bad data. The majority of systems simply regurgitate custodial data – garbage in, garbage out. In the family office market, basis points matter and it can mean the difference between a manager being fired or receiving a higher allocation to manage. Trust in the data means trust in the relationship. Although capturing and correcting data is critical, it must be done with hyper-efficiency and operating scale. Ultra-high net worth individuals need information that is tax level accurate, comprehensive enough to support their entire balance sheet regardless of the type of investment, currency or ownership structure, and timely enough to be relevant and actionable.

Historically, the few family offices that did attempt to create a consolidated view of their balance sheets relied on large operations teams and manual effort to manage the data. The problem is that manual effort is not scalable, is error-prone and is very expensive over the long term, especially when considering training costs and operational security. To solve the industry's structural issue with scale we ensured our system was hyper-efficient for processing data without sacrificing quality or comprehensiveness. For example, one reconciliation analyst on our system can support 5.4 times more transactions than other systems in our industry. We took the time to build a proprietary accrual calculator that supports all day count basis across all instruments and jurisdictions so that we can calculate total market value each day systematically without requiring manual entry from month-end statements, thereby providing values and performance calculations that are more timely and more accurate for better decision making without operational burden. Our efficiency allows us to provide more data, faster, more accurately and at a lower total cost for even the most complex wealth.

6. What sets Private Wealth Systems apart

The following client case study demonstrates our differentiation. A multi-billion-dollar family office hired one of the largest accounting firms in the world to perform a global search for a system that could support their complexity across financial instruments, currencies and complex partnership structures. After reviewing 22 systems across the Americas, Asia and Europe, the family selected Private Wealth Systems. A year after enrolment the family hired an accounting firm to perform a transaction-level audit of their data on our system. We proved that we systematically matched back to each system of record across all custodian banks and private investment managers. We are working with another family office that did not know they had direct exposure to seven emerging currencies until they enrolled onto our platform. Another example is a family that has over 400 holdings in a single account and 10% of those holdings have market values under US$500, highlighting the fact that the account is not being managed efficiently. Wealth owners must engage and take an active role in how their wealth is managed.

Of equal importance to speed and accuracy is data privacy and personal security. Because we work with several of the top global private banks in the United States and Europe, we must adhere to the collective cyber security and operational security protocols of the world's largest banks.

Because ultra-high net worth individuals are by nature very exacting, we created a data model unlike any data model in the industry, enabling individuals to create their own personal attributes at the holding level for infinite personalisation but with global scale. Private Wealth Systems empowers each individual with the ability to classify, structure and format their data any way they want whenever they want – true personalisation at scale.

Personalisation also drives engagement because people will want to interact with data on their terms. To help facilitate active engagement we have developed an enhanced design that can support the most sophisticated financial professional while equally informing someone with little to no financial sophistication at all. To help our clients who have balance sheets over 100 pages long engage with their data, we enable them to start at a summary view and drill all the way down to individual tax lots. For example, you can view performance or allocation at the entity level across 20 related or unrelated entities. You notice one entity had a material change in market value or performance, so you click on that entity and drill down to see performance across all the managers for that entity. You then see the increase in performance is from Goldman Sachs and JP Morgan, so you drill through Goldman Sachs and JP Morgan to see which accounts, styles or strategies drove the performance and you then see which holding or holdings contributed to the performance gains taking into account volatility, risk and fees. We are making complex data more manageable regardless of financial sophistication.

Again, the purpose of our platform is to empower wealth owners to gain oversight and take control over their financial destiny. We are supporting family offices that are becoming more sophisticated and are starting to offer services that are banking related. For example, more family offices are starting to make direct investments and offer special purpose vehicles to offer their investment expertise to other family offices. We are working with families that are creating internal loan products, using cash from entity A to create a loan for entity B. This trend will continue and foundationally change global finance.

7. The trillion dollar question

The industry's trillion-dollar question is what does an empowered consortium of ultra-high net worth individuals with a collective US$31.7 trillion in global wealth and dominant expertise in building new business models mean to the established banking, wealth and asset management industries? Who can serve unbanked markets such as India faster and more efficiently – a large commercial bank that requires regulatory approval and massive infrastructure, or a consortium of ultra-high net worth individuals who have the capital and network to create, distribute and manage financial products and services in India and around the world? Whatever the future holds, our team is determined to help drive meaningful transformation with our digital infrastructure that will eliminate the risks associated with friction of information and action that exist across global finance today.

About the authors

Jeremy Arnold
Consultant, Withersworldwide
jeremy.arnold@withersworldwide.com

Jeremy Arnold is a consultant at Withers LLP which is a global law firm acting for successful people and their businesses. Mr Arnold has over 30 years' experience in the wealth advisory business working as a solicitor in private practice in the UK, as a managing director in a major international bank and as general counsel in a leading family office. This experience enables him to provide a commercial and strategic perspective when advising clients.

Charlie Bain
Chief operating officer, Digitalis
charlie.bain@digitalis.com

Digitalis is a technology company that specialises in online reputation management, crisis communications and digital privacy and risk. Charlie Bain has 25 years' experience within the sectors of risk consulting, communications and journalism. He is widely recognised as a leading expert in advising clients on their digital footprint and the effect this has on their reputation. During his career, he has helped a number of leading families, global corporates and prominent individuals understand the nascent field of internet risk and digital crisis communications.

Following a career in journalism for several UK newspapers covering crime and foreign news, including the war in Afghanistan in 2001 and the 9/11 attacks on New York, Mr Bain was appointed deputy chief executive at risk management firm G3 Good Governance Group.

Mr Bain is on the advisory board of VALUEworks, a multi-family office based in Zurich and a senior adviser to Dallington Associates, a company that offers pastoral care to foreign students in the UK.

Melissa Berman
President and CEO, Rockefeller Philanthropy Advisors, Inc
mberman@rockpa.org
Melissa Berman is the founding president and CEO of Rockefeller Philanthropy Advisors, Inc, an innovative non-profit philanthropy service launched by the Rockefeller family in 2002, whose mission is to help donors create thoughtful, effective philanthropy throughout the world. Rockefeller Philanthropy Advisors provides services in planning, research, foundation management, donor collaboratives, regranting and fiscal sponsorship. Rockefeller Philanthropy Advisors also publishes, convenes and

speaks about innovations in thoughtful, effective philanthropy.

Ms Berman has led Rockefeller Philanthropy Advisors since its inception, building it into one of the world's leading philanthropy services. An adjunct professor at Columbia University's Business School, she is also a director/trustee of Rockefeller Philanthropy Advisors, the Adrian Brinkerhoff Foundation and Candid, formerly the Foundation Center and Guidestar. She serves on the advisory boards of the Marshall Center for Philanthropy and Social Entrepreneurship at the London School of Economics and the Tamer Center for Social Enterprise at Columbia University. Ms Berman holds a BA from Harvard University and a PhD from Stanford University.

Linda Bourn
Director, Family Enterprise Risk Practice
Crystal, Alliant Private Client
linda.bourn@alliant.com

Linda Bourn leads the Family Enterprise Risk Practice. She is a recognised expert in advising family enterprise boards, directors, officers and trustees on enterprise risk management for their organisations and guiding generational families on aligning risks with insurance strategy.

She specialises in working alongside wealthy families and their advisers to help them evaluate family risk exposures using holistic assessment tools and to help them develop customised strategies to manage risk.

Ms Bourn is a fellow of the Family Firm Institute (FFI) and serves on the Babson College Board of Advisors of the Institute for Family Entrepreneurship. She holds an MBA and a BA and the Advanced Certificate in Family Business Advising from FFI Global Education Network.

Gail E Cohen
Chair and general trust counsel, Fiduciary Trust Company International
gcohen@ftci.com

Gail E Cohen has over 40 years of experience in the area of trusts and estates. Before joining Fiduciary Trust in 1994, Ms Cohen was a trusts and estates associate at the law firm of Debevoise & Plimpton. She is a former chair of the New York Bankers Association and has the distinction of having served as its first woman chair. Ms Cohen is a fellow of the American College of Trust and Estate Counsel (ACTEC), has also been elected into the NAEPC Estate Planning Hall of Fame and holds that association's distinguished accredited estate planner designation. Ms Cohen chairs the fiduciary professions editorial committee of *Trusts and Estates Magazine*. She is a former member of the New York City Bar Association's committee on estate and gift tax, which she chaired from 1998 to 2001. Ms Cohen has served as an adjunct professor of law at Brooklyn Law School. She received her BA from Mount Holyoke College and her JD, *summa cum laude*, from Brooklyn Law School.

John Deverell
Founder, www.thepreparedmind.net
john@thepreparedmind.net

John Deverell, CBE, works with family clients on issues of governance, leadership and risk mitigation. His company – www.thepreparedmind.net – provides internationally recognised bespoke crisis management plans and checks existing plans; and it writes and runs scenario-based workshops for family offices and other clients. Mr Deverell used his experience over four decades of crisis resolution and risk mitigation as a basis for establishing this company for the benefit of clients. He has appeared many times on TV and radio, advising on risk, security and strategy.

Keith Drewery
Director, Drewery Consulting
keith@dreweryconsulting.com

Keith Drewery has been an adviser inside professional services firms and the wealth management industry for over 35 years. Latterly, his work has included being part of KPMG's family office services team in Sydney. Mr Drewery's focus of work is to help manage the transition of ownership of family capital and how to consider the allocation of their resources including through the use of a family office.

Mr Drewery's work has involved the development of governance models to help families make decisions around the ownership of family capital and helping families develop policies and procedures. He is engaged by wealth owners, family offices and professional service firms, all keen to understand the dynamics of wealth, its effect on family relationships and how other families have dealt with these challenges.

Mr Drewery is a contributing editor to *The International Family Offices Journal* and co-author of the Special Report *Setting Up a Family Office*, both published by Globe Law and Business.

Joseph A Field
Senior counsel, Pillsbury Winthrop Shaw Pittman LLP
joseph.field@pillsburylaw.com

Joseph A Field has worked with international families for over 40 years. His specialty is dealing with tax and structuring issues when families or family offices invest, migrate or send children to different countries. He is active with a number of international planning groups and, of late, has been fascinated by the crossover between issues relating to families and a plethora of new legislation which would seek to destroy their privacy and make their information public; it is possible that the acts of these families, and indeed their advisers, may give rise to criminal sanctions. In addition, Mr Field has an interest in the concerns of these families in regard to the unwelcome gathering of information by cyber attackers and how they can best protect their most intimate and personal data.

Barbara R Hauser
Independent family adviser
BRHauser@gmail.com

Barbara R Hauser has worked with wealthy clients for more than 40 years in a number of countries. A private client lawyer based in the United States, she had the honour of clerking at the US Supreme Court. She is the author of *International Estate Planning* and *International Family Governance* and the consulting editor for *Family Offices: The STEP Handbook for Advisers* and *Trusts in Prime Jurisdictions*. She is the editor-in-chief of *The International Family Offices Journal*. Ms Hauser has been named on the Spears 500 list.

Gerard F Joyce
Managing director, deputy general trust counsel and national head of trusts & estates, Fiduciary Trust Company International
gerry.joyce@ftci.com

Gerard F Joyce is responsible for trust and estates planning and administration at Fiduciary Trust Company International. Mr Joyce works closely with domestic and international clients to develop customised trust and estates strategies. Prior to joining Fiduciary Trust Company International, he was at HSBC Private Bank. He is a member of the New York City and New York State Bar Associations. He has been involved with STEP and has experience in international estate planning, especially cross-border families passing a legacy to US family members. Mr Joyce is on the board of the Samuel Waxman Cancer Research Foundation. He has lectured on family and closely held business planning, international estate and fiduciary investments. He received a BS in finance from Lehigh University and his JD degree from Fordham University School of Law, where he was on the editorial board of *Fordham Law Review*.

Todd D Mayo
Executive director, senior wealth strategist, UBS
todd.mayo@ubs.com

Todd D Mayo is an executive director, senior wealth strategist, at UBS. Mr Mayo works with ultra-high net worth families, helping them to design and implement wealth strategies that reflect their values and goals. He helps families and individuals to create multi-generational structures for managing their wealth, fulfilling their philanthropic visions and optimising tax effects. Mr Mayo is the consulting editor of *Private Trust Companies: A Handbook for Advisers* published by Globe Law and Business. He was a principal author of the New Hampshire Family Trust Company Act (which governs private trust companies) and the New Hampshire Foundation Act (which was the first act recognising civil law-type foundations in the US).

Jeremy McGivern
Founder, Mercury Homesearch
jeremy@mercuryhomesearch.com

Jeremy McGivern is the leading expert on acquiring residential property in prime central London having inspected over 20,000 properties and seen the details of over 153,400 more. He founded Mercury Homesearch in 2001 because he was frustrated by the advice he was receiving from estate agents.

He has featured on Bloomberg Television, CNBC, Reuters, *Forbes India*, *The Financial Times*, *The Sunday Times*, *MoneyWeek* and *BusinessWeek*, among others. He is also an internationally recognised speaker having given talks for firms of solicitors, accountants, private banks and multi-family offices in London, India and the UAE.

Mr McGivern has helped many of the world's most successful families and businesspeople find their ideal homes and investments while negotiating prices that they had not thought possible through his knowledge of the market and negotiation techniques.

Mr McGivern was educated at Eton College. He is married with two children and still plays football and golf and runs marathons for charity.

Asher Noor
Chief investment officer, AlTouq Group
asher@altouq.com

Asher Noor is the chief investment officer for AlTouq Group, a Saudi Arabian single family office. He previously worked for PricewaterhouseCoopers and Banque Saudi Fransi. His last position was chief financial officer for Morgan Stanley in Saudi Arabia.

His role includes managing the investment portfolio of the family, which is allocated in the traditional and alternative asset classes globally. He also sits on the boards of several companies. His achievements include taking a company public, executing the first equity swap on the Saudi stock exchange and several M&A transactions and exits.

He is a well-known speaker and is on the board of the Family Firm Institute (FFI) and the editorial board of the Society of Trusts and Estate Practitioners (STEP) Journal. He holds an MBA from EDHEC Business School, France.

Mr Noor is a qualified trust and estate practitioner and a fellow chartered accountant. He chaired the STEP global special interest group on business families in 2018 and was profiled as a top 30 global family office investor by Trusted Insight.

Natasha Pearl
CEO and founder, Aston Pearl
Npearl@astonpearl.com

Natasha Pearl founded Aston Pearl in 2003, providing highly objective and confidential consulting services to single family offices and families. Areas of focus include single family office structure and residential operations. The firm has developed a proprietary approach and significant intellectual capital in Wealth Preservation Infrastructure™.

Aston Pearl was awarded "Best Family Office Consulting Firm" in 2014 by *Private Asset Management*, the family office industry publication, and was "Highly Commended" in 2019. In 2015, *Private Asset Management* named Ms Pearl one of "The 50 Most Influential Women in Private Wealth". Ms Pearl's expertise has been cited in numerous articles, including "Battling for Billionaires", *Bloomberg Markets* and "The Billionaire Service Industry", *The Atlantic*. Prior to founding Aston Pearl, Ms Pearl served as a senior vice president and worldwide director at Sotheby's, and as a principal at Mercer Management Consulting (now Oliver Wyman). She received her undergraduate and MBA degrees from Harvard University.

Craig Pearson
CEO, Private Wealth Systems
cpearson@privatewealthsystems.com

Craig Pearson, CEO, co-founded Private Wealth Systems 45 days after restructuring and selling a leading investment reporting company. With the backing of three prominent family offices, Mr Pearson started Private Wealth Systems intent on solving the structural industry challenges that continue to plague legacy software systems and the global financial services industry in terms of data capture, data processing and data presentation.

Beginning his career as an investment banker and later transitioning into financial technology, he has held leading positions at several of the largest fintech companies with direct experience in trade order management, multi-asset portfolio management, compliance and reporting. Private Wealth Systems is now the industry leader in delivering multi-asset, multi-manager, multi-currency consolidated financial intelligence to family offices across four continents. Mr Pearson is a chartered financial analyst (CFA) and holds a master's degree in finance.

Amy Radnor
Counsel, Farrer & Co
amy.radnor@farrer.co.uk

Amy Radnor qualified as a family lawyer in 2008. She has extensive experience advising clients on all aspects of relationship breakdown and wealth protection, including financial claims on divorce, international and jurisdictional issues, and issues relating to children. She has a particular interest and expertise in drafting and negotiating prenuptial and postnuptial agreements and in cross-border children work.

Nicola Saccardo
Partner, Maisto e Associati
n.saccardo@maisto.it

Nicola Saccardo is a partner at Maisto e Associati. He graduated from the Bocconi University in Milan and holds an LLM in International Taxation from the University of Leiden in the Netherlands. He is admitted to the Italian Bar and is also qualified as an Italian chartered accountant.

Mr Saccardo is a member of the International Academy of Estate and Trust Law, as well as its vice president for Europe and chair of its tax committee. He is an international fellow of the American College of Trust and Estate Counsel (ACTEC) and is also a member of STEP and some of its global committees, such as the international client global SIG steering committee and the EU public policy committee.

He leads the EU tax law course of the LLM at King's College in London, has authored many publications on Italian tax matters and is a frequent speaker at conferences. His areas of expertise include taxation of trusts, estates and high net worth individuals; estate planning in general; and international and EU tax law.

Rose Spencer-Longhurst
Senior associate, Farrer & Co
rose.spencer-longhurst@farrer.co.uk

Rose Spencer-Longhurst enjoys working on a broad range of private family law matters, both contentious and non-contentious, including resolving complex financial issues further to a marital or relationship breakdown, disputes relating to children, prenuptial and postnuptial agreements and cohabitation. Ms Spencer-Longhurst has experience of working for a wide range of clients including entrepreneurs, bankers and other professionals, and homemakers and wealthy international couples – and for both mothers and fathers in children-related matters – and draws on her background in commercial law to inform and guide her approach in the family law arena. Many of her cases involve an international element. Ms Spencer-Longhurst is a member of Resolution and of the International Bar Association.

About Globe Law and Business

Globe Law and Business was established in 2005, and from the very beginning, we set out to create law books which are sufficiently high level to be of real use to the experienced professional, yet still accessible and easy to navigate. Most of our authors are drawn from Magic Circle and other top commercial firms, both in the UK and internationally.

Our titles are carefully produced, with the utmost attention paid to editorial, design and production processes. We hope this results in high-quality books which are easy to read, and a pleasure to own. All our new books are also available as ebooks, which are compatible with most desktop, laptop and tablet devices. We have recently expanded our portfolio to include a new range of journals and Special Reports, available both digitally and in hard copy format, and produced to the same high standards as our books.

We'd very much like to hear from you with your thoughts and ideas for improving what we offer. Please do feel free to email me at sian@globelawandbusiness.com with your views.

Sian O'Neill
Managing director
Globe Law and Business
www.globelawandbusiness.com

Related titles

Globe Law and Business

Go to **www.globelawandbusiness.com**
for full details including free sample chapters

www.ingramcontent.com/pod-product-compliance
Ingram Content Group UK Ltd.
Pitfield, Milton Keynes, MK11 3LW, UK
UKHW062251150926
8656IPUK00007B/40

9 781787 42330